1,000,000 Books

are available to read at

---◆---

www.ForgottenBooks.com

---◆---

Read online
Download PDF
Purchase in print

ISBN 978-1-334-94621-9
PIBN 10780787

This book is a reproduction of an important historical work. Forgotten Books uses
state-of-the-art technology to digitally reconstruct the work, preserving the original format
whilst repairing imperfections present in the aged copy. In rare cases, an imperfection in
the original, such as a blemish or missing page, may be replicated in our edition. We do,
however, repair the vast majority of imperfections successfully; any imperfections that
remain are intentionally left to preserve the state of such historical works.

Forgotten Books is a registered trademark of FB &c Ltd.
Copyright © 2018 FB &c Ltd.
FB &c Ltd, Dalton House, 60 Windsor Avenue, London, SW19 2RR.
Company number 08720141. Registered in England and Wales.

For support please visit www.forgottenbooks.com

1 MONTH OF
FREE
READING

at
www.ForgottenBooks.com

By purchasing this book you are eligible for one month membership to ForgottenBooks.com, giving you unlimited access to our entire collection of over 1,000,000 titles via our web site and mobile apps.

To claim your free month visit:
www.forgottenbooks.com/free780787

* Offer is valid for 45 days from date of purchase. Terms and conditions apply.

English
Français
Deutsche
Italiano
Español
Português

www.forgottenbooks.com

Mythology Photography **Fiction**
Fishing Christianity **Art** Cooking
Essays Buddhism Freemasonry
Medicine **Biology** Music **Ancient
Egypt** Evolution Carpentry Physics
Dance Geology **Mathematics** Fitness
Shakespeare **Folklore** Yoga Marketing
Confidence Immortality Biographies
Poetry **Psychology** Witchcraft
Electronics Chemistry History **Law**
Accounting **Philosophy** Anthropology
Alchemy Drama Quantum Mechanics
Atheism Sexual Health **Ancient History**
Entrepreneurship Languages Sport
Paleontology Needlework Islam
Metaphysics Investment Archaeology
Parenting Statistics Criminology
Motivational

Their appetites, to taste of the fruit that
Is forbidden.

Beaumont and *Fletcher's Elder Brother.*

Oh, the blindness of a cov'tous wretched
Father, that is led only by the ears,
And in love with sounds ! Nature had done well
To have thrust him into the world without
An eye, that like a mole is so affected
To base earth ; and there means to dig for paradise.
Fathers their children, and themselves abuse ;
That wealth, a husband, for their daughters chuse.

Shirley's School of Compliments.

Honour thy parents to prolong thine end ;
With them, though for a truth, do not contend :
Though all should truth defend, do thou lose rather
The truth a while, than lose their loves for ever :
Whoever makes his father's heart to bleed ;
Shall have a child that will revenge the deed.

Randolph.

P A R T I N G.

And by the way, she sundry purpose found
  Of this or that, the time for to delay ;
And of the perils whereto he was bound,
  The fear whereof seem'd much her to affray :
  But all she did, was but to wear out day.
Full oftentimes she leave of him did take ;
  And eft again deviz'd somewhat to say,
Which she forgot ; whereby excuse to make :
So loth she was his company for to forsake.

Spenser's Fairy Queen.

Parting is such sweet sorrow,
That I shall say good night, till it be morrow.

Shakespear's Romeo and Juliet.

———— I would have thee gone,
And yet no further than a wanton's bird,
That lets it hop a little from her hand,
Like a poor pris'ner in his twisted gyves ;
And with a silk thread plucks it back again,

So

So loving jealous of his liberty.

Shakespear's Romeo and Julie

With his head over his shoulder turn'd,
He seem'd to find his way without his eyes:
For out of doors he went without their help,
And, to the last, bended their light on me.

Shakespear's Hamlet

————————————1. So long,
As he could make me with this eye, or ear,
Distinguish him from others, he did keep
The deck, with glove, or hat, or handkerchief,
Still waving, as the fits and stirs of's mind
Could best express how slow his soul sail'd on,
How swift his ship.
2. Thou should'st have made him
As little as a crow, or less; ere left
To after eye him.
1. Madam, so I did.
2. I would have broken mine eye strings, crack'd 'em, bu
To look upon him; till the diminution
Of Space had pointed him sharp as my needle;
Nay, follow'd him, till he had melted, from
The smallness of a gnat, to air; and then
Have turn'd mine eye, and wept.

Shakespear's Cymbelin

Did not take my leave of him, but had
Most pretty things to say: Ere I could tell him,
How I would freely think on him, at certain hours;
Such thoughts, and such; or, I could make him swea
The flies of *Italy* should not betray,
Mine int'rest and his honour; or have charg'd him
At the sixth hour of the morn, at noon, at midnight
T'encounter me with orisons; for then
I am in heav'n for him; or ere I could
Give him that parting kiss, which I had set
'Twixt two charming words, comes in my father;
And, like the tyrannous breathing of the north,
Shake all our buds from growing.

Shakespear's Cymbelin

With that, wringing my hand, he turns away ;
  And tho' his tears would hardly let him look,
Yet such a look did through his tears make way ;
  As show'd how sad a farewel there he took.

Daniel's Arcadia.

Sweetest love, I do not go,
  For weariness of thee ;
Nor in hope the world can show
  A fitter love for me :
But since that I
  Must die at last, 'tis best,
  Thus to use myself in jest
By feigned death to die.

Yesternight the sun went hence,
  And yet is here to day ;
He hath no desire nor sense,
  Nor half so short a way :
Then fear not me,
  But believe that I shall make
  Hastier journeys, since I take
More wings and spurs than he.

Dr. *Donne.*

As in *September*, when our year resigns
The glorious sun to the cold watry signs,
Which through the clouds looks on the earth in scorn,
The little bird, yet to salute the morn,
Upon the naked branches sets her foot,
The leaves then lying on the mossy root ;
And there a silly chirriping doth keep,
As though she fain would sing, yet fain would weep,
Praising fair summer, that too soon is gone,
Or sad for winter, too fast coming on :
In this strange plight, I mourn for thy depart,
Because that weeping cannot ease my heart.

Drayton's Queen Margaret to Duke of Suffolk.

I make no doubt, as I shall take the course,
Which she shall never know, till it be acted ;

And

And when she wakes to honour, then she'll thank
    for't
I'll imitate the pities of old surgeons
To this lost limb; who ere they shew their art,
Cast one asleep, then cut the diseas'd part:
So out of love to her I pity most,
She shall not feel him going till he's lost;
Then she'll commend the cure.
        Middleton's Women beware Wo.

P A S S I O N S.

Behold the image of mortality,
And feeble nature cloth'd with fleshly tire;
When raging passion with fierce tyranny,
    Robs reason of her due regality,
And makes it servant to her basest part!
    The strong it weakens with infirmity,
And with bold fury arms the weakest heart;
The strong, through pleasure soonest falls, the w
    through smart.
        Spenser's Fairy Q

But though the apprehensive pow'r do pause,
    The motive virtue then begins to move;
Which in the heart below doth passions cause,
    Joy, grief, and fear, and hope, and hate, and

These passions have a free commanding might,
    And divers actions in our life do breed;
For all acts done without true reason's light,
    Do from the passions of the sense proceed.

But since the brain doth lodge the pow'rs of sense,
    How makes it in the heart those passions spring?
The mutual love, the kind intelligence
    'Twixt heart and brain, this sympathy doth bri

From the kind heat which in the heart doth reign,
    The sp'rits of life do their beginning take;
These sp'rits of life ascending to the brain,
    When they come there, the spirits of sense do n
                  7

These sp'rits of sense, in fantasy's high court,
  Judge of the forms of objects, ill or well;
And so they send a good or ill report
  Down to the heart, where all affections dwell.

If the report be good, it causeth love,
  And longing hope, and well-assured joy:
If it be ill, then doth it hatred move,
  And trembling fear, and vexing griefs annoy.
                          Sir *John Davies*.

Most necessary 'tis, that we forget
To pay ourselves what to ourselves is debt:
What to ourselves in passion we propose,
The passion ending, doth the purpose lose:
The violence of either grief or joy,
Their own enactors with themselves destroy:
Where joy most revels, grief doth most lament;
Grief joys, joy grieves on slender accident.
                          Shakespear's Hamlet.

——————————— Passions are desperate,
And tempt with uncouth woe, as well as joy:
It evil is, that glories to destroy.
                          Lord *Brooke's Alaham*.

Passions are oft mistaken, and misnam'd;
Things simply good, grow evil with misplacing.
                          Lord *Brooke's Mustapha*.

Who would the title of true worth were his,
Must vanquish vice, and no bare thoughts conceive:
The bravest trophy ever man obtain'd;
Is that, which o'er himself, himself hath gain'd.
                          E. of *Sterline's Darius*.

Fear seeing all, fears it of all is spy'd:
Like to a taper lately burning bright,
But wanting matter to maintain his light;
The blaze ascending, forced by the smoke,
Living by that, which seeks the same to choke:
The flame still hanging in the air doth burn,
Until drawn down, it back again return:

                          Then

Then clear, then dim; then spreadeth, and then close
Now getteth strength, and now its brightness loseth
As well the best discerning eye may doubt,
Whether it yet be in, or whether out :
Thus in my cheek, my sundry passions shew'd ;
Now ashy-pale, and now again it glow'd.
　　　　Drayton's Lady Geraldine to the Earl of Sur

The grief that melts to tears, by't self is spent :
Passion resisted, grows more violent.
　　　　Tourneur's Atheist's Trag

————Each small breath
Disturbs the quiet of poor shallow waters :
But winds must arm themselves, ere the large sea
Is seen to tremble.
　　　　Habbington's Queen of Arra

——————Passions without power,
Like seas against a rock, but lose their fury.
　　　　Denham's So

The gods from passions might have made us free ;
Or gave us only those, which best agree.
　　　　Sir R. *Howard's Vestal Vir*

These starts, are the convulsions of weak reason,
When fits of passion grow too strong upon you :
We have all our haggard passions, but none so wild
Or so unmann'd as yours. ————
They may be tam'd and brought from their excess,
And watch'd by reason, into gentleness.
　　　　I

——Passions are like thieves
That watch to enter undefended places ;
And rob you too, of all that puts a difference
Between wild beasts and man.
　　　　Sir R. *Howard's Blind La*

—————— Oh ! these passions
Are but the cracks and splinters of the soul ;
Shatter'd and bruis'd by some external pow'r, .
Which might securely lie in its own haven.
Mens minds, like kingdoms, never so much flourish

As when they raife the price of native goods ;
And fet low values upon foreign wares.

Fane's Love in the dark.

'Tis hard to fay, what men, whom reafon ghides
Intend to do ; much more, whom paffion rides.

Fountain's Rewards of Virtue.

We oft by light'ning read in darkeft nights ;
And by your paffions, I read all your natures,
Though you at other times can keep them dark.

Crown's Firft Part of Henry VI.

Oh, fir! your paffion's dead ; and you are weaving
Garlands of fine expreffions for it's funeral.

Crown's Second Part of Henry VI.

PATIENCE.

What cannot be preferv'd when fortune takes,
Patience her injury a mock'ry makes.
The robb'd, that fmiles, fteals fomething from the thief;
He robs himfelf, that fpends a bootlefs grief.

Shakefpear's Othello.

Patience unmov'd——no marvel though fhe paufe ;
They can be meek, that have no other caufe :
A wretched foul, bruis'd with adverfity,
We bid be quiet, when we hear it cry ;
But were we burden'd with like weight of pain ;
As much, or more, we fhould ourfelves complain.

Shakefpear's Comedy of Errors.

What fortune hurts, let fuff'rance on'y heal ;
No wifdom with extremities to deal.

Drayton's Duke of Suffolk to Queen Margaret.

1. For he whofe breaft is tender, blood fo cool,
That no wrong heat it, is a patient fool :
What comfort do you find in b'ing fo calm ?

2. That which green wounds receive from fov'reign
   balm ;
Patience, my lord ; why, 'tis the foul of peace :
Of all the virtues 'tis neareft kin to heaven ;
It makes men look like gods : The beft of men
That eer wore earth about him, was a fufferer,

A fufo

A soft, meek, patient, humble, tranquil spirit,
The first true gentleman that ever breath'd.
The stock of patience then cannot be poor;
All it desires, it has; what monarch more?
It is the greatest enemy to law
That can be; for it doth embrace all wrongs;
And so chains up lawyers, and womens tongues.
'Tis the perpetual pris'ner's liberty,
His walks and orchards; 'tis the bond-slave's freed
And makes him seem proud of each iron chain,
As though he wore it more for state, than pain:
It is the beggar's musick; and thus sings,
Although their bodies beg, their souls are kings.
O my dread liege! It is the self same bliss
Rears us aloft, makes men and angels kiss:
And last of all, to end a houshold strife;
It is the honey 'gainst a waspish wife.
         Dekker's First Part of the Honest Wh

'Tis an easy thing for him that has no
Pain, to talk of patience.
         Tourneur's Atheist's Trag

Patience grows fury that is often stirr'd;
When conquerors wax calm, and cease to hate;
The conquer'd should not dare reiterate.
         Goffe's Couragious T

I have heard you with that patience,
(And with no better) as the troubled pilot
Endures a tempest, or contrary winds:
Who, finding nevertheless his tackling sure,
His vessel tight, and sea-room round about him,
Plays with the waves, and vies his confidence
Above the blasts of fortune, till he wins
His way, through all her threatnings, to his port.
         Richard Brome's Damoi

He that's besotted to his fear, or ease;
Will make his patience prove his worst disease.
         Tatham's Distracted St

Patience in cowards is tame hopeless fear ;
But in brave minds, a scorn of what they bear.

Sir R. Howard's Indian Queen.

PATRON.

How many great ones may remember'd be,
  Who in their days most famously did flourish ;
Of whom no word we hear, no sign we see,
  But as things wip'd out with a sponge they perish ;
  Because they, living, cared not to cherish
Some gentle wit, thro' pride, or covetize,
Which might their names for ever memorize ?

Spenser's Ruins of Time.

O grief of grief! O gall of all good hearts !
  To see that virtue should despised be
Of such, as first were raised for virtuous parts ;
  And now, broad-spreading, like an aged tree,
  Let none shoot up, that nigh them planted be :
O let not those of whom the muse is scorn'd,
Alive, or dead, be by the muse adorn'd.

Spenser, Ibid.

Who grac'd the muses, which her times became :
For they who give them comfort, must have fame.

Daniel's Civil War.

And to invite great men from foreign parts,
  Guests worthy of this table, he did add
Rich salaries to sublimate their hearts
  For high designs : Some guerdon must be had
To raise a great, and a dejected soul :
Virtue steers bravely, where there's such a pole.

Antiquity the arts so flourishing saw,
  Chear'd by their patron's sweet and temp'rate air :
'Twas hope of meed that made *Apelles* draw
  Such an unvalu'd piece of *Philip's* heir ;
And well he might : Rewards not only can
Draw such a picture, but make such a man.

Aleyn's Crescey.

PEACE.

P E A C E.

A peace is of the nature of a conqueſt;
For then both parties nobly are ſubdu'd,
And neither party loſer.

Shakeſpear's Second Part of King Henry IV.

Let me have war, ſay I; it exceeds peace,
As far as day does night; it's ſprightly, waking,
Audible, and full of vent.   Peace is a
Very apoplexy, lethargy, mull'd,
Deaf, ſleepy, inſenſible, a getter   ]
Of more baſtard children, than war's a deſtroyer
Of men.
2. 'Tis ſo; and as war in ſome ſort
May be ſaid to be a raviſher, ſo
It cannot be denied, but peace is
A great maker of cuckolds.
1. Ay, and it makes men hate one another.
2. Reaſon, 'cauſe they then leſs need one another.

Shakeſpear's Coriolanus.

1. Now all's peace, no danger: Now what follows?
Idleneſs ruſts us; ſince no virtuous labour
Ends ought rewarded, eaſe, ſecurity,
Now all the palm wears; we made war before
So to prevent war; men with giving gifts
More than receiving, made our country ſtrong:
Our matchleſs race of ſoldiers then would ſpend
In publick wars, not private brawls, their ſp'rits;
In daring enemies, arm'd with meaneſt arms;
Not courting ſtrumpets, and conſuming birth-rights
In apiſhneſs, and envy of attire:
No labour then was harſh, no way ſo deep,
Nor rock ſo ſteep, but if a bird could ſcale it,
Up would our youth fly to.   A foe in arms,
Stirr'd up a much more luſt of his encounter,
Than of a miſtreſs never ſo be-painted:
Ambition then, was only ſcaling walls,
And over-topping turrets: Fame was wealth;
Beſt parts, beſt deeds, were beſt nobility;

Honour

Honour with worth ; and wealth well got, or none.
Countries we won, with as few men as countries.
Virtue fubdu'd all.

2. Juft : And then our nobles
Lov'd virtue fo, they prais'd and us'd it too ;
Had rather do, than fay : their own deeds hearing
By others glorify'd, than be fo barren,
That their parts only ftood in praifing others.

1. Who could not do, yet prais'd, and envy'd not :
Civil behaviour flourifh'd ; bounty flow'd ;
Avarice to upland boors, flaves hang-men banifh'd.

2. 'Tis now quite otherwife ; but to note the caufe
Of all thefe foul digreffions, and revolts
From our firft natures ; this 'tis, in a word :
Since good arts fail, craft and deceit are us'd :
Men ignorant are idle ; idle men
Moft practice, what they moft may do with eafe,
Fafhion, and favour : All their ftudies aiming
At getting money, which no wife man ever
Fed his defires with.

Chapman's Revenge of Buffey D'ambois.

Thus mighty rivers quietly do glide,
And do not by their rage their pow'rs profefs,
But by their mighty workings ; when in pride
Small torrents roar more loud, and work much lefs :
Peace greatnefs beft becomes.   Calm pow'r doth guide
With a far more imperious ftatelinefs,
Than all the fwords of violence can do ;
And eafier gains thofe ends fhe tends unto.

Daniel's Panegyrick to the King.

The people thus in time of peace agree
To curb the great men ftill ; ev'n in that form,
As in calm days they do disbranch the tree,
Which fhrowded them of late againft a ftorm.

E. of Sterline's Julius Cæfar.

The mifery of peace ! Only outfides
Are then refpected : As fhips feem very
Great upon the river, which fhew very

Little

Little upon the feas; fo fome men in
The court, feem *Coloſſuſſes* in a chamber;
Who if they came into the field, would appear
Pitiful pigmies.

Webſter's *White Devil.*

———————— Pox of peace ——
It fills the kingdom full of holydays;
And only feeds the wants of whores and pipers;
And makes th' idle drunken rogues get fpiniters:
By heav'n it is the furfeit of all youth,
That makes the toughneſs, and the ſtrength of nations
Melt into women.   'Tis an eaſe that broods
Thieves, and baſtards only.

Beaumont and *Fletcher*'s *Captain.*

————————In this plenty,
And fat of peace, your young men ne'er were train'd
In martial difcipline; and your ſhips unrigg'd,
Rot in the harbour; nor defence prepar'd,
But thought unuſeful: as if that the gods
Indulgent to your ſloth, had granted you
A perpetuity of pride and pleaſure;
Nor change fear'd, or expected.

Maſſinger's *Bondman.*

———————— States that never knew
A change but in their growth, which a long peace
Hath brought unto perfection, are like ſteel;
Which being neglected, will confume itſelf
With its own ruſt: fo doth fecurity
Eat through the hearts of ſtates, while they're ſleeping
And lull'd in her falfe quiet.

Nabbs's *Hannibal and Scipio.*

Men are unhappy when they know not how
To value peace, without its lofs:
And from the want learn how to ufe,
What they could fo ill manage when enjoy'd.

Sir R. Howard's *Blind Lady.*

Surfeited with fulfome eaſe and wealth,
Our luſcious hours are candy'd up for women;

Whilſt

Whilft our men lofe their appetite to glory;
Our pilots all their skill, for want of ftorms.

Crown's *Ambitious Statefman*.

PERSEVERANCE.

Perfeverance keeps honour bright :
To have done, is to hang quite out of fafhion,
Like rufty mail in monumental mockery.
For honour travels in a ftraight fo narrow,
Where one but goes abreaft ; keep then the path ;
For emulation hath a thoufand fons,
That one by one purfue ; if you give way,
Or turn afide from the direct forth-right,
Like to an entred tide, they all rufh by,
And leave you hindermoft ; and there you lie,
Like to a gallant horfe fall'n in firft rank,
For pavement to the abject near, o'er-run
And trampled on : then what they do in prefent,
Tho' lefs than yours in paft, muft o'er-top yours.
For time is like a fafhionable hoft,
That flightly fhakes his parting gueft by th' hand ;
But with his arms outftretch'd, as he would fly,
Grafps in the comer ; welcome ever fmiles,
And farewel goes out fighing. O, let not virtue feek
Remuneration for the thing it was !
For beauty, wit, high birth, defert in fervice,
Love, friendfhip, charity, are fubjects all
To envious and calumniating time.
One touch of nature makes the whole world kin ;
That all, with one confent, praife new-born gawds,
Tho' they are made and moulded of things paft,
And give to duft, that is a little gilt,
More laud than they will give to gold o'er-dufted :
The prefent eye praifes the prefent object.
Then marvel not, thou great and compleat man,
That all the *Greeks* begin to worfhip *Ajax* ;
Since things in motion fooner catch the eye,
Than what not ftirs.

Shakefpear's Troilus and Creffida.
Know

Know mortals, that the men the gods most love,
In hard and dang'rous arts they always prove;
When men live brave at first, then fall to crimes,
Their bad is chronicle to future times:
For who begins good arts, and not proceeds;
He but goes backward in all noble deeds.

Goffe's Couragious Turk

Not to promote what we do once commence,.
Argues a weakness, and a diffidence.

When great ones, for great actions are bound,
    And sailed far i'th' voyage, they will not
Turn for their honour, but be rather drown'd;
    Nor can, perhaps: as those the gulph have shot.
Or not begin, or finish, is a rule,
    As well in *Mars's*, as in *Venus'* school.

Nerves would be cramp'd, the lazy blood would freeze,
    Limbs be unactive, should they longer lie;
And if they still should sacrifice to ease,
    Valour would fall into a lethargy:
Dull lakes are choak'd with melancholick mud;
    Motions do clear, and christallize a flood.

Aleyn's Poictiers

Revolt is recreant, when pursuit is brave;
Never to faint, doth purchase what we crave.

Machen's Dumb Knight.

Attempt the end, and never stand to doubt;
Nothing's so hard, but search will find it out.

Herrick

PETITION.

You hurt your innocence, suing for the guilty.

Johnson's Volpone

Virtue is either lame, or not at all;
And love a sacrilege, and not a saint,
When it bars up the way to mens petitions.

Beaumont and Fletcher's Valentinian.

How wretched is that suppliant, who must
Make suit to obtain that, which he fears to take?

Richard Brome's Mad couple well match'd

———————— They have robb'd me
Of all means to prefer my juſt complaints
With any promiſing hope to gain a hearing ;
Much leſs redreſs : Petitions not ſweetned
With gold, are but unſav'ry ; oft refus'd :
Or if receiv'd, are pocketted, not read.
A ſuitor's ſwelling tears by the glowing beams
Of chol'rick authority are dry'd up,
Before they fall ; or if ſeen, never pity'd.

Maſſinger's Emperor of the Eaſt.

———————— Petitions ſhall be drawn,
Humble in form ; but ſuch for matter
As the bold *Macedonian* youth would ſend
To men he did deſpiſe for luxury :
The firſt begets opinion of the world,
Which looks not far, but on the outſide dwells :
Th' other enforces courage in our own ;
For bold demands muſt boldly be maintain'd.

Suckling's Brennoralt.

P L A Y E R.

Is it not monſtrous that this player here,
But in a fiction, in a dream of paſſion,
Could force his ſoul ſo to his own conceit,
That, from her working, all his viſage warm'd :
Tears in his eyes, diſtraction in his aſpect,
A broken voice, and his whole function ſuting
With forms to his conceit ? and all for nothing ?
For *Hecuba* ?
What's *Hecuba* to him, or he to *Hecuba*
That he ſhould weep for her ? what would he do,
Had he the motive, and the cue for paſſion,
That I have ? he would drown the ſtage with tears,
And cleave the gen'ral ear with horrid ſpeech ;
Make mad the guilty, and appall the free,
Confound the ignorant, and amaze, indeed,
The very faculty of eyes and ears. ———————

Shakeſpear's Hamlet.

1. Speech

1. Speak the speech, I pray you, as I pronounc'd
It to you, trippingly on the tongue. But
If you mouth it, as many of our players
Do, I had as liefe, the town crier had
Spoke my lines: and do not faw the air too
Much with your hand thus, but ufe all gently;
For in the very torrent, tempeft, and,
As I may fay, whirl-wind of your paffion,
You muft acquire, and beget a temp'rance
That may give it fmoothnefs.   Oh, it offends
Me to the foul, to hear a robufticus
Periwig-pated fellow tear a paffion
To tatters, to very rags, to fplit the
Ears of the groundlings: who, for the moft part,
Are capable of nothing, but inexplicable
Dumb fhews, and noife: I could have fuch a fellow
Whip'd for o'erdoing termagant; it
Out-*Herods Herod.*   Pray you, avoid it.
2. I warrant your honour.
1. Be not too tame neither; but let your own
Difcretion be your tutor, fute the action
To the word, the word to the action;
With this fpecial obfervance, that you o'erftep
Not the modefty of nature; for any
Thing fo overdone is from the purpofe
Of playing; whofe end, both at the firft and
Now, was and is, to hold as 'twere the mirror
Up to nature; to fhew virtue her own
Feature, fcorn her own image, and the very
Age and body of the time, his form and
Preffure   Now this o'erdone, or come tardy
Of, tho' it makes th' unfkilful laugh, cannot
But make the judicious grieve: the cenfure
Of which one, muft in your allowance o'er weigh
A whole theatre of others.   Oh, there be
Players that I've feen play, and heard others
Praife, and that highly, not to fpeak it prophanely,
That neither having the accent of chriftian,

N

e gait of chriſtian, pagan, nor man,
'o ſtrutted, and bellow'd, that I have
ght ſome of nature's journeymen had made
and not made them well ; they imitated
nity ſo abominably !
hope, we have reform'd that indiff'rently
us,
! reform it altogether.
t thoſe that play your clowns, ſpeak no more
is ſet down for them : for there be of
i, that will themſelves laugh, to ſet on ſome
ity of barren ſpectators to
too ; though, in the mean time, ſome
ary queſtion of the play be
to be conſider'd : that' villainou ;
ews a moſt pitiful ambition
fool that uſes it.

       Shakeſpear's Hamlet.

—————Players
never more uncertain in their lives :
know not when to play, where to play, nor
to play; not when to play, for fearful fools ;
e to play, for puritan fools ; nor what
ay, for critical fools.

    Middleton's Mad World my Maſters.
——————— They abuſe our ſcene,
ay we live by vice, indeed 'tis true ;
e phyſicians by diſeaſes do,
to cure them : they do live we ſee
:ooks by pamp'ring prodigality ;
h are our fond accuſers. On the ſtage.

And [illegible] : hence the cause doth rise,
[illegible] are not won by th' ears, so well as eyes.
Partidge's Mirror Looking-Glass.

———————— To better in a play
Be [illegible] than himself indeed ;
How oft with danger of the field beset,
Or with some mountain would he unite
Himself? or over crucifixion weeping,
With, that with putting off a vizard, he
May put true inward sorrow lay aside?
The shews of things are better than themselves :
How does it stir within every part of us,
To hear our poets tell imagin'd fights,
And the strange blows that feigned courage gives !
When I'd *Achilles* near upon the stage
Speak honour, and the greatness of his soul,
Methinks, I too could on a *Phrygian* spear
Run boldly, and make tales for after times :
But when we come to act it in the deed,
Death mars this bravery, and th' ugly fears
Of the other world, fit on the proudest brow ;
And boasting valour loseth it's red cheek.

Nero.

P L E A S U R E.

Ease dulls the sp'rit ; each drop of fond delight
Allays the thirst, which glory doth excite.

Mirror for Magistrates,

All these fond pleasures, if fond things
Deserve so good a name,
Should not seduce a noble mind,
To stain itself with shame.
The time shall come, when all these same,
Which seem so rich with joy :
Like tyrants, shall torment thy mind,
And vex thee with annoy.

Brandon's Octavia to Antonius.

Pleasure is like a building, the more high,

The

The narrower still it grows; cedars die
Soonest at top.

Shakespear and Rowley's Birth of Merlin.

Since all earth's pleasures are so short and small;
The way t' enjoy 'em, is t' abjure 'em all.

Chapman's Bussy D'ambci..

Long lull'd asleep with scornful fortune's lies,
 A slave to pleasure, drown'd in base delights;
I made a cov'nant with my wand'ring eyes,
 To entertain them still with pleasant sights;
My heart enjoy'd all that was wish'd of late,
 Whilst it the height of happiness did cloy;
Still serv'd with dainty, but suspected meat,
 My soul with pleasure sick, was faint for joy:
All, with much care, what might procure mine ease,
 My will divin'd, obsequiously devis'd;
And who my fancy any way could please,
 As prais'd by me, was by all others priz'd.
Save serving me, none else could have deserv'd,
 Of whom whatever came, was held of weight;
My words and looks were carefully observ'd,
 And whom I grac'd, were had in honour straight;
For pomp and pow'r, far passing other kings
 Whilst too secure with drowsy thoughts i slumber'd,
My coffers still were full of precious things,
 Of which, as wealth least weigh'd, gold scarce was
          numb'red;
rear'd rare buildings, all emboss'd with gold;
 Made ponds for fishes; forests for wild beasts;
And with vain thoughts which could not be controul'd,
 Oft spent the day in sport, the night in feasts.
toss'd the elements with pow'r like Jove's;
 Driv'd water up, air down; a pleasant change:
or stately fountains, artificial groves,
 As common things, were not accounted strange.
With me; what more could any monarch crave?
 In all the parts of pomp, none could compare:
Myminions gallant councellors were grave;
 My guards were strong, my concubines were fair:

Yea, whilst light fortune my defects supply'd,
  I had all that could breed, as now I find,
In others wonder, in the owner pride:
  So puffing up the flesh to spoil the mind.
Thus with delight, long pressing pleasure's grapes,
  With fortune I carous'd, what men dear hold:
But ah! from misery none always scapes:
  One must be wretched once, or young, or old.
                              E. of *Sterline's Crasu*

Like dew upon the grass, when pleasure's sun
Shines on your virtues, all your virtue's done.
                    Marston's Insatiate County.

That pleasure is of all
  Most bountiful and kind,
That fades not straight, but leaves
  A living joy behind.
    T. Campion's Masque, at the E. of Somerset's Marriage
Thus grief and gladness still by turns do come,
But pleasure least while doth possess the room:
Long nights of grief may last; but lo, one day
Of shining comfort slideth soon away.
                              Goffe's Orestes

Farewell to thy enticing vanity,
Thou round gilt box, that doll deceive man's eye!
The wise man knows, when open thou art broke,
The treasure thou includ'st, is dust and smoke.
          Beaumont and *Fletcher's Four Plays in One*
——————————————— What is pleasure,
More than a lustful motion in the sense?
The prosecution full of anxious fears;
The end repentance.   Though content be call'd
The soul of action, and licentious man
Propounds it as the reason of his life;
Yet if intemp'rate action pursue it,
The pure end's lost, and ruin must attend it.
                              Nabbs's Microcosmus

Pleasure whose means are easy, in the end
Do lose themselves.   Things only are esteem'd

                                          And

And valu'd by their acquifition.
Should you win her delights without fome pains,
They would not relifh.

Nabbs's Microcofmus.

As dogs of *Nilus* drink a fnatch, and gone :
Sweets muft be tafted, and not glutted on.

Aleyn's Crefcay.

Henceforth, I'll ftrive to fly the fight of pleafure,
As of an harpy or a bafilisk ;
And when the flatt'rers, feal my ears with wax,
Took from that boat, that row'd with a deaf oar,
From the fweet tunes of the *Sicilian* fhore.

Marmyon's Holland's Leaguer.

Pleafure's a courtly miftrefs, a conceit
That fmiles and tickles without worth or weight :
Whofe fcatter'd reck'ning, when 'tis to be paid,
Is but repentance, lavifhly inlaid.

Cleveland.

Why ? would not eating, drinking, fleeping,
Education of children be half neglected,
Were it not for pleafure ? would underftanding
Embrace the truth, if it took not pleafure
In it ? what kind of men are thofe that oppugn
Pleafure ? doth not the courtier take pleafure
In honour ; the citizen in wealth ; the
Countryman in delights of health ; the
Academick in the myfteries of
Learning ? is there not ev'n in angels, a
Certain incomprehenfible pleafure ?

Parthomachia : Or Love's Load-ftone.

———————————— I defpife
Thefe fhort and empty pleafures, and how low
They ftand in my efteem ; which ev'ry peafant,
The meaneft fubject in my father's empire,
Enjoys as fully, in as high perfection
As he or I ; and which are had in common
By beafts as well as men, wherein they equal,
If not exceed us.   Pleafures to which we're led

C 2

Only

Only by fenfe, thofe creatures which have leaft
Of reafon, moft enjoy.

Denham's Sopby.

Ye gods, was it man's nature or his fate,
Betray'd him with fweet pleafure's poifon'd bait?
Which he, with all defigns of art, or pow'r,
Doth with unbridled appetite devour:
And as all poifons fuck the nobleft part,
Pleafure poffeffes firft the head and heart,
Intoxicating both: By them, fhe finds,
And burns the facred temples of our minds.

Denham.

Pleafures like wonders, quickly lofe their price,
When reafon or experience makes us wife.

Bifhop *King.*

In my delights I can no limits bear.
But, for what reafon never could be known,
Our joys have bounds, and our defires have none.

Crown's Caligula.

POETS. POETRY.

O facred poefy, thou fp'rit of *Roman* arts,
The foul of fcience, and the queen of fouls!
What prophane violence, almoft facrilege,
Hath here been offer'd thy divinity,
That thine own guiltlefs poverty fhould arm
Prodigious ignorance to wound thee thus?
For thence is all their force of argument
Drawn forth againft thee; or from the abufe
Of thy great powers in adult'rate brains:
When fp'rits, would men learn but to diftinguifh
And fet true diff'rence 'twixt thofe jaded wits
That run a broken pace for common hire,
And the high raptures of a happy mufe,
Bone on the wings of her immortal thought,
That kicks at earth with a difdainful heel,
And beats at heav'n's gates with her bright hoofs;
They would not then with fuch diftorted faces,
And defp'rate cenfures, ftab at poefy.

They

ey would admire bright knowledge, and their minds
ould ne'er defcend on fo unworthy objects
 gold or titles: they would dread far more,
 be thought ignorant, than be known poor.

Johnfon's Poetaſter.

rfe hath a middle nature; heav'n keeps fouls,
e grave keeps bodies, verfe the fame enrolls.

Dr. *Donne.*

hen heav'n would ſtrive to do the beſt it can,
d put an angel's ſpirit into man,
e utmoſt pow'r it hath, it then doth fpend,
hen to the world a poet it doth intend:
at little diff'rence 'twixt the gods and us,
 them confirm'd, diſtinguiſh'd only thus:
hom they in birth ordain to happy days,
e gods commit their glory to our praiſe;
 eternal life when they diſſolve their breath,
e likewiſe ſhare a fecond pow'r by death.

Drayton's E. *of Surry to Lady Geraldine.*

verfe may find him who a fermon flies;
d turn delight into a facrifice.

Herbert.

u dare not, fir, blaſpheme the virtuous ufe
 facred poetry; nor the fame traduce
 poets; who not alone immortal be,
t can give others immortality.
ts that can men into ſtars tranſlate,
d hurl men down under the feet of fate:
was not *Achilles*' fword, but *Homer*'s pen,
at made brave *Hector* die the beſt of men:
d if that pow'rful *Homer* likewiſe would,
llen had been a hag, and *Troy* had ſtood.

Richard Brome's 'Sparagus Garden.*

w ſhall my debts be paid? or can my fcores
 clear'd with verfes to my creditors?
xameter's no ſterling; and I fear
hat the brain coins, goes fcarce for currant there.

C 3
Can

Can meter cancel bonds? is there a time
Ever to hope to wipe out chalk with rhime?
Or if I now were hurrying to a jail,
Are the nine mules held sufficient bail?
Would they to any composition come,
If we should mortgage our *Elysium*,
Tempe, Parnassus, and the golden streams
Of *Tagus*, and *Pactolus*, those rich dreams
Of active fancy?

Randolph

Clowns for posterity may cark and care;
That cannot out-live death but in an heir:
By more than wealth we propagate our names,
That trust not to successions, but our fames.

Ibid

A poet's then exact in ev'ry part
That is born one by nature, nurst by art:
Whose happy mixture both of skill and fate,
Makes the most sudden thought elaborate:
Whose easy strains a flowing sense does fit;
Unforc'd expressions, and unravish'd wit:
Words fill'd with equal subject, such as brings
To chosen language, high and chosen things.
Harsh reason clear as day, as smooth as sleep,
Glide here like rivers, even still though deep:
Discords grow musick; grief itself delight;
Horror when he describes, leaves off t'affright.
Sullen philosophy does learn to go
In lightest dressings, and becomes them too.

Dr. *Lluellin*

Poets are truly poor; but only then,
When each a hero lacks for his own pen.
They pine when mighty arguments are scant;
And not, when they that trifle, treasure, want.
As at such dearth they languish, so they seem
To swell, when they have got a plenteous theme;
For rashly then the muses take their flight:
Yet as a man, o'erjoy'd at sudden sight

Of treasure found, grows jealous, and through care,
Lest others in his prize should claim a share,
Bears hastily from that which he did find
Much less away, than what he leaves behind :
So, whilst thus rashly I convey to fame
Your virtues, I so few of them proclaim,
That many more are left behind unprais'd,
Than those, which on this poem's wings are rais'd.
How glad will all discreeter poets be,
Because, whilst in their choice they disagree,
They this imperfect present shall prevent,
Which darkens you, to whom it lustre meant ;
Or rather it does quite extinguish me ;
Who looking up to you, do only see
I by a fainting taper lose my aim,
And lifting it too high, put out the flame.

Sir W. Davenant to the King.

Th' eternal cause, in their immortal lines
Was taught ; and poets were the first divines :
And *Moses*, in the old original,
Ev'n God, the poet of the world doth call.

Denham.

Poets by dangers, like old soldiers taught,
Grow wise ; and shun the fame which once they fought.

Prologue to Sir R. Howard's Vestal Virgin.

With equal eagerness contend
Some to cry down, and others to commend :
So easy 'tis to judge, so hard to do ;
There's so much frailty, yet such prying too ;
That who their poetry to view expose,
Must be prepar'd to be abus'd in prose.

Alexander Brome on Richard Brome.

A poem's life and death dependeth still
Not on the poet's wit, but reader's will.

Alex. Brome.

POLICY. POLITICIAN.

For this chaos,
This lump of projects, ere it be lick'd o'er,

C 4

Is

Is like a bear's conception : Stratagems
B'ing but begot, and not got out ; are like
Charg'd cannons not difcharg'd ; they do no harm
Nor good : True policy, breeding in the brain,
Is like a bar of iron, whofe ribs b'ing broken,
And fotten'd i'th' fire, you then may forge it
Into a fword to kill, or to a helmet,
To defend life : 'Tis therefore wit to try
All fafhions, ere y' apparel villany.

Marlo s Luft's Dominion.

———————————— A precifian
In ftate, is a ridic'lous miracle ;
Friendfhip is but a vizor, beneath which
A wife man laughs to fee whole families
Ruin'd ; upon whofe miferable pile
He mounts to glory.

Chapman and *Shirley's* Admiral of France.

Juftice to live, doth nought but juftice need,
But policy muft ftill on mifchief feed :
Untruth, for all his ends, truth's name doth fue in ;
None fafely live, but thofe that ftudy ruin.

Chapman's Revenge of Buffey D'ambois.

For who obferves ftrict policy's true laws,
Shifts his proceeding to the varying caufe.

Drayton's Barons Wars.

A politician, *Proteus*-like, muft alter
His face and habit ; and like water, feem
Of the fame colour that the veffel is
That doth contain it ; varying his form
With the camelion at each object's change.
My tongue muft
With paffionate oaths and proteftations,
With fighs, fmooth glances, and officious terms,
Spread artificial mifts before the eyes
Of cred'lous fimplicity : He that will be high,
Muft be a parafite, to fawn and lie.

Mafon's Mulcaffes.

He

He that deals all by ſtrength, his wit is ſhallow :
When a man's head goes thro', each limb will follow
Webſter's White Devil.

He that can compaſs me, and know my drift ,
May ſay he hath put a girdle 'bout the world,
And ſounded all her quick ſands.
Webſter's Dutcheſs of Malſy.

————— ————This 'tis for a puny
In policy's Protean ſchool, to try concluſions
With one that hath commenc'd and gone out doctor.
If I diſcover what but now he bragg'd of,
I ſhall not be believ'd : If I fall off
From him, his threats and actions go together ;
And there's no hope of ſafety, till I get
A plummet, that may ſound his deepeſt councils.
I muſt obey and ſerve him.   Want of skill
Now makes me play the rogue againſt my will.
Maſſinger's Duke of Milan.

The greateſt politician may be
Deceiv'd ſometimes ; wit without brains we ſee.
Shirley's Witty Fair One.

————— So politicians thrive,
That with their crabbed ſaces, and ſly tricks
Legerdemain, ducks, cringes, formal beards,
Criſp'd hairs, and punctual cheats, do wriggle in
Their heads firſt, like a fox, to rooms of ſtate,
Then the whole body follows.
John Ford's Lover's Melancholy.

Policy will, ſome ſeeming cauſe be had,
To make that good, which juſtice knows for bad
Jones's Adraſta.

——————————Theſe great ſtateſmen,
When time has made bold with the king and ſubject,
Throwing down all fence that ſtood 'twixt their pow'r
And others right; are, on a change,
Like wanton ſalmons coming in with floods,
That leap o'er wires and nets ; and make their way,
To be at their return, to ev'ry one a prey.
Suckling's Aglaura.

—————————— Your politicians
Have evermore a taint of vanity ;
As hasty still to shew, and boast a plot,
As they are greedy to contrive it.
               Sir W. Davenant's Fair Fave

P O P U L A R I T Y.

—————— I love the people ;
But do not like to stage me to their eyes :
Though it do well, I do not relish well
Their loud applause and *Ave's* vehement :
Nor do I think the man of safe discretion,
That does affect it.
              Shakespear's Measure for Mea

Ourself, and *Bushy, Bagot* here, and *Green*
Observ'd his courtship to the common people :
How he did seem to dive into their hearts,
With humble and familiar courtesy ;
What rev'rence he did throw away on slaves ;
Wooing poor craftsmen with the craft of smiles,
And patient under-bearing of his fortune,
As 'twere to banish their affects with him.
Off goes his bonnet to an oyster-wench ;
A brace of draymen bid, God speed him well :
And had the tribute of his supple knee,
With——Thanks, my countrymen, my loving frie
As were our *England* in reversion his,
And he our subjects next degree in hope.
              Shakespear's King Richar

Who hates not the vulgar, deserves not love
Of the virtuous : And to affect praise of
That we despise, how ridiculous is it ?
              Chapman's Widow's T

Look how *Thames*, enrich'd with many a flood,
   And goodly river, (that have made their graves,
And bury'd both their names, and all their good,
   Within his greatness, to augment his waves)
Glides on with pomp of waters, unwithstood,
   Unto the ocean ; which his tribute craves,

And lays up all his wealth within that pow'r,
Which in itself all greatnefs doth devour :

So flock the mighty, with their foll'wing train,
  Unto the all-receiving *Bullingbroke* ;
Who wonders at himfelf, how he fhould gain
  So many hearts as now his party took ;
And with what eafe, and with how flender pain,
  His fortune gives him more than he could look :
What he imagin'd never could be wrought,
Is pour'd upon him far beyond his thought :

So, often, things which feem at firft in fhew,
  Without the compafs of accomplifhment ;
Once ventur'd on, to that fuccefs do grow,
  That ev'n the authors do admire th'event :
So many means which they did never know,
  Do fecond their defigns, and do prefent
Strange unexpected helps ; and chiefly then,
When th'actors are reputed worthy men.
               Daniel's Civil War.

——————————Popular men,
They muft create new monfters, and then quell 'em,
To make their arts feem nothing.   Would you have
Such an *Herculean* actor in the fcene,
And not his *Hydra ?* They mut fweat no lefs
To fit their properties, than to exprefs their parts.
               Johnfon's Catiline.

I never courted popular applaufe ;
Feafted the men of action ; or labour'd
By prodigal gifts to draw the needy foldier,
The tribunes or centurions to a faction ;
Of which, I would rife up the head gainft him.
I hold no place of ftrength, fortrefs, or caftle
In my command, that can give fanctuary
To malcontents, or countenance rebellion :
I've built no palaces to face the court ;
Nor do my follow'rs brav'ry fhame his train ;
And though I cannot blame my fate for want,
        C 6   My

My competent means of life deferves no envy ;
In what then am I dangerous?
Maffinger's Emperor of the

1. How full of hidden ambiguities
Grow thefe diftracted times?
The factious common's giddy cenfure ftand
So ftrange and doubtful, that 'twere policy indeed
To found 'em to the bottom ;
2. To be a crouching, crawling, fawn'ng cur,
To lick the lazy hands of prating priefts,
With proteftations of integrity
Devoted wholly to them;
With true compunction of unfeigned grief,
Submiffively to crave their gracious pardon :
To paw the ragged multitude with praife
Of their ingenious care and fervent love
For prefervation of the commonwealth ;
To promife fair rewards to froward fools ;
Perhaps, with dirty feet to mire with fawnings,
And then be beaten with the fhameful ftaff
Of foul reproach :
To do all this, were to be born a fool ;
To live a flave, and die a coward.
Death! I will ftand between the counter-buffs
Of thefe devouring ftorms in fpite of hell ;
Nor prieft, nor peafant fhall inforce me ftoop
An inch to either : As I have liv'd, I'll fall ;
Or freed from both, or rent up root and all.
Hemmings's Jews Tr

P O V E R T Y.

——————— O known evil,
Rich fly the poor, as good men fhun the devil!
Heywood's Woman kill'd with Kin

Poverty, thou bane of chaftity,
Poifon of beauty, broker of maidenheads!
I fee when force, nor wit can fcale the hold,
Wealth muft ; fhe'll ne'er be won, that defies gold
But lives there fuch a creature? Oh, 'tis rare,

To find a woman chaste, that's poor and fair !

Dekker and *Webster's Westward Hoe.*

————————A poor spirit,
Is poorer than a poor purse.

Tourneur's Atheist's Tragedy.

————————The rich
Have wakeful nights, whilst the poor man's turf
Begets a peaceful sleep ; in which they're blest
From frigid fears all day, at night with rest.

Goffe's Careless Shepherdess.

Poor men are born to wrongs; low are their ranks ;
The more they're trod on, the more they must give
thanks.

Dauborne's Poor Man's Comfort.

With poverty in love we only close,
Because our lovers it most truly shews ;
When they who in that blessed age did move,
Knew neither poverty, nor want of love ;
The hatred which they bore was only this,
That ev'ry one did hate to do amiss :
Their fortune still was subject to their will ;
Their want, O happy ! was the want of ill.

Brown's Pastorals.

1. Our want with this philosophy doth well
Agree ; but yet I hope your constancy
Will yield it a far less uneasy task
To commend poverty, than suffer it.
2. Not so, for wit is heav'n's gift to those
Are shap'd of purer clay; but patience
Each noble mind bestows upon itself.

Marriage-Broker.

To mortal men great loads allotted be ;
But of all packs, no pack like poverty.

Herrick.

P O W E R.

When pow'r, that may command, so much descends ;
Their bondage, whom it stoops to, it intends.

Johnson's Sejanus.

————Oh,

—————————Oh, 'tis excellent
To have a giant's ftrength! but it is tyrannous
To ufe it like a giant.

Shakefpear's Meafure for Meafu

For pow'r is proud, till it look down to fear;
Though only fafe, by ever looking there.

Lord Brooke's Alaba

In all ftates, pow'r which oppreffeth fpirits,
Imprifons nature, empire difinherits.

Lord Brooke's Muftaph

Pow'r, doth what likes, in her inferiors move;
As we are fefs'd, fo pay we hate, or love.

Lord Brooke's Alaba

Inftead of thefe, I faw the veils of pow'r,
Practice, and pomp, fpecious hypocrify,
Rent from her face, ev'n while fhe did devour:
I faw thofe glorious ftiles of government,
God, laws, religion, (wherein tyrants hide
The wrongs they do, and all the woes we bide,)
Wounded, prophan'd, deftroy'd: pow'r is unwife,
That thinks in pomp to mafk her tyrannies.

Ibi

The violent thunder is ador'd by thofe
Are dafh'd in pieces by it.

Webfter's White Dev

Pow'r's a ftrange thing, which ev'n additions make
    Weak, and difpos'd to fall: Few can digeft
The fwelling cheer of fortune: If you take
    But one difh more, you prejudice the reft:
Some fortunes, that have flow'd gently before,
Run over, if you add one honour more.

Aleyn's Henry VI

With what a diff'rence nature's palate taftes
    The fweeter draught which art provides her, pow'r
Since pow'r, pride's wine, but high in relifh lafts
    Whilft funning new; for time does turn it four?

Y

Yet pow'r, earth's tempting fruit, heav'n firſt did plant,
  From man's firſt ſerpent ſ ſe, ambition's reach ;
Elſe *Eden* could not ſerve ambition's want ;
  Whom no command can rule, nor council teach.

Pow'r is that luſcious wine, which does the bold,
  The wiſe, and noble moſt intoxicate ;
Adds time to youth, and takes it from the old ;
  Yet I by ſurfeit this elixir hate.
Sir *W*. *Davenant's Gondibert*.

Yield not in ſtorms of ſtate to that diſlike
  Which from the people does to rulers grow ;
Pow'r, fortune's ſail, ſhould not for threat'nings ſtrike ;
  In boats beſtorm'd, all check at thoſe that row.
Ibid.

For he who ſecrets, pow'r's chief treaſure, ſpends,
To purchaſe friendſhip, friendſhip dearly buys :
Since pow'r ſeeks great confed'rates, more than friends.
Ibid.

———— My reward is pow'r ;
An outward trifle, bought with inward peace ;
Got in an age, and rifled in an hour ;
When ſev'riſh love, the people's ſit ſhall ceaſe.
Ibid.

But how men gain their pow'r, the gods do not
So much regard ; as how 'tis us'd, when got
E. of *Orrery's Tryphon*.

Oh wretched he, who call'd abroad by pow'r,
To know himſelf can never find an hour !
Strange to himſelf, but to all others known ;
Lends ev'ry one his life, and uſes none :
So ere he taſted life, to death he goes ;
And himſelf loſes, ere himſelf he knows.
Crown's Thyeſtes.

But pow'r, it ſeems, can change the names of things ;
Call treaſon virtue, and make rebels kings.
Crown's Charles VIII. *of France*.

P R A I S E.

PRAISE.

Or who would ever care to do brave deed,
   Or strive in virtue others to excel;
If none should yield him his deserved meed,
   Due praise, that is the spur of doing well?
For if good were not praised more than ill,
None would chuse goodness, of his own free will.
Spenser's Tears of the Muse.

One good deed, dying tonguelefs,
Slaughters a thousand waiting upon that:
Our praises are our wages.
Shakespear's Winter's Tale.

The worthiness of praise distains his worth;
If he that's prais'd, himself bring the praise forth:
What the repining enemy commends,
'That breath, fame blows; that praise, sole pure tran-
   scends.
Shakespear's Troilus and Cressida.

Your praise is come too swiftly home before you:
Know you not, master, to some kind of men,
'Their graces serve them but as enemies?
No more do yours; your virtues, gentle master,
Are sanctify'd and holy traitors to you.
Oh, what a world is this, when what is comely
Envenoms him that bears it!
Shakespear's As you like it.

'Tis grown almost a danger to speak true
Of any good mind; now, there are so few.
'The bad, by number are so fortify'd,
As what they've lost t' expect, they dare deride:
So both the prais'd and praiser suffer: yet
For others ill, ought none their good neglect.
Johnson's Forest.

That praise contents me more which one imparts,
   Of judgment found, though of a mean degree;
Than praise from princes, void of princely parts,
   Who have more wealth, but not more wit than he.
E. of *Sterline's Cræsus.*

And

…at is moſt commended at this time,
…ing ages may account a crime.

E. of Sterline's Darius.

…ch vain minds, it may be truly ſaid,
…ve falſe praiſe, of falſe ſcorns are afraid.

Lord Brooke on Fame and Honour.

…ger a defence argues a ſtrong
…ion ; and too veh'ment a praiſe,
…a ſuſpicion of others worthy diſparagement.
…rs to bright day, it ill befits ;
…ines can vent themſelves, and not good wits.

Marſton's What you will.

…aiſe, the brow of common men doth ring ;
…nly girts the temples of a king

Marſton's Second Part of Antonio and Mellida.

…nade ſhort the hours that time made long ;
…ain'd mine ears to his moſt pleaſing tongue :
…have waited on your praiſes worth,
…tch'd his words ere he could get them forth:
…e had ſpoke, and ſomething by the way
…roke off, that he was about to ſay,
…n mind where from his tale he fell,
…on him the reſidue to tell.
…would ſay, how ſweet a prince is he !
…have prais'd him, but for praiſing thee ;
…proceed, I would entreat and wooe ;
…t to eaſe him, help to praiſe thee too.

rayton's Counteſs of Salisbury to the Black Prince.

…htens them with commendation : Praiſe
…reflection doth from virtue riſe :
…air encomiums do virtue raiſe
…igher acts : to praiſe is to adviſe.
…men what they are, we let them ſee,
…reſent to them, what they ſhould be.

Aleyn's Poictiers.

——————— To refuſe juſt praiſe,
…treme, worſe, than man's over-weening
…of himſelf.

Nabbs's Hannibal and Scipio.

A *Venus* and *Diana* mixt in one
　　She was; whose wit was ev'n in greenest years
Flowing as nectar; ripe as autumn shewn.
　　And crown'd with graces, envy'd by white hairs:
Which who can tell? and yet who cannot tell?
Well may I praise her, but not praise her well.

To do it meanly, were no less disgrace,
　　Than a coarse garment to a princely dame;
Or homely painting to a lovely face;
　　Or a brass setting to a precious gem.
Think not weak muse by thy low song to raise her;
'Tis praise enough, that none enough can praise her.
　　　　　　　　　　　　　　　　　　　Bar

Praise is but virtue's shadow; who court her,
Doth more the handmaid than the dame admire.
　　　　　　　　　　　　　Heath's Clarast
This is new court thrift; they are not able
To maintain flatterers, therefore bely
Each other, with their own praises.
　　　　　　　　　　Sir *W. Davenant's Si*

———————————— Now he brings
　　The youths to view the temple built for praise;
Where olive for th' *Olympian* victor springs;
　　Myrtle, for lovers; and for war's triumph, bays.

These, as rewards of praise, about it grew;
　　For lib'ral praise, from an abundant mind,
Does ev'n the conqueror of fate subdue;
　　Since heav'n's good king is captive to the kind.
　　　　　　　　　　Sir *W. Davenant's Gondib*
Commend but sparingly whom thou dost love;
But less condemn whom thou dost not approve;
Thy friend like flatt'ry, too much praise doth wrong
And too sharp censure shews an evil tongue.
　　　　　　　　　　　　　　　　　Denb

Hark how they bandy praise, and flatt'ry round!
Each takes her turn to catch it at rebound;
　　　　　　　　　　　　　　　　　W1

Whilst we defertlefs fools muft patience feign,
And praife ourfelves, if any praife we'll gain.

Crown's Calife.

PRAYER.

We, ignorant of ourfelves,
Beg often our own harms ; which the wife pow'rs
Deny us for our good ; fo find we proft
By lofing of our prayers.

Shakefpear's Antony and Chefatra.

That high all-feer, which I dallied with,
Hath turn'd my feigned prayer on my head,
And giv'n in earneft, what I begg'd in jeft.
Thus doth he force the fwords of wicked men,
To turn their own points on their mafters bofoms.

Shakefpear's King Richard III.

———————————————— Pray I cannot,
Though inclination be as fharp as will ;
My ftronger guilt defeats my ftrong intent :
And, like a man to double bufinefs bound,
I ftand in paufe where I fhall firft begin,
And both negleft. What if this curfed hand
Were thicker than itfelf with brother's blood ?
Is there not rain enough in the fweet heav'ns
To wafh it white as fnow ? whereto ferves mercy,
But to confront the vifage of offence ?
And what's in prayer, but this two-fold force,
To be foreftalled ere we come to fall,
Or pardon'd being down ? then I'll look up ;
My fault is paft ——— But oh ! what form of pray'r
Can ferve my turn ? forgive me my foul murther !
That cannot be, fince I am ftill poffeft
Of thofe effefts, for which I did the murther ;
My crown, my own ambition, and my queen.
What then ? what refts ?
Try, what repentance can : what can it not ?
Yet what can it, when one cannot repent ?
Oh wretched ftate ! oh bofom, black as death !
Oh limed foul, that, ftruggling to be free,

Art

Art more engag'd! help, angels! make aſſay!
Bow, ſtubborn knees; and, heart, with ſtrings of ſt
Be ſoft as ſinews of the new-born babe!
All may be well ――――

Shakeſpear's Ham

When we of hopes, or helps, are quite bereaven,
Our humble pray'rs have entrance into heaven.

John Ford's Lover's Sacri

Temporal bleſſings heav'n doth often ſhare
Unto the wicked, at the good man's pray'r.

Qua

Man's plea to man, is, that he never more
Will beg; and that he never begg'd before:
Man's plea to God is, that he did obtain
A former ſuit, and therefore ſues again.
How good a God we ſerve; that when we ſue,
Makes his old gifts th' examples of his new!

1

―――――― She will out pray
A preacher at ſaint *Ant'lin's*, and divides
The day in exerciſe; I did commend
A great preciſian to her, for her woman;
Who tells me, that her lady makes her quilt
Her ſmocks before for kneeling.

Main's City-Ma

Mark, *Birtha*, this unrighteous war of pray'r!
  Like wrangling ſtates, you ask a monarch's aid
When you are weak, that you may better dare
  Lay claim, to what your paſſion would invade.

Long has th' ambitious world rudely preferr'd
  Their quarrels, which they call their pray'rs, to hea
And thought that heav'n would like themſelves have e
  Depriving ſome, of what's to others giv'n.

Thence modern faith becomes ſo weak and blind,
  Thinks heav'n in ruling other worlds employ'd,
And is not mindful of our abject kind,
  Becauſe all ſutes are not by all enjoy'd.

I

How firm was faith, when humble futes for need,
  Not choice were made ? then, free from all defpair,
As mod'rate birds, who fing for daily feed :
  Like birds, our fongs of praife included pray'r.
Sir *W Davenant's Gondibert.*

He who this builder's building did create,
  Has an apartment here triangular ;
Where *Aftragon* three fanes did dedicate,
  To days of praife, of penitence and pray'r.

To thefe, from diff'rent motives, all proceed ;
  For when difcov'ries they on nature gain,
They praife high heav'n, which makes their works
    fucceed :
  But when it fails, in penitence complain.

If after praife, new bleffings are not giv'n,
  Nor mourning penitence can ills repair ;
Like practis'd beggars, they follicit heav'n,
  And will prevail by violence of pray'r.

The temple built for pray'r, can neither boaft
  The builder's curious art, nor does declare,
By choice materials he intended coft ;
  To fhew, that nought fhould need to tempt to pray'r.

No bells are here ; unhing'd are all the gates :
  Since craving in diftrefs is natural,
All lies fo ope, that none for entrance waits ;
  And thofe whom faith invites, can need no call.

The great have by diftinction here no name ;
  For all fo cover'd come, in grave difguife,
To fhew none come for decency or fame,
  That all are ftrangers to each others eyes.
Id.

How far is it to heav'n, that yet this lady's
Mournings are not heard ? for if they were, my
Suff'rings and my guilt would cefe ; or cannot
Our petitions climb, and get accefs as
Nimbly as our faults ? O this is it, that

So

So emboldens vex'd humanity; makes
Us complain. Those undiscern'd, immortal
Governors, are often in
Their bounty flow, in justice too severe;
And give not what we beg, but what we fear.

Sir *W. Davenant's Platonick*

Can pray'rs to all alike so gentle be,
Since all the world's devotions disagree?
None beg the same; the pray'rs of all the best
Are little more than curses for the rest.

Sir *Robert Howard's Vesta*

P R E F E R M E N T

When a noble nature's rais'd,
   It brings friends joy, foes grief, posterity fam
In him the times, no less than prince, are prais
   And by his rise, in active men, his name
      Doth emulation stir:
      To the dull, a spur
It is: to th' envious meant
A mere upbraiding grief, and tort'ring punishm

Johnson's Und

———— Whoe'er is rais'd,
For worth he has not; he is tax'd, not prais'd.

Johnson's Ep

Many such ends have fall'n on such proud honou
No more because the men on whom they fell
Grew insolent, and left their virtue's state;
Than for their hugeness, that procur'd their hat
And therefore little pomp in men most great,
Makes mightily and strongly to the guard
Of what they win by chance or just reward:
Great and immodest braveries again,
Like statues, much too high made for their base
Are overturn'd as soon as giv'n their places.

Chapman's Revenge of Bussy D'

There is a deep nick in time's restless wheel
For each man's good; when which nick con
   strikes:

As rhetorick, yet works not perfuafion,
But only is a mean to make it work ;
So no man rifeth by his real merit,
But when it cries clink to his raier's fpirit.
Many will fay, that cannot rife at all,
Man's firft hour's rife is firft ftep to his fall :
I'll venture that ; men that fall low muft die,
As well as men caft headlong from the sky.

Chapman's Buffy D'ambois.

For when that men of merit grow ungrac'd,
  And by her fautors, ignorance held in,
And parafites in good mens rooms are plac'd,
  Only to footh the higheft in their fin ;
From thofe whofe skill and knowledge is debas'd,
  There many ftrange enormities begin.

Drayton's Barons Wars.

Others that ftemm'd the current of the time,
Whence I had fall'n, ftrove fuddenly to climb.

Like the camelion, whilft time turns the hue,
  And with falfe *Proteus* puts on fundry fhapes ;
This change fcarce gone, a fecond doth enfue ;
  One fill'd, another for promotion gapes :
Thus do they fwarm like flies about the brim ;
Some drown'd, and fome do with much danger fwim.

Drayton's Pierce Gaveffen.

When knaves come to preferment, they rife as
Gallows are rais'd in the *Low Countries,* one
Upon another's fhoulders.

Webfter's White Devil.

For places in the court, are but like beds
In the hofpital ; where this man's head lies
At that man's foot, and fo lower and lower.

Webfter's Duchefs of Malfi.

If on the fudden he begins to rife ;
No man that lives can count his enemies

Middleton's Trick to catch the Old One.

'Tis

'Tis not advancement that I love alone;
'Tis love of shelter, to keep shame unknown.
Middleton's *Mayor of Quinborou*

———————— All preferment
That springs from sin and lust shoots up quickly;
As gard'ners crops do in the rott'nest grounds:
So is all means rais'd from base prostitution,
Ev'n like a sallad growing upon a dunghill.
Middleton's *Women beware Wom*

————He who cannot merit
Preferment by employments; let him bare
His throat unto the *Turkish* cruelty;
Or die or live a slave without redemption.
John Ford's *Lady's Tri*

What throngs of great impediments besiege
The virtuous mind? So thick, they jostle
One another as they come.   Hath vice a
Charter got, that none must rise, but such, who
Of the devil's faction are? The way to
Honour is not evermore the way to
Hell: A virtuous man may climb   Let the
Flatterer sell his lies elsewhere; it is
Unthrifty merchandize to change my gold
For breath.
Sir *W. Davenant*'s *Cruel Broth*

P R I D E.

So proud she shined in her princely state,
  Looking to heav'n, for earth she did disdain;
And sitting high, for lowly she did hate.
  Lo! underneath her scornful feet, was lain
  A dreadfull dragon with a hideous train:
And in her hand she held a mirror bright,
  Wherein her face she often viewed fain,
And in her self-lov'd semblance took delight;
For she was wond'rous fair, as any living wight.

Of grisly *Pluto* she the daughter was,
  And sad *Proserpina*, the queen of hell;
Yet did she think her peerless worth to pass
  That parentage, with pride so did she swell:
And thund'ring *Jove* that high in heav'n doth dwell,
And wield the world, she claimed for her sire;
  Or if that any else did *Jove* excell;
For to the highest she did still aspire·
Or, if ought higher were than that, did it desire.
And proud *Lucifera* men did her call.——
Spencer's Fairy Queen.

He that is proud eats up himself. Pride is
His own glass, his own trumpet, his own chronicle;
And whatever praises itself but in
The deed, devours the deed in the praise.
Shakespear's Troilus and Cressida.

——Pride hath no other glass
To shew itself, but pride; for supple knees
Feed arrogance, and are the proud man's fees.
Ibid.

Let this example move th'insolent man,
Not to grow proud, and careless of the gods:
It is an odious wisdom to blaspheme,
Much more to slighten or deny their pow'rs.
For whom the morning saw so great and high;
Thus low, and little, 'fore the eve doth lie.
Johnson's Sejanus.

How blind is pride! What eagles are we still
In matters that belong to other men,
What beetles in our own?
Chapman's All Fools.

How poor a thing is pride! When all as slave,
Differ but in their fetters, not their graves.
Daniel's Civil War.

Pride by presumption bred, when at a height,
  Encount'ring with contempt, both march in ire;
And 'twixt 'em bring base cruelty to light;
  The loathsome off-spring of a hated sire.
E. of *Sterline's Alexandrean Tragedy.*

'Tis not advancement that I love alone :
'Tis love of shelter, to keep shame unknown.
Middleton's Mayor of Quinborough.

——————— All preferment
That springs from sin and lust shoots up quickly ;
As gard'ners crops do in the rott'nest grounds :
So is all means rais'd from base prostitution,
Ev'n like a sallad growing upon a dunghill.
Middleton's Women beware Women.

————He who cannot merit
Preferment by employments ; let him bare
His throat unto the *Turkish* cruelty ;
Or die or live a slave without redemption.
John Ford's Lady's Trial.

What throngs of great impediments besiege
The virtuous mind ? So thick, they jostle
One another as they come.   Hath vice a
Charter got, that none must rise, but such, who
Of the devil's faction are ? The way to
Honour is not evermore the way to
Hell : A virtuous man may climb   Let the
Flatterer tell his lie elsewhere ; it is
Unthrifty merchandize to change my gold
For breath.
Sir *W Davenant's Cruel Brother.*

P R I D E.

So proud she shined in her princely state,
  Looking to heav'n, for earth she did disdain ;
And sitting high, for lowly she did hate.
  Lo ! underneath her scornful feet, was lain
  A dreadfull dragon with a hideous train :
And in her hand she held a mirror bright,
  Wherein her face she often viewed fain,
And in her self-lov'd semblance took delight ;
For she was wond'rous fair, as any living wight.

Of

Of grifly *Pluto* fhe the daughter was,
   And fad *Proferpina*, the queen of hell;
Yet did fhe think her peerlefs worth to pafs
   That parentage, with pride fo did fhe fwell:
And thund'ring *Jove* that high in heav'n doth dwell,
And wield the world, fhe claimed for her fire;
   Or if that any elfe did *Jove* excell;
For to the higheft fhe did ftill afpire:
Or, if ought higher were than that, did it defire.
And proud *Lucifera* men did her call.————
Spenfer's Fairy Queen.

He that is proud eats up himfelf. Pride is
His own glafs, his own trumpet, his own chronicle;
And whatever praifes itfelf but in
The deed, devours the deed in the praife.
Shakefpear's Troilus and Creffida.

————————Pride hath no other glafs
To fhew itfelf, but pride; for fupple knees
Feed arrogance, and are the proud man's fees.
Ibid.

Let this example move th'infolent man,
Not to grow proud, and carelefs of the gods:
It is an odious wifdom to blafpheme,
Much more to flighten or deny their pow'rs.
For whom the morning faw fo great and high;
Thus low, and little, 'fore the eve doth lie.
Johnfon's Sejanus.

How blind is pride! What eagles are we ftill
In matters that belong to other men,
What beetles in our own?
Chapman's All Fools,

How poor a thing is pride! When all as flave,
Differ but in their fetters, not their graves.
Daniel's Civil War.

Pride by prefumption bred, when at a height,
   Encount'ring with contempt, both march in ire;
And 'twixt 'em bring bafe cruelty to light;
   The loathfome off-fpring of a hated fire.
E. of Sterline's Alexandrean Tragedy.

1. Are you not proud of your cloaths?
Why then you were never proud of any thing;
For therein chiefly confisteth pride ; for you
Never faw pride pictur'd, but in gay attire.
2. True ; but in my opinion, pride might as well
Be pourtray'd in any other shape ; being
The caufes thereof are fo fev'ral and
Divers : as fome are proud of their ftrength, although
That pride coft them the lofs of a limb or
Two, by over-daring : Some are proud of
Their humour ; although in that humour, they
Be often knock'd for being fo : Some are
Proud of their drink, although that liquid
Operation caufe them to wear a night-cap
Three weeks after : Some are proud of their good
Parts, although they were never put to better
Ufes, than the enjoying of a common
Strumpet's company : And fome are only
Made proud, by the favour of a waiting-woman.

Taylour's Hog hath loft his Pearl.

————————I believe cunning
Court ladies chufe fome pretty venial errors,
To fet perfection off: For fhould you not
Ufurp a handfome pride, your fame would lie
Like unwall'd cities, open to the prey
Of each invading youth. Did you not fhew
A fcorn, you would deferve it.

Habbington's Queen of Arragon.

He like a high-fwol'n and impetuous tide,
Bore all before him ; rais'd to fuch a pride
As did his own approaching ruin fhew,
And draw it on : Plethorick bodies fo,
From whence difeafes of themfelves do breed,
The feeds of death in that ftrong fulnefs feed.

May's Edward III.

I'll offer, and I'll fuffer no abufe,
Becaufe I'm proud ; pride is of mighty ufe.

Th;

e affectation of a pompous name,
s oft set wits and heroes in a flame :
lumes, and buildings, and dominions wide,
e oft the noble monuments of pride.

Crown's Caligula.

PRODIGALITY.

hat will this come to ? He commands us to
wide, and give great gifts, and all out of
empty coffer : Nor will he know
is purse, or yield me this——
shew him what a beggar his heart is,
'ng of no pow'r to make his wishes good ;
is promises fly so beyond his state,
hat what he speaks is all in debt ; he owes for ev'ry
  word :
e is so kind, that he pays inter'st for't :
is land's put to their books. Well, would I were
ntly put out of office, ere I were forc'd.

Shakespear's Timon.

——————————Prodigal men
el not their own stock wasting.

Johnson's Catiline.

at which made him gracious in your eyes,
d gilded over his imperfections,
wasted and consumed ev'n like ice,
hich by the vehemence of heat dissolves,
d glides to many rivers ; so his wealth,
at felt a prodigal hand, hot in expence,
lted within his gripe, and from his coffers,
n like a violent stream to other mens.

Cook's Green's Tu quoque.

ung heirs, left in this town, where sin's so rank,
d prodigals gape to grow fat by them,
e like young whelps, thrown in the lion's den,
ho play with them a while, at length devour them.

Wilkins's Miseries of enforc'd Marriage.

us like a fever that doth shake a man
m strength to weakness, I consume myself:

D 2

I know

I know this company, their custom wild,
Hated, abhorr'd of good men; yet, like a child,
By reason's rule instructed how to know
Evil from good, I to the worser go.

Wilkins's Miseries of enforced Marriage.

What is a prodigal? Faith, like a brush,
That wears himself, to flourish others cloaths;
And having worn his heart ev'n to the stump,
He's thrown away like a deformed lump:
Oh such am I! I have spent all the wealth
My ancestors did purchase; made others brave
In shape and riches, and myself a knave:
For tho' my wealth rais'd some to paint their door,
'Tis shut 'gainst me, saying, I am but poor.
Nay, ev'n the greatest arm, whose hand had grac'd
My presence to the eye of majesty, shrinks back,
His fingers clutch, and like to lead
They're heavy to raise up my state, b'ing dead:
By which I find spend thrifts, and such am I,
Like strumpets flourish, but are foul within;
And they like snakes, know when to cast their skin.

Ibid.

My old master kept a good house, and twenty
Or thirty tall sword and buckler-men about
Him; and in faith his son differs not much,
He will have metal too; tho' he has no
Store of cutlers blades, he will have plenty
Of vintners pots. His father kept a good
House for honest men, his tenants, that brought
Him in part: And his son keeps a bad house
With knaves that help to consume all: 'Tis but
The change of time: Why should any man repine
At it? Crickets, good loving and lucky worms,
Were wont to feed, sing, and rejoice in the
Father's chimney: And now carrion-crows build
In the son's kitchen.

Ibid.

—Our

—————————Our eyes
See daily prefidents: hopeful gentlemen
Being trufted in the world with their own will,
Divert the good is look'd from them, to ill:
Make their old names forgot, or not worth note;
Such company they keep, fuch revelling
With panders, parafites, prodigies of knaves,
That they fell all, ev'n to their old fathers graves.

Wilkins's Miferies of enforced Marriage.

—————————He has not felt
The weight of need, that want is virtue's clog;
Of what neceffity, refpect and value
Wealth is; how bafe and how contemptible
Poverty makes us: liberality
In fome circumftances, may be allow'd;
As when it has no end but honefty;
With a refpect of perfon, quantity,
Quality, time, and place: but this profufe,
Vain, injudicious fpending makes him idiot:
And yet, the beft of liberality
Is to be lib'ral to ourfelves: And thus
Your wifdom is moft liberal, and knows
How fond a thing it is for difcreet men
To purchafe with the lofs of their eftate
The name of one poor virtue, liberality,
And that too, only from the mouths of beggars!
One of your judgment would not, I am fure,
Buy all the virtues at fo dear a rate.

Randolph's Mufes Looking-Glafs.

1. Two thoufand pounds a year
Cannot be melted fuddenly; when 'tis,
Men can but fay, her prodigality
Has done an act of juftice, and tranflated
That wealth which fortune's blindnefs had mifplac'd
On fuch a fellow: what fhould he do with it?
2. And thou fay'ft right. Some men were made to be
The conduit-pipes of an eftate; or rather
The fieves of fortune, thro' whofe leaking holes

She

She means to scatter a large flood of wealth,
Besprinkling many with refreshing show'rs :
So usurers, to dying aldermen
Pour at once upon their sieve like heirs
Whole puffs of envy'd wealth ; which they together
Through many holes let out again in show'rs,
And, with their ruin water a whole country.

May's Old Couple.

P R O J E C T O R.

1. What is a projector, I would conceive ?
2 Why, one, sir, that projects
Ways to enrich men ; or to make 'em great,
By suits, by marriages, by undertakings :
According as he sees they humour it

Johnson's Devil is an Ass.

Money's a whore, a bawd, a drudge ;
Fit to run out on errands : Let her go.
Via pecunia ! When she's run and gone,
And fled, and dead ; then will I fetch her again
With *Aqua vitæ,* out of an old hogshead !
While there are lees of wine, or dregs of beer,
I'll never want her! coin her out of cobwebs,
Dust, but I'll have her ! raise wool upon Egg-shells,
Sir, and make grass grow out o'marrow bones !

Ibid.

—————————————He shall not draw
A string of 's purse.   I'll drive his patent for him.
We'll take in citizens, commoners, and aldermen,
To bear the charge ; and blow them off again,
Like to many dead flies, when 'tis carry'd :
The thing is for recov'ry of drown'd land,
Whereof the crown's to have a moiety,
If it be owner ; else the crown and owners
To share that moiety, and the recoverers
T 'enjoy the other moiety for their charge.

Ibid.

It shall be no shame to me, to confess
To you, that we poor gentlemen, that want acres,

Must

luſt for our needs, turn fools up, and plough ladies
ſometime, to try what glebe they are ; and this
no unfruitful piece. She and I now
are on a project, for the fact, and venting
Of a new kind of fucus, paint for ladies,
To ſerve the kingdom : wherein ſhe herſelf
hath travell'd, 'ſpecially, by way of ſervice
Into her ſex ; and hopes to get the whole monopoly,
As the reward of her invention.

Johnson's Devil is an Aſs.

1. I meant to have offer'd it
Your ladyſhip on the perfecting the patent.
2. How is it ?
1. For ſerving the whole ſtate with tooth-picks ;
ſomewhat an intricate buſineſs to diſcourſe, but
I ſhow how much the ſubject is abus'd ;
Firſt, in that one commodity : then what diſeaſes
And putrefactions in the gums are bred,
By thoſe are made of adulterate and falſe wood ;
My plot, for reformation of theſe fellows,
To have all tooth-picks brought unto an office,
There ſeal'd ; and ſuch as counterfeit 'em mulcted :
And laſt, for venting 'em, to have a book
Printed, to teach their uſe ; which ev'ry child
Shall have throughout the kingdom that can read,
And learn to pick his teeth by : which beginning
Early to practiſe, with ſome other rules,
Of never ſleeping with the mouth open, chawing
ſome grains of maſtick, will preſerve the breath
Pure, and ſo free from taint.

Ibid.

Theſe are my old projectors, and they make me
The ſuperintendent of their buſineſs :
But ſtill they ſhoot two or three bows too ſhort,
For want of money and adventurers.
They have as many demurrs as the chancery ;
And hatch more ſtrange imaginations
Than any dreaming philoſopher ; one of them

D 4

Will

Will undertake the making of bay-salt,
For a penny a bushel, to ferve the ftate;
Another dreams of building water-works,
Drying of fens and marfhes, like the *Dutch men:*
Another ftrives, to raife his fortunes, from
Decay'd bridges, and would exact a tribute
From ale houfes, and hyn-pofts: fome there are,
Would make a thorough fare for the whole kingdom,
An office, where nature fhould give account
For all the tools, and fent into the world:
For they were born in an unlucky hour,
For fome unfortunate mifchief or other,
Still comes athwart them! well I muft in to them,
And fall them with new hopes; 'twill be good fport
To hear how they difpute it *pro* and *con*

            Marmyon's Holland's Leaguer.

PROMISE.

Promifing is the very air of the
Time; it opens the eyes of expectation.
Performance is ever the duller for
His act; and, but in the plainer and fimpler
Kind of people, the deed is quite out of
Ufe   To promife, is moft courtly, and fafhionable;
Performance is a kind of will or teftament,
Which a goes a great fieknefs in his judgment
That makes it.

               Shakefpear's Timon.

Our promife muft not prejudice our good:
And that it is no reafon that the tongue
Tie the whole body to eternal wrong.

               Daniel's Arcadia.

1. We think your promifes fpring tide; but we
Fear you'll ebb in your performance.
2. My deed, and fpeeches, fir,
Are lines drawn from one center; what I promife
To do, I'll do

           Dekker's Match me in London.

                      Court

t promises ! let wife men count them curst ;
while you live, he that scores best, pays worst.
Webster's White Devil.

ly your promises with deeds ;
know that painted meat no hunger feeds.
Ibid.

ls promises are mortal, and commonly
within half an hour they are spoken.
Middleton's Mad World my Masters.

ises of princes must not be
fter-arts evaded. Who dares punish
breach of oaths in subjects ; and yet slight
faith he hath made them ?
Habbington's Queen of Arragon.

cannot lose your virtue, sir, and then
sure my courtesy will never fail :
romise more, would make me seem too prodigal
vhat you can't in nobleness receive.
Sir W. Davenant's Platonick Lovers.

———————— 'Tis apparent,
wilt not fail thy friend in great engagements,
art so punctual in a promis'd trifle.
he man that is not in th' enemy's pow'r,
fetter'd by misfortune, and breaks promises,
ades himself ; he never can pretend
onour more.
Sir Robert Stapleton's Slighted Maid.

PROSPERITY.

erity's the very bond of love,
e fresh complexion, and whose heart together,
tion alters.
Shakespear's Winter's Tale.

and hourly proof
us, prosperity is at highest degree,
fount and handle of calamity :
dust before a whirlwind those men fly,
prostrate on the ground of fortune lie ;

D 5   And

And being great, like trees that broadest sprout,
Then own top heavy state grub up their root.
                    Chapman's First Part of Byron's Conspi

Things over rank do never kindly bear,
    As in the corn the flexure, when we see
Fill but the straw, when it should feed the ear;
    Rotting that time in rip'ning it should be,
And be'ng once down, itself can never rear:
    With us well doth this simile agree
Of the wise man, due to the great in all,
By their own weight b'ing broken in their fall.

Self loving man, what sooner doth abuse;
    And more than his prosperity doth wound?
Into the deep but fall how can he chuse
    That over strides whereon his foot to ground?
Who sparingly prosperity doth use,
    And to himself doth after ill propound;
Unto his height who happily doth climb,
Sits above fortune, and controuleth time.
                    Drayton in the Mirror for Magist

Lo, when prosperity too much prevails,
    Above the judgment thus of vulgar minds;
As little barges burden'd with great sails,
    They move in state, all swoln with fortune's win
                    E. of *Sterline's Alexandrean Tra*

Prosperity doth bewitch men, seeming clear;
But seas do laugh, shew white, when rocks are nea
                    Webster's White L

——————   Knaves will thrive,
When honest plainness knows not how to live.
                    Shirley's Maid's Rev

He that suffers
Prosperity to swell him 'bove a mean;
Like those impressions in the air, that rise
From dunghill vapours, scatter'd by the wind,
Leaves nothing but an empty name behind.
                    Nabbs's Hannibal and S

Of both our fortunes good and bad, we find
Prosperity more searching of the mind :
Felicity flies o'er the wall and fence,
While misery keeps in with patience.

Herrick.

More in prosperity is reason tost,
Than ships in storms, their helms and anchors lost :
Before fair gales not all our sails we bear,
But with side winds into safe harbours steer.
More ships in calms on a deceitful coast,
Or unseen rocks, than in high storms are lost.

Denham.

None violent empires long enjoy secure ;
They're mod'rate conditions that endure.
When fortune raiseth to the greatest height,
The happy man should most suppress his state ;
Expecting still a change of things to find,
And fearing, when the gods appear too kind.

Sir *Robert Howard.*

PROVIDENCE.

Thus doth th' all working providence retain,
And keep for good effects the seed of worth ;
And so doth point the stops of time thereby,
In periods of uncertain certainty.

Daniel's Panegyrick to the King.

So blind's the sharpest councils of the wise
　This over-shadowing providence on high,
And dazzleth all their clearest-sighted eyes,
　That they see not how nakedly they lie:
There where they little think the storm doth rise,
　And over-casts their clear security :
When Man hath stopp'd all ways, save only that,
Which, as least doubted, ruin enters at.

Daniel's Civil War.

What man, not wondring, can by deeds behold
　The providence of all commanding Jove,
Whose brazen edicts cannot be controul'd :
　Firm are the statutes of the states above :

D 6

That

'That mortal whom a deity's favour shields,
  No worldly force is able to confound;
He may securely walk through danger's fields;
  Times and occasions are to serve him bound.
                 E. of Sterline's Crœsus

O all preparing providence divine !
  In thy large book what secrets are enroll'd !
What kindly help doth thy great pow'r assign,
  To prop the course which thou intend'st to hold !
What mortal tongue is able to define
  Thy mysterys, thy councils manyfold !
It is thy wisdom strangely that extends
Obscure proceedings to apparent ends
               Drayton's Barons War

———— ———— Wise princes
Fight not alone with forces; providence
Directs and tutors through ' elle elephants
And barbed horses might as well prevail,
As the most labid stratagems of war.
             John Ford's Perkin Warbeck

———— ———— Wisdom and virtue be
The only defences set for a man to follow.
The heav'nly pow'rs are to be reverenc'd,
Not search'd into; their mercies rather be
By humble prayers to be sought, than their
Hidden counsels by curiosity.
               Baron's Mirza

Who is it, that will doubt
The care of heaven, or think th' immortal
Pow'rs are slow, 'cause they take the priviledge
To chuse their own time, when they will lend their
Blessings down !
           Sir W. Davenant's Fair Favourit

P R U D E N C E.

She's a majestick ruler, and commands
Ev'n with the terror of her awful brow.
As in a throng, sedition being rais'd,
Th' ignoble multitude inflam'd with madness.
               Virebram

ands and stones fly ; fury shews them weapons :
ying some grave man, honour'd for wisdom,
straight are silent, and erect their ears ;
he with his sage council doth asswage
minds disorder, and appease their rage :
dence, when rebellious appetites
rais'd temptations, with their batteries
ting reason, then doth interpose,
eep it safe.   Th' attempts of sense are weak,
eir vain forces wisdom deign to break.

Nabbs's Microcosmus.

ce, thou virtue of the mind, by which
consult of all that's good or evil,
cing to felicity ; direct
oughts and actions by the rules of reason :
me contempt of all inferior vanities ;
in a marble portal gilded o'er,
w carpets, chairs of ivory,
uxury of a stupendous house,
ents perfum'd, gems valu'd not for use,
edless ornament : a sumptuous table,
ll the baits of sense.   A vulgar eye
ot the dangers which beneath them lie.

Ibid.

———————— A wise man,
he does found his happiness, forecasts
efs, that fate had never practis'd yet ;
h if they happen, if they prove too true,
meet, not overtake him ; and so find
rn, because a preparation.

Gomersail's Lodovick Sforza.

forward what's to come, and back what's past ;
ife will be with praise and prudence grac'd :
loss or gain may follow, thou may'st guess ;
then wilt be secure of the success.

Denham.

P U-

P U N I S H M E N T.

Ye princes all, and rulers ev'ry one,
  In punifhment, beware of hatred's ire.
Before you fcourge, take heed ; look well thereon :
  In wrath's ill will, if malice kindle fire,
  Your hearts will burn in fuch a hot defire,
That in thofe flames, the fmoke fhall dim your fight,
Ye fhall forget to join your juftice right.

You fhould not judge, till things be well difcern'd ;
  Your charge is ftill to maintain upright laws :
In confcience rules ye fhould be throughly learn'd,
  Where clemency bids wrath and rafhnefs paufe ;
  And further faith, ftrike not without a caufe :
And when ye fmite, do it for juftice fake ;
Then in good part, each man your fcourge will take.
           Churchyard in the *Mirror for Magiftrates*
Unpunifh'd 'fcape for heinous crime fome one ;
But unaveng'd in mind or body, none.
                Mirror for Magiftrates

All have not offended :
For thofe that were, it is not fquare to take
On thofe that are, revenge : crimes, like to lands,
Are not inherited.
                 Shakefpear's Timon
Yet muft we not put the ftrong law on him ;
He's lov'd of the diftracted multitude,
Who like not in their judgment, but their eyes :
And where 'tis fo, th' offendor's fcourge is weigh'd,
But never the offence.
                Shakefpear's Hamlet.
Reck'ning it better, fince his end is meant,
  And muft be wrought, at once to rid it clear,
And put it to the fortune of th' event,
  'Than by long doing to be long in fear :
When in fuch courfes of high punifhment,
The deed and the attempt like danger bear.
              Daniel's Civil War

                        W here

e fits the offence,
ne fault's punifhment be deriv'd from thence.
Middleton's Game at Chefs.

nce of death when it is mildly fpoke,
promifes life ; but when your doom you mix
fuch rough threats, what is't but twice to kill ?
Heywood's Royal King.

ould not dare to kill, that dares not die ;
needy mifchief, and he's bafely bent,
dares do ill, yet fears the punifhment.
W. Rowliy's All's Loft by Luft.

nftom, nor example, nor vaft numbers
ich as do offend, make lefs the fin ;
ach particular crime a ftrict account
be exacted ; and that comfort which
damn'd pretend, follows in mifery,
s nothing from their torments : ev'ry one
fuffer in himfelf, the meafure of
wickednefs.
Maffinger's Picture.

———— The land wants fuch
are with rigour execute her laws ;
fefter'd members muft be lanc'd and tented :
a bad furgeon that for pity fpares
part corrupted, 'till the gangrene fpread,
all the body perifh : he that's merciful
o the bad, is cruel to the good.
pillory muft cure the ear's difeafe ;
ftocks the foot's offences ; let the back
her own fin, and her rank blood purge forth
he phlebotomy of a whipping poft :
yet the fecret and purfe-punifhment
ld the wifer courfe ; becaufe at once
elps the virtuous, and corrects the vicious.
not the fword of juftice fleep, and ruft
hin her velvet fheath ; preferve her edge,
keep it fharp with cutting ; ufe muft whet her:
Tame

'Tame mercy is the breaſt that ſuckles vice,
Till *Hydra*-like ſhe multiply her heads.

Randolph's Muſes Looking·

1. —————Think not of pardon, ſir.
Rigour and mercy us'd in ſtates uncertainly
And in ill times, look not like th' effects
Of virtue, but neceſſity : nor will
They thank your goodneſs, but your fears ?——
2. Revenge in princes ſhould be ſtill imperfect ;
It is then handſomeſt, when the king comes to
Reduce, not ruin—————
1. Who puts but on the face of puniſhing,
And only gently cuts, but primes rebellion ;
He makes that flouriſh, that he wou'd deſtroy.
Who wou'd not be a rebel, when the hopes
Are vaſt, the fears but ſmall ?
2. Why, I wou'd not ;
Nor you, my lord, nor you, nor any here.
Fear keeps low ſpirits only in, the brave
Do get above it, when they do reſolve.
Such puniſhments in infancy of war
Make men more deſp'rate ; not the more yielding
The common people are a kind of flies ;
They're caught with honey, not with wormwoo
Severity exaſperates the ſtirr'd humour ;
And ſtates diſtempers turn into diſeaſes.

Suckling's Brenn

The laws are ſinfully contriv'd.   Juſtice
Should weigh the preſent crime, not future
Inference on deeds ; but now they cheapen
Blood : 'tis ſpilt
To puniſh the example, not the guilt.

Sir *W. Davenant's Juſt Ita*

Do not, if one but lightly thee offend,
The puniſhment beyond the crime extend ;
Or after warning the offence forget ;
So God himſelf our failings did remit.

De

Who would, unblamed, ſtrike,
Muſt what he ſeems to do, not ſeem to like.
Orgula, or the Fatal Error.

Q U A C K.

1. PITY his ignorance !
They are the only knowing men of *Europe*;
Great gen'ral ſcholars, excellent phyſicians,
Moſt admir'd ſtateſmen, profeſt favourites,
And cabinet counſellors to the greateſt princes !
The only languag'd men of all the world !
2. And, I have heard, they are moſt lewd impoſtors ;
Made all of terms and ſhreds ; no leſs believers
Of great mens favours, than their own vile med'cines ;
Which they will utter upon monſtrous oaths :
Selling that drug for two pence ere they part,
Which they have valu'd at twelve crowns before.
Johnſon's Volpone.

1. Good doctor *Alcon*, I am come to crave
Your counſel to adviſe me for my health ;
For I ſuppoſe, in troth, I am not well ;
Methinks I ſhould be ſick, yet cannot tell :
Something there is amiſs that troubles me,
For which I would take phyſick willingly.
2. Welcome, fair nymph ; come, let me try your pulſe.
I cannot blame you, t' hold yourſelf not well.
Something amiſs, quoth you ; here's all amiſs !
The whole fabrick of yourſelf diſtemp'red is ;
The *ſyſtole* and *diaſtole* of your pulſe
Do ſhew your paſſions moſt *hyſterical :*
It ſeems you have not careful been
T' obſerve the *prophylactick* regimen
Of your own body ; ſo that we muſt now
Deſcend unto the *therapheutical ;*
That ſo we may prevent the *ſyndrome*
Of ſymptoms, and may afterwards apply

Some

Some *analeptical alexipharmacum*,
That may be proper for your malady :
It feems, fair nymph, you dream much in the nigh
1. Doctor, I do indeed.
2. I know you do ;
You're troubled much with thought.
1. I am indeed.
2. I know you are ;
You have great heavinefs about your heart.
1. Now truly fo I have.
2. I know you have ;
You wake oft in the night.
1. In troth I do.
2. All this I know you do ;
And this unlefs by phyfick you prevent,
Think whereto it may bring you in the end ;
And therefore you muft firft evacuate
All thofe *colaxical* hot humours which
Difturb your heart, and then refrigerate
Your blood by fome *menakhian* cordials,
Which you muft take, and you fhall ftraight find
And in the morning I will vifit you.

                       Daniel's Arc

——————— Out you impoftors,
Quackfalving-cheating mountebanks,——your ski
Is to make found men fick, and fick men kill !

              Maffinger and *Dekker's Virgin Ma*

QUALIFICATIONS.

Good parts in youth and manhood are the fame ;
They're the fame picture in a fmaller frame.

                            Lier

——————— 'Tis ftrange to fee
How gen'rally this gentleman doth take :
For my part, as I fee not any thing
In him that I much miflike, fo truly
Naught that I admire : he has fome graceful
And becoming parts and qualities ; a
Handfome way in talk ; yet when I mark it

                              Seri

Serioufly, methinks it is as curious
Pictures, which although they make a pleafing
Shew, yet, for the moft part are drawn on coarfe
And ordinary matter.   I needs muft fay,
He has this happinefs, that if he excel
In aught, it is in things of that familiar
Nature, that each place and company
He comes in, afford him opportunity
To fhew it : and this certainly is the
Only thing that makes him make a greater
Blaze than fome of far more worth ; whofe eminence
Lying in that which is more choice, cannot
So frequently difcover itfelf ; nor
Is their value proftituted unto
Every eye ; but they, as great bells, who
Are not eafily, nor on all flight occafions,
Raifed, yet being up, will far out-found
Any of thefe tinckling ting-tang blades.

The Hectors.

For as when fome common metals will ferve
For good fubftantial ufe, yet if you ftrive
To force them to more curious fhapes, they only
Such rude draughts will take, as will render them
More deformed : fo this gentleman, had
His coarfer foul but had the luck to have
Acted in fome downright way, to have manag'd
Some plodding trade, he might by long experience
Have underftood himfelf within his fphere ;
Nay, have had wit enough to have got a
Good eftate, and through the repute of that,
Have been look'd upon by the world as wife :
But this by his father's induftry being
Left to his hand ; the common courfe of the
World, unhappily doth fling him upon
Things fit only for more refined minds ;
Which although he cannot mafter, yet fome
Odd grudges and imperfect ftamps have

Trans-

Transformed him from what he was, nor can
He be what he would.

The He

Q U A R R E L.

———————————————— Beware
Of entrance to a quarrel : But being in,
Bear it, that the oppofed may beware of thee.

Shakefpear's *Ha*

But yefterday, thou waft the common fecond
Of all that only know thee ; thou hadft bills
Set up on ev'ry poft, to give thee notice
Where any diff'rence was, and who were parties ;
And as to fave the charges of the law
Poor men feek aibitrators, thou wert chofen
By fuch as knew thee not, to compound quarrels :
But thou wert fo delighted with the fport,
That if there were no juft caufe, thou wouldft make
Or be engag'd thyfelf : This goodly calling
Thou haft follow'd five and twenty years, and ftud
The criticifms of contentions, and art thou
In fo few hours transform'd ?

Beaumont and *Fletcher*'s *Little French Lar*

There's a mifchief greater than all thefe ;
A bafe and fordid provocation,
Us'd among gentlemen they cannot quarrel
About a glafs of wine, but out flies ftraight
Son of a whore : dead mothers muft be torn
Out of their graves, or living, have their names
Poifon'd by a prodigious breath : It were
A brave and noble law to make this tongue
Be cut for't ; it would fave much blood i'th'year,
That might be fpent more honourably.

Shirley's *Gam*

———See the fate of traytors !
How wonderfully heav'n does bring about
Their punifhment, that like to canibals,
The one doth eat the other !

Tatham's *Diftracted S.*

———————— Surely one
Of the winds got him ; his cradle was a drum,
And he was nurs'd upon a belfry.
He hath more rage and noife than a winter-ftorm :
Only his virtue is, he will not out-laft it.

Sir W. Davenant's News from Plymouth.

QUEEN.

A dow'r, my lords ! difgrace not fo your king,
That he fhould be fo abject, bafe and poor,
To chufe for wealth, and not for perfect love.
Henry is able to inrich his queen ;
And not to feek a queen, to make him rich :
So worthlefs peafants bargain for their wives,
As market-men for oxen, fheep or horfe :
But marriage is a matter of more worth,
Than to be dealt in by attorneyfhip :
Not whom we will, but whom his grace affects,
Muft be companion of his nuptial-bed.
And therefore, lords, fince he affects her moft,
It moft of all thefe reafons bindeth us,
In our opinions fhe fhould be preferr'd :
For what is wedlock forced, but a hell,
An age of difcord, and continual ftrife ?
Whereas the contrary bringeth forth blifs,
And is a pattern of celeftial peace.
Whom fhould we match with *Henry*, b'ing a king,
But *Marg'ret*, that is daughter to a king ?
Her peerlefs feature, joined with her birth,
Approves her fit for none, but for a king.
Her valiant courage, and undaunted fpirit,
More than in woman commonly is feen,
Anfwer our hope in iffue of a king :
For, *Henry*, fon unto a conqueror,
Is likely to beget more conquerors,
If with a lady of fo high refolve,
As is fair *Marg'ret*, he be link'd in love.

Shakefpear's Firft Part of King Henry VI.

When

When you are made my confort,
All the prerogatives of my high birth cancell'd,
I'll practice the obedience of a wife,
And freely pay it. Queens themselves, if the
Make choice of their inferiors, only aiming
To feed their fenfual appetites, and to reign
Over their husbands, in fome kind commit
Authoriz'd whoredom.

Maffinger's Maid of

Q U E S T I O N S.

She now with jealous queftions, utter'd faft,
Fills *Orgo*'s ear, which there unmark'd are gon
As throngs through guarded gates, when all mal
Not giving warders time t'examine one.

Sir W. Davenant's G

R A P E.

YOUR brother did with vicious loofenefs,
    Corrupt the chafte ftreams of my fpotlefs
And left me foiled like a long-pluck'd rofe,
Whofe leaves diffever'd, have foregone their fw

Chapman's Revenge for

——————————————Woman's forced ufe,
Like unripe fruits, no fooner got, but wafte;
They have proportion, colour, but no tafte.

Marfton's Sof

If he, from heav'n that filch'd that living fire,
    Condemn'd by *Jove* to endlefs torment be;
    I greatly marvel how you ftill go free,
That far beyond *Prometheus* did afpire:

The fire he ftole, although of heav'nly kind,
    Which from above he craftily did take
    Of lifelefs clods, us living men to make,
He did beftow in temper of the mind:

you broke into heav'n's immortal ftore,
Where virtue, honour, wit, and beauty lay;
Which taking thence, you have efcap'd away,
ftand as free as e'er you did before :

old *Prometheus* punifh'd for his rape :
as poor thieves fuffer, when the greater 'fcape.

Drayton's Ideas.

——She longs to be ravifh'd :
e have no pleafure but in violence ;
be torn in pieces is their paradife :
ordinary in our country, fir, to ravifh all ;
ey will not give a penny for their fport
lefs they be put to it, and terribly ;
d then they fwear they'll hang the man comes
      near 'em,
l fwear it on his lips too.

Beaumont and Fletcher's Maid in the Mill.

How like a hill of fnow fhe fits, and melts
ore the unchafte fire of others luft ?
at heart can fee her paffion, and not break ?
Take comfort, gentle madam, you know well
n actual fins committed without will,
: neither fins nor fhame, much more compell'd ;
ur honour's no whit lefs, your chaftity
 whit impair'd, for fair *Merione*
aore a virgin yet than all her fex :
as 'tis done ! why burn thefe tapers now ?
cked and frantick creatures joy in night.
agine fair *Merione* had dream'd
: had been ravifh'd, would fhe fit thus then
cruciate ? Fie, fie, how fond is this ?
iat reafon for this furfeit of remorfe ?
w many that have done ill and proceed,
omen that take degrees in wantonnefs,
mmence, and rife in rudiments of luft,
iat feel no fcruple of this tendernefs ?
 Wherefore fits

My

My *Phæbe* shadow'd in a sable cloud?
'Those pearly drops which thou let'st fall like beads,
Numb'ring on them thy vestal orisons,
Alas, are spent in vain; I love thee still,
In 'midst of all these show'rs thou sweetlier scents't,
Like a green meadow on an *April* day;
In which the sun and west wind play together,
Striving to catch, and drink the balmy drops.
Beaumont and *Fletcher's Queen of Corinth.*

—— He amongst all the ladies
Singled out that dear form, who ever liv'd,
As cold in lust, as she is now in death.
O vicious minute!
Unfit but for relation to be spoke of——
Then with a face more impudent than his vizard
He hurry'd her amidst a throng of panders,
That live upon damnation of both kinds,
And fed the rav'nous vulture of his lust:
O death to think on't! She, her honour forc'd,
Deem'd it a nobler dowry for her name,
To die with poison, than to live with shame.
Tourneur's Revenger's Tragedy.

Lucrece was chaste after the rape; but where
The blood consents, there needs no ravisher.
Shirley's Royal Master.

What foolish thief would rob an altar,
Be guilty of the sacrilege, to gain
A brazen censor? Why should you then affect
A sin so great, as spoiling me of honour,
For such a poor gain, as the satisfying
Your sensual appetite? Think, good my lord,
The pleasures you so covet, are but like flatt'ring
      mornings,
That shew the rising sun in his full brightness;
Yet do ere night bury his head in tempests.
Glapthorne's Albertus Wallenstein.

Kill me, oh kill me! rather let me die
Than live to see the jewel that adorns

The

The souls of virtuous virgins ravish'd from me.
Do not add sin to sin, and at a price
That ruins me, and not inriches you,
Purchase damnation : Do not, do not do't ;
Sheath here your sword, and my departing soul
Like your good angel, shall sollicit heav'n
To dash out your offences ; let my flight
Be pure and spotless : Do not injure that,
Manhood would blush to think on : It is all
A maid's divinity : Wanting her life,
She's a fair coarse; wanting her chastity,
A spotted soul of living infamy.

Rawlins's Rebellion.

Methinks I stand like *Tarquin*, in the night,
When he defil'd the chastity of *Rome*,
Doubtful of what to do; and like a thief
I take each noise to be an officer.
She has a ravishing feature, and her mind
Is of a purer temper than her body :
Her virtues more than beauty ravish me,
And I commit ev'n with her piety,
A kind of incest with religion :
Though I do know it is a deed of death,
Condemn'd to torments in the other world.
Such tempting sweetness dwells in ev'ry limb,
That I must venture my essential parts,
For the fruition of a moment's lust ;
A pleasure dearly bought——

Hemmings's Fatal Contract.

1. Accuse tyrannick heav'n that made you bright,
Accuse those killing eyes ; not my weak sight :
I did a crime, without my own consent ;
And justice pardons, where there's no intent :
When love commands, who dares be innocent ?
Blame not the ship that falls foul on another ;
But blame the winds that blow it : Neighbourly streams
Keep in their destin'd bounds, till show'rs from heav'n
Constrain them to invade the friendly earth

With as unqueſtion'd power
As that which gives it from the higheſt cauſe :
Celeſtial viſions cancel written laws.
2. If man may act whate'er he's mov'd to do;
The ſame man is both judge and party too :
Bodies and ſouls are ſo in marriage ty'd,
Their diſtinct iſſues hardly are deſcry'd ;
But well known body is the ſurer ſide.
Inſpir'd thoughts may flow from heav'n or hell,
But *Æthiop*'s baſtards will their fathers tell :
Charge not the gods with thy infernal ſins ;
Murder and piety cannot paſs for twins.
1. I urg'd their pow'r, but now defend their juſtice:
Impartial heav'n, not robbing all the reſt,
Could not permit by one to be poſſeſs'd
So great a joy too long :
But, if you call a crime, what heav'n commands,
Tho' clear'd above, yet I have loſt my cauſe.
In vain the priſ'ner pleads his innocence.
Who'd rather die, than anger his accuſer.

Fane's Sacrifice.

Beauty I love, but I hate toilſome rapes ;
I love good wine, but would not tread the grapes.

Crown's Caligula.

R A S H N E S S.

————————————To be too raſh,
Without both care and will to ſhun the worſt ;
It b'ing in pow'r to do well, and with chear,
Is ſtupid negligence, and worſe than fear.

Chapman's Revenge of Buſſy D'ambois.

————————————Men by timidity
Are on more dang'rous reſolutions caſt,
Than by the wildneſs of temerity :
Virtue's defects nothing of her poſſeſs,
But raſhneſs may ; for that is an exceſs.

Aleyn's Poictiers.

Raſhneſs her heat but to firſt onſets brings ;
Then ſtugs, like waſps, when they have loſt their ſtings.

Ibid.

—————————Rashness, gentlemen,
Gives the first onset fiercely ; then recoils,
As wasps, when they have lost their stings.
Glapthorne's Albertus Wallenstein.

R E A S O N.

This spark of reason is not ours,
But lent us from above :
The gods do give and take the same,
And make us loath and love.
Brandon's Antony to Octavia.

If the beam of our lives had not one scale
Of reason to poize another of sensuality ;
The blood and baseness of our natures would
Conduct us to most prepost'rous conclusions :
But we have reason, to cool our raging
Motions, our carnal stings, our unbitted lusts.
Shakspear's Othello.

—————————— Oh accursed reason !
How many eyes hast thou to see thy shame,
And yet how blind once to prevent defame.
Marston's Courtezan.

Hence do we out of words create us arts ;
  Of which the people notwithstanding be
Masters, and without rules do them impart :
  Reason we make an art, yet none agree
What this true reason is ; nor yet have pow'rs,
To level others reason unto ours.
Lord Brooke of Human Learning.

Oh most imperfect light of human reason,
Thou mak'st us so unhappy, to foresee
What we can least prevent !
Webster's Dutchess of Malfy.

—————————Accursed man
Thou bought'st thy reason at too dear a rate ;
For thou hast all thy actions bounded in
With curious rules, when ev'ry beast is free.
Beaumont and *Fletcher's King and No King.*

'There's nothing done, but there is reason for it,
If a man could find it ; For what's the reason
Your citizens wives continually wear hats,
But to shew the desire they always have
'To be cover'd ? Or why do your sempsters
Spend their time in pricking, and your ladies
In poking of ruffs, but only to shew
They do as they would be done unto ? Or why
Does your inns of-court man lie with his landress
In a long vacation, but because he
Hath no money to go abroad ? Or why do
Your old judges widows always marry
Young gentlemen, but to shew that they love
Execution better than judgment.

Cupid's Whirligig

Man is not the prince of creatures,
But in reason ; fail that, he is worse
Than horse, or dog, or beast of wilderness.

Field's Amends for Lad

Those fond philosophers that magnify
Our humane nature, and did boast we had
Such a prerogative in our rational soul,
Convers'd but little with the world ; confin'd
To cells and unfrequented woods, they knew not
The fierce vexation of community ;
Else they had taught, our reason is our loss ;
And but a privilege that exceedeth sense,
By nearer apprehension, of what wounds,
To know ourselves most miserable.

Shirley's Brother

Where men have sev'ral faiths, to find the true,
    We only can the aid of reason use ;
'Tis reason shews us which we should eschew,
    When by comparison we learn to chuse.
But though we there on reason must rely,
    Where men to sev'ral faiths their minds dispose ;
Yet after reason's choice, the schools are shy
    To let it judge the very faith it chose.

Howe'

Howe'er 'tis call'd to conftrue the records
　　Of faith's dark charter, wrapt in facred writ;
And is the only judge ev'n of thofe words,
　　By which faith claims that reafon fhould fubmit.

Since holy text bids faith to comprehend
　　Such myfteries as nature may fufpect,
And faith muft reafon as her guide attend,
　　Left fhe miftake what fcripture doth direct.

Since from the foul's far country, heav'n, God fent
　　His law, an embaffy to few reveal'd,
Which did thofe good conditions reprefent
　　Of our eternal peace, ere it was feal'd.

Since to remote ambaffadors are giv'n
　　Interpreters, when they with things confer;
Since to that law, God's embaffy fiom heav'n,
　　Our reafon ferves as an interpreter;

Since juftly clients pay that judge an awe,
　　Who laws loft fenfe interprets and reftores;
Yet judges are no more above the laws,
　　Than truchmen are above ambaffadors.

Since reafon as a judge, the trial hath
　　Of diff'ring faiths, by adverfe pens perplex'd;
Why is not reafon reckon'd above faith,
　　Though not above her law, the facred text?

If reafon have fuch worth, why fhould fhe ftill
　　Attend below, whilft faith doth upward climb?
Yet common faith feems but unftudy'd will,
　　And reafon calls unftudy'd will a crime.

Slave reafon, ev'n at home in prifon lies;
　　And by religion, is fo watch'd, and aw'd,
That though the prifon-windows, both her eyes
　　Stand open, yet fhe fcarce dares look abroad.

E 3　　　　　　　　　　　Faith

Faith thinks, that reason is her adverse spy ;
   Yet reason is, through doubtful ways, her guide ;
But like a scout, brought in from th'enemy,
   Must, when she guides her, bound and guarded ride.

Or if by faith, not as her judge disdain'd,
   Nor, as her guide suspected, but is found
In ev'ry sentence just to the arraign'd,
   And guides her right unguarded, and unbound.

Why then should such a judge be still deny'd
   T'examine, since faith's claims still publick are,
Her secret pleas ? Or why should such a guide
   Be hinder'd, where faith goes, to go as far ?

And, yet as one bred humbly, who would shew
   His monarch's palace to a stranger, goes
But to the gates ; as if to let him know
   Where so much greatness dwells, not what it does ;

Whilst strait the stranger enters undeny'd,
   As one whose breeding has much bolder been ;
So reason, though she were at first faith's guide
   To heav'n, yet waits without, when faith goes in.

But though at court, bold strangers enter, where
   The way is to their bashfull guide forbid ;
Yet he, when they come back, is apt to hear
   And ask them, what the king then said, and did :

And so, though reason, which is faith's first guide
   To God, is stopt where faith has entrance free,
As nature's stranger ; though 'tis then deny'd
   To reason, as of nature's family ;

Yet strait, when from her vision and her trance
   Faith does return, then reason quits that awe
Enjoin'd when priests impos'd our ignorance ;
   And asks how much she of the Godhead saw ?
     Sir *W. Davenant's Philosopher* to the *Dying Christian.*

I see

I fee the errors that I would avoid,
And have my reafon ftill, but not the ufe on't :
It hangs upon me like a wither'd limb
Bound up and numb'd by fome difeafe's froft ;
The form the fame, but all the ufe is loft,
Sir R. Howard's Great Favourite.

R E B E L L I O N.

1 There was a time, when all the body's members
Rebell'd againft the belly ; thus accus'd it ; ——
That only, like a gulf, it did remain
I'th' midft o'th' body, idle and unactive,
Still cupboarding the viand, never bearing
Like labour with the reft ; where th'other inftruments
Did fee, and hear, devife, inftruct, walk, feel,
And mutually participate, did minifter
Unto the appetite, and affection common
Of the whole body.   The belly anfwer'd, ——
(For, look you, I may make the belly fmile,
As well as fpeak) it tauntingly reply'd
To th' difcontented members, th' mutinous parts,
That envy'd his receit ; even fo moft fitly,
As you malign our fenators, for that
They are not fuch as you ——
2. Your belly's anfwer —— What !
The kingly crown'd *head*, the vigilant *eye*,
The counfellor *heart*, the armour foldier,
Our fteed, the *leg* the *tongue* our trumpeter ;
With other muniments and petty helps
In this our fabrick, if that they
Should by the cormorant belly be reftrain'd,
Who is the fink of the body,
The former agents, if they did complain,
What could the belly anfwer ?
1. Your moft grave belly was deliberate,
Not rafh, like his accufers ; and thus anfwer'd ;
True it is, my incorp'rate friends, quoth he,
That I receive the gen'ral food at firft,
Which you do live upon ; and fit it is,

E 4

Becaufe

Becaufe I am the ftore-houfe, and the fhop
Of the whole body.　But, if you do remember,
I fend it through the rivers of your blood,
Ev'n to the court, the heart ; to th' feat o'th' brain;
And, through the cranks and offices of man,
The ftrongeft nerves, and fmall inferior veins,
From me receive that natural competency,
Whereby they live.　And though that all at once,
You, my good friends, this fays the belly, mark me——
Though all at once cannot
See what I do deliver out to each,
Yet I can make my audit up, that all
From me do back receive the flow'r of all,
And leave me but the bran.　What fay you to't ?
2. It was an anfwer ; —— how apply you this ?
1. The fenators of *Rome* are this good belly,
And you the mutinous members ; for examine
Their counfels, and their cares ; digeft things rightly,
Touching the weal o'th' common ; you fhall find,
No publick benefit, which you receive,
But it proceeds, or comes, from them to you,
And no way from yourfelves.　What do you think ?
You, the great toe of this affembly ! ——
2. I the great toe ! Why, the great toe ?
1. For that, being one of the loweft, bafeft, pooreft,
Of this moft wife rebellion, thou goeft foremoft ;
Thou rafcal, that art worft in blood to run,
Lead'ft firft, to win fome 'vantage. ——

Shakefpear's Coriolanus

1. If we can make our peace
Upon fuch large terms and fo abfolute,
As our conditions fhall infift upon ;
Our peace fhall ftand as firm as rocky mountains.
2. Ay, but our valuation fhall be fuch,
That ev'ry flight and falfe-derived caufe,
Yea, ev'ry idle, nice, and wanton reafon,
Shall to the king tafte of this action :
That, were our royal faiths martyrs in love,

W,

We shall be winnow'd with so rough a wind,
That ev'n our corn shall seem as light as chaff,
And good from bad find no partition.
1. No, no, my lord, note this; the king is weary
Of dainty, and such picking grievances :
For he hath found, to end one doubt by death,
Revives two greater in the heirs of life :
And therefore will he wipe his tables clean,
And keep no tell-tale to his memory,
That may repeat and history his loss
To new rememb'rance. For full well he knows,
He cannot so precisely weed this land,
As his misdoubts present occasion ;
His foes are so inrooted with his friends,
That, plucking to unfix an enemy,
He doth unfasten so and shake a friend:
So that this land, like an offensive wife,
That hath enrag'd him on to offer strokes,
As he is striking, holds his infant up.
And hangs resolv'd correction in the arm
That was uprear'd to execution.
2. Besides, the king hath wasted all his rods
On late offenders, that he now doth lack
The very instruments of chastisement :
So that his pow'r, like to a fangless lion,
May offer. but not hold.
1. 'Tis very true :
And therefore be assur'd, my good lord marshal,
If we do now make our atonement well,
Our peace will, like a broken limb united,
Grow stronger for the breaking.
          Shakespear's Second Part of King Henry IV.
My lord, your son, had only but the corps,
But shadows, and the shews of men to fight.
For that same word, rebellion, did divide
The action of their bodies from their souls ;
And they did fight with queasiness, constrain'd,
As men drink portions, that their weapons only

Seem'd on our fide : But for their fpirits and fouls,
This word, rebellion, it had froze them up,
As fifh are in a pond.

Shakefpear's Second Part of King Henry IV

Want made them murmur ; for the people, who
To get their bread do wreftle with their fate,
Or thofe who in fuperfluous riot flow,
Seemeft rebel : Convulfions in a ftate,
Like thofe, which nat'ral bodies do oppress ;
Rife from repletion, or from emptinefs,

Aleyn's Henry VII

But well weigh'd reafon told him, that when law
Either's renounc'd, or mifapply'd by th'awe
Of falfe nam'd patriots ; that when the right
Of king and fubject is fuppreffd by might ;
When all religion either is refus'd
As mere pretence, or merely as that us'd ;
When thus the fury of ambition fwells,
Who is not active, modeftly rebels.

Cartwright

This late commotion in your kingdom, fir,
Is like a growing wen upon the face ;
Which as we cannot look on but with trouble,
So take't away we cannot but with danger.

Suckling's Brennorall

The vulgar in rebellion, are like
Unknown lands ; thofe that firft poffefs them, have them

Ibid

———————————————— There is gain
In mighty rebels.   Flies and moths may buzz
About our beard, and are not worth the notice ;
Or if we crufh them, they but foul our fingers :
'Tis noble prey deferves a prince's ftroak.

Baron's Mirza

——————————————— Sedition walks
With claws bow'd in, and a clofe mouth, which only
She keeps for opportunity of prey.

Killegrew's Confpirac

ot such favour to rebellion shew,
vear a crown the people do bestow;
when their giddy violence is past,
from the king th' ador'd, revolt at last:
then the throne they gain, they shall invade,
scorn that idol which themselves have made.
Crown's Charles VIII. *of France.*

R E D R E S S.

1 swelling floods have overflown the town,
late it is to save them that shall drown.
G. Ferrers in the *Mirror for Magistrates.*

ive me your hands all over, one by one.
1d let us swear our resolution.
o, not an oath: if that the face of men,
uff'rance of our souls, the time's abuse ——
se be motives weak, break off betimes;
v'ry man hence to his idle bed:
t high-sighted tyranny rage on,
ich man drop by lott'ry. But if these,
m sure they do, bear fire enough
ndle cowards, and to steel with valour
ielting spirits of women; then countrymen,
need we any spur, but our own cause,
ck us to redress? what other bond,
secret *Romans*, that have spoke the word,
ill not palter? and what other oath,
honesty to honesty engag'd,
his shall be, or we will fall for it?
priests and cowards, and men cautelous,
ble carrions, and such suff'ring souls
elcome wrongs: unto bad causes, swear
eatures as men doubt; but do not stain
en virtue of our enterprize,
insuppressive mettle of our spirits;
1k, that or our cause, or our performance,
d an oath: when ev'ry drop of blood,
v'ry *Roman* bears, and nobly bears,
y of a several bastardy,

If he doth break the fmalleft particle
Of any promife that haft paft from him.

Shakefpear's Julius Cæfar.

The better, loathing courfes fo impure,
Rather will like their wounds, than fuch a cure.

Daniel's Civil War.

After this fhipwrack, I again muft try
  Some happier voyage, hopeful ftill to make :
The plots that barren long we fee did lie,
  Some fitting feafon plentifully take ;
One fruitful harveft fiankly doth reftore,
What many winters hindred had before.

Drayton in the *Mirror for Magiftrates.*

The only way to falve a deep difeafe
Is to give what may cure, not what may pleafe ;
Wherein delays prove worft : artifts apply
Receipts, before diftempers grow too high.

Lady Alimony.

Are you here, fir ? does it become a king
To look upon afflicftion, and not ftrait
Redrefs it ? the poor phyfician is fo nice
In the honour of his fcience, that he ne'er
Will vifit dying men : as if he were
Afham'd to look upon thofe inward wounds
He hath not skill to cure

Sir *W. Davenant's Fair Favourite.*

1. Sir, I am pre-engag'd, let that fuffice.
2. The antidote's too late, to him who dies :
Too late we take the taper from the fly,
When he is burnt fo, that he needs muft die.

Dover's Roman Generals.

REFORMATION.

The king is full of grace and fair regard,
And a true lover of the holy church.
2. The courfes of his youth promis'd it not ;
The breath no fooner left his father's body,
But that his wildnefs, mortify'd in him,
Seem'd to die too ; yea, at that very moment,

Confidederation, like an angel, came,

vhipp'd th'offending *Adam* out of him ;

ng his body as a paradise,

elope and contain celeftial fpirits.

' was fuch a fudden fcholar made :

' came reformation in a flood

fuch a heady current, fcow'ring faults:

ver *Hydra*-headed wilfulnefs

n did lofe his feat, and all at once,

his king.

're bleffed in the change.

ar him but reafon in divinity,

all-admiring, with an inward wifh

ould defire, the king were made a prelate :

him debate of commonwealth affairs,

fay, it hath been all in all his ftudy ;

is difcourfe of war, and you fhall hear

ful battle render'd you in mufick.

him to any caufe of policy,

ordian knot of it he will unloofe,

iar as his garter.   When he fpeaks,

ir, a charter'd libertine, is ftill ;

he mute wonder lurketh in mens ears,

al his fweet and honied fentences :

t the act, and practick part of life,

be the miftrefs to this rhetorick.

h is a wonder how his grace fhould glean it,

his addition was to courfes vain ;

mpanies unletter'd, rude and fhallow ;

ours fill'd up with riots, banquets, fports ;

never noted in him any ftudy,

etirement, any fequeftration,

open haunts and popularity.

he ftraw-berry grows underneath the nettle,

vholefome berries thrive, and ripen beft,

nbour'd by fruit of bafer quality:

o the prince obfcur'd his contemplation

r the veil of wildnefs ; which, no doubt,

Grew

Grew like the summer-grafs, faftest by night,
Unfeen, yet crefcive in his faculty.
2. It muft be fo ; for miracles are ceas'd :
And therefore we muft needs admit the means,
How things are perfected.

Shakefpear's King Henr.

I know you all, and will awhile uphold
The un-yok'd humour of your idlenefs,
Yet herein will I imitate the fun,
Who doth permit the bafe contagious clouds
To fmother up his beauty from the world
That when he pleafes again to be himfelf ;
Being wanted, he may be more wonder'd at,
By breaking through the foul and ugly mifts
Of vapours, that did feem to ftrangle him.
If all the year were playing holidays,
The fport would be as tedious as to work ;
But when they feldom come, they wifh'd-for come,
And nothing pleafeth but rare accidents :
So when this loofe behaviour I throw off,
And pay the debt I never promifed ;
By how much better than my word I am,
By fo much fhall I falfify men's hopes ;
And, like bright metal on a fullen ground,
My reformation, glitt'ing o'er my fault,
Shall fhew more goodly, and attract more eyes,
Than that which hath no foil to fet it off.
I'll fo offend, to make offence a fkill ;
Redeeming time, when men think leaft I will.

Shakefpear's Firft Part of King Henry

Formlefs themfelves, reforming do pretend ;
As if confufion could diforder mend.

Daniel's Civil W

For never headftrong reformation will
   Reft, till to th' extreme oppofite it run,
And over-run, the mean diftrufted ftill,
   As b'ing too near of kin to that men fhun :
For good and bad, and all, muft be one ill,
   When once there is another truth begun.

R E F 87

So hard it is an even hand to bear,
  In temp'ring with such maladies as these :
Lest that our forward passions lance too near,
  And make the cure prove worse than the disease :
For with the worst, we will not spare the best,
  Because it grows with that which doth displease.

And faults are easier look'd in, than redress'd :
  Men running with such eager violence,
At the first view of errors, fresh in quest ;
  As they, to rid an inconvenience,
Stick not to raise a mischief in the stead,
  Which after mocks their weak improvidence :
And therefore do not make your own sides bleed,
To prick at others.

Daniel's Musophilus.

Indeed a prince need not travel farther
Than his own kingdom, if he apply himself
Faithfully, worthy the glory of himself
And expectation of others : and it
Would appear far nobler industry in
Him, to reform those fashions that are
Already in his country ; than to bring
New ones in, which have neither true form nor
Fashion : To make his court an owl,
City an ape, and the country a wolf,
Preying upon the ridiculous pride
Of either : And therefore I hold it a
Safer stern upon this lucky advantage,
Since my father is near his setting, and
I upon the eastern hill to take my rise,
To look into the heart and bowels of dukedom,
And in disguise, mark all abuses ready
For reformation or punishment.
So much have the complaints and suits of men,
Seven, nay, seventeen years neglected, still
Interpos'd by coin and great enemies,
Prevail'd with pity, that I cannot otherwise

Think,

Think, but there are infectious dealings
In moſt offices, and foul myſteries
Throughout all profeſſions : And therefore I
Nothing doubt, but to find travel enough
Within myſelf, and experience I fear
Too much : Nor will I be curious to fit
My body to the humbleſt form and bearing,
So the labour may be fruitful : For how
Can abuſes that keep low, come to the
Right view of a prince, unleſs his looks lie
Level with them, which elſe will be longeſt
Hid from him, he ſhall be the laſt man ſees them?
For oft between kings eyes, and ſubjects crimes,
Stands there a bar of bribes ; the under office
Flatters him next above it ; he the next,
And ſo of moſt, or many . ev'ry abuſe will chuſe a
          brother,
'Tis through the world, this hand will rub the other.
                              Middleton's Phœnix.

Who labours to reform, is fit to reign :
How can the king be ſafe that ſtudies not
The profit of his people?
                                        Ibid.

———————————————Wiſe experience
Gives us to know, that in th'lopping of trees,
The ſkillful hand prunes but the lower branches,
And leaves the top ſtill growing, to extract
Sap from the root ; as meaning to reform,
Not to deſtroy.
                    Tatham's Diſtracted State.

R E L I G I O N.

He wears his faith but as the faſhion of
His hat, it ever changes with the next block.
                    Shakeſpear's Much ado about Nothing.

Religion is a branch, firſt ſet and bleſt
By heav'n's high finger in the hearts of kings ;
Which whilome grew into a goodly tree,
Bright angels ſat and ſung upon the twigs,

                                        And

And royal branches for the heads of kings
Were twisted of them : But since squint-ey'd envy
And pale suspicion dash'd the heads of kingdoms
One 'gainst another, two abhorred twins
With two foul tails, stern war and liberty
Enter'd the world ; the tree that grew from heav'n
Is over-run with moss; the chearful musick
That heretofore hath sounded out of it,
Begins to cease; and as she casts her leaves,
By small degrees, the kingdoms of the earth
Decline and wither ; and look whensoever
That the pure sap in her, is dry'd up quite,
The lamp of all authority goes out,
And all the blaze of princes is extinct.
Thus as the poet sends a messenger
Out to the stage, to shew the sum of all
That follows after : So are kings revolts,
And playing both ways with religion,
Fore-runners of afflictions imminent ;
Which, like a chorus, subjects must lament.

Chapman's *Second Part of Byron's Conspiracy.*

Sacred religion ! mother of form and fear !
   How gorgeously sometimes dost thou sit deck'd ?
What pompous vestures do we make thee wear ?
   What stately piles we prodigal erect ?
How sweet perfum'd art thou, how shining clear ?
   How solemnly observ'd ; with what respect ?

Another time all plain, all quite thread-bare ;
   Thou must have all within, and nought without ;
Sit poorly without light, disrob'd : No care
   Of outward grace t'amuse the poor devout ;
Pow'rless, unfollow'd : Scarcely men can spare
   The necessary rites to set thee out.

Daniel's Musophilus.

He whom God chuseth, out of doubt doth well ;
What they that chuse their God do. who can tell ?

Lord *Brooke*'s *Mustapho.*

Seek

Seek true religion : O where ! *Mirreus*,
Thinking her unhous'd here, and fled from us,
Seeks her at *Rome* ; there, because he doth know
That she was there a thousand years ago :
He loves the rags so, as we here obey
The state cloth, where the prince sate yesterday
Grants to such brave loves will not be enthrall'd,
But loves her only, who at *Geneva* is call'd
Religion ; plain, simple, sullen, young,
Contemptuous, yet unhandsome : As among
Letch'rou humours, there is one that judges
No wenches wholesome, but coarse country drudges.
Grajus stays still at home here ; and because
Some preachers, vile ambitious bawds, and laws
Still new, like fashions, bid him think that she
Which dwells with us, is only perfect ; he
Embraceth her, whom his godfather's will
Tenders to him, being tender ; as wards still
Take such wives as their guardians offer, or
Pay values.   Careless *Phrygius* doth abhor
All, because all cannot be good ; as one,
Knowing some women whores, dares marry none.
Gracchus loves all as one, and thinks that so,
As women do in divers countries go
In divers habits, yet are still one kind,
So doth, so is religion : And this blind,
Ness too much light breeds.   But unmoved thou
Of force must one, and forc'd but one allow,
And the right ; ask thy father which is she,
Let him ask his.   Though truth and falshood be
Near twins, yet truth a little elder is :
Be busy to seek her ; believe me this,
He's not of none, nor worst, that seeks the best
T'adore, or scorn an image, or protest,
All may be bad.

Dr. Do

Divinity, wrested by some factious blood,
Draws swords, swells battles, and o'er throws all
Webster's White

Religion is the fool's bridle, worn by policy,
As horse wear trappings, to seem fair in shew;
And make the world's eye doat on what we seem.

Mason's Mulcasses.

———————————— Turn christian?
If it be but for three qualities they have,
I'll be none of their society; first,
They suffer their wives to be their masters; secondly,
They make men thieves for want of maintenance,
And then hang them up for stealing: Lastly,
They're mad four times a year, which they call terms;
And then they're so purg'd by their physicians,
Which they call lawyers, that some never are
Their own men after.

Dauborne's Christian turned Turk.

'Twere happy for our holy faith to bleed;
The blood of martyrs is the churches seed.

Shirley's St. Patrick for Ireland.

As men, for fear the stars should sleep and nod,
    And trip at night, have spheres supply'd,
As if a star were duller than a clod,
    Which knows his way without a guide:

Just so the other heav'n they also serve,
    Divinity's transcendent sky:
Which with the edge of wit they cut and carve;
    Reason triumphs, and faith lies by.

Could not that wisdom which first broach'd the wine,
    Have thicken'd it with definitions?
And jagg'd his seamless coat, had that been fine,
    With curious questions and divisions?
But all the doctrine which he taught and gave
    Was clear as heav'n, from whence it came:
At least those beams of truth, which only save,
    Surpass in brightness any flame.
Love God, and love your neighbour; watch and pray;
    Do as you would be done unto:
O dark instructions, ev'n dark as day!
    Who can these gordian knots undo?   But

But he doth bid us take his blood for wine;
  Bid what he pleaſe; yet I am ſure,
To take and taſte what he doth there deſign,
  Is all that ſaves, and not obſcure.

'Then burn thy *Epicycles*, fooliſh man;
  Break all thy ſpheres, and ſave thy head:
Faith needs no ſtaff of fleſh, but ſtoutly can
  To heav'n alone both go and lead.
                                      Herbert

Religion, ere impos'd, ſhould firſt be taught;
  Not ſeem to dull obedience ready lay'd,
'Then ſwallow'd ſtraight with eaſe; but long be ſough
  And be by reaſon counſell'd, though not ſway'd.
  Sir *W. Davenant*'s *Chriſtian's Reply to the Philoſophe*

Philoſophy doth ſeem to laugh upon
Our hopes; and wiſe divinity belies
Our knowledge, with our faith: Jealous
Nature hath lock'd her ſecrets in a cabinet,
Which time ne'er ſaw: And he that in it pries,
Unto religion forſeits his bold eyes.
                        Sir *W. Davenant*'s *Juſt Italia*

True piety, without ceſſation, toſt
By theories; the practick part is loſt:
And like a ball bandy'd 'twixt pride and wit,
Rather than yield, both ſides the prize will quit:
Then whilſt his foe the gladiator foils,
The atheiſt looking on, enjoys the ſpoils.
                                      Denba

Religion's veil'd in types from vulgar eyes;
None e'er return'd to tell celeſtial joys:
If heav'n were left for ev'ry one to ſee,
Heav'n would be hell, with too much company.
                        Fane's *Love in the Da*

Zeal againſt policy maintains debate;
Heav'n gets the better now, and now the ſtate:
The learned do by turns the learn'd confute,
Yet all depart unalter'd by diſpute.

ly office cannot be deny'd;
av'n's liv'ry, and is made our guide:
ould we be punish'd if we stray;
ur guides dispute, which is the way?

E. Of *Orrery's Muſtapha.*

h religion ſtill will be ſevere;
think much, ſhould I as harſh appear
iend love. 2. would it not pity breed,
e climbing mountains for a weed?
ce *Prometheus* rather to the brow
rocks, for ever clad in ſnow;
religion gnawing of thee ſtill:
d not the devouring vulture kill?
or *Cymmerians* to the ſun unknown,
ry land all darkneſs, like their own!
retched lands with fables overflown,
ntains of the moon, and ſprings unknown,
of falſhood rank their fertile earth,
ing elſe but prieſts and prophets birth!
's *Second Part of the Deſtruction of Jeruſalem.*

R E P E N T A N C E.

fly up, my thoughts remain below;
ithout thoughts, never to Heaven go.

Shakeſpear's Hamlet.

epentance is not ſatisfy'd,
Heav'n, nor Earth; for theſe are pleas'd:
ace, th' eternal wrath's appeas'd.

Shakeſpear's Two Gentlemen of Verona.

the chaos of eternal night,
e I aſcend,
the cold damp of this piercing air;
he juſtice, whoſe almighty word
the bloody acts of impious men
al pennance; who in th' act it ſelf
h' infliction; which, like chain'd ſhot,
ether ſtill: though, (as the thunder
mens duller hearing than their ſight,
a great time after light'ning forth,

Yet

Yet both at one time tear the lab'ring cloud:
So men think pennance of their ills is flow,
'Though th' ill and pennance still together go.
Chapman's Revenge of Bussy D'ambois.

The drunkard, after all his lavish cups,
Is dry, and then is sober: so at length,
When you awake from this lascivious dream,
Repentance then will follow, like the sting
Plac'd in the adder's tail.
Webster's White Devil.

Heaven and Angels
Take great delight in a converted sinner.
Why should you then a servant and professor,
Differ so much from them? If ev'ry woman
That commits evil, should be therefore kept
Back in desires of goodness, how should virtue
Be known and honour'd? From a man that's blind,
To take a burning taper, 'tis no wrong:
He never misses it: But to take light
From one that sees, that's injury and spight.
Pray whether is religion better serv'd,
When lives that are licentious are made honest,
Or when they still run through a sinful Blood?
'Tis nothing, vertue's temples to deface:
But build the ruins, there's a work of grace.
Middleton's Women beware Women.

Man should do nothing that he should repent:
But if he have, and say that he is sorry:
It is a worse fault, if he be not truly.
Beaumont and Fletcher's Honest Man's Fortune.

This brittle glass of life, already broken
With misery, the long and quiet sleep
Of Death would be most welcome. Yet before
We end our pilgrimage, 'tis fit that we
Should leave corruption and foul sins behind us,
But with wash'd feet and hands, the heathens dar'd not
Enter their prophane Temples: and for me
To hope my passage to eternity

Can

nade eafy, till I have fhook off
then of my fins in free confeffion,
ith forrow, and repentance for them
t reafon. Tis not laying by
l ornaments, or putting on
ment of humility, and contrition,
wing duft, and afhes on my head,
ls to tame my proud flefh, that can make
nt for my foul; that muft be humbled;
rd figns of penitence elfe are ufelefs.

Maffinger's Emperor of the Eaft.

r paft ills, doth reftore frail man
rft innocence.

Nabbs's Microcofmus.

th forrow; greateft faults are fmall,
at alone may make amends for all.

Ibid.

to cry God mercy, or to fit
roop, or to confefs that thou haft fail'd:
ewail the fins thou didft commit;
ot commit thofe fins thou haft bewail'd.
bewails, and not forfakes them too;
rather what he means to do.

Quarles.

is fins hath paid with death and forrow;
it's more that pays, than doth not borrow.

Killegrew's Confpiracy.

repents e're he commits a fault;
e a thirfty finner ftore his foul
rcy, to abfolve that fin himfelf,
c may afterwards more fecurely

Sir *W. Davenant's Cruel Brother.*

ence appears unnatural;
e repent what nature did perfwade:
lamenting man's continu'd fall,
: what nature neceffary made.

Since

Since the requir'd extreme of penitence
    Seems so severe, this temple was design'd
Solemn and strange without, to catch the sense;
    And dismal shew'd within, to awe the mind.

Of sad black marble, was the outward frame,
    (A mourning monument to distant sight):
But by the largeness, when you near it came,
    It seem'd the palace of eternal night.

Black beauty (which black *Meroens* had prais'd
    Above their own) fully adorn'd each part;
In stone from *Nile*'s hard quarrys, slowly rais'd,
    And slowlier polish'd by *Numidian* art.

Hither a loud bell's toll rather commands
    Than seems t'invite the persecuted ear;
A summons nature hardly understands;
    For few, and slow are those who enter here:

Within a dismal majesty they find;
    All gloomy, great, all silent does appear,
As Chaos was, e're th' elements were design'd;
    Man's evil fate seems hid and fashion'd here.

Here all the ornament is rev'rend black;
    Here the check'd sun his universal face
Stops bashfully, and will no entrance make;
    As if he spy'd night naked through the glass.

Black curtains hide the glass; whilst from on high,
    A winking lamp, still threatens all the room;
As if the lazy flame just now would die:
    Such will the sun's last light appear at doom.

This lamp was all, that here inform'd all eyes;
    And by reflex, did on a picture gain
Some few false beams, that then from *Sodom* rise;
    Where pencils feign the Fire which Heav'n did r

T

This on another tablet did reflect,
   Where twice was drawn the am'rous *Magdaline*;
Whilst beauty was her care, then her neglect,
   And brightest through her tears she seem'd to shine.

Near her, seem'd crucify'd, that lucky thief
   (In heav'n's dark lott'ry prosp'rous more than wife);
Who grop'd at last, by chance, for heav'n's relief,
   And throngs undoes with hope, by one drawn prize.

In many figures by reflex were sent,
   Through this black vault instructive to the mind,
That early, and this tardy penitent;
   For with *Obsidian* stone 'twas chiefly lin'd.

The seats were made of *Ethiopian* wood;
   The polish'd ebony, but thinly fill'd:
For none this place by nature understood;
   And practice, when unpleasant, makes few skill'd.

Yet these, whom heav'n's mysterious choice fetch'd in,
   Quickly attain devotion's utmost scope;
For having softly mourn'd away their sin,
   They grow so certain, as to need no hope.

At a low door they enter, but depart
   Through a large gate, and to fair fields proceed:
Where *Astragon* makes nature last by art,
   And such long summers shew, as ask no seed.
               Sir *W. Davenant*'s *Gondibert.*

Tis not too late yet, to recant all this;
And there is oft more glory in repenting
Us of some errors, than never to have err'd:
Because we find there are more folks have judgment
Than ingenuity,
               Fountain's *Rewards of Virtue.*
A limb by being broke gets strength, they say,
If set with art; so broken vertue may.
               Crown's *Married Beau.*

R E P O R T.

For seldom shall a ruler lose his life,
 Before false rumours openly be spread :
Whereby this proverb is as true as rife,
 That rulers rumours hunt about a head :
 Frown fortune once, all good report is fled :
For present shew doth make the many blind,
And such as see dare not disclose their mind.

Mirror for Magistrate

Reason with the fellow,
Before you punish him, where he heard this ;
Lest you should chance to whip your Information,
And beat the messenger, who bids beware
Of what is to be dreaded.

Shakespear's Coriolan

Open your ears: For which of you will stop
The vent of hearing, when loud rumour speaks?
I from the orient to the drooping west,
Making the wind my post horse, still unfold
The acts commenced on this Ball of earth.
Upon my tongue continual slanders ride,
The which in ev'ry language I pronounce ;
Stuffing the ears of men with false reports.
I speak of peace, while covert enmity,
Under the smile of safety, wounds the world :
And who but rumour, who but only I,
Make fearful musters, and prepar'd defence ;
Whilst the big year, swoln with some other griefs,
Is thought with child by the stern tyrant war,
And no such matter? Rumour is a pipe,
Blown by surmises, jealousies, conjectures,
And, of so easy and so plain a stop,
That the blunt monster, with uncounted heads,
The still discordant wav'ring multitude,
Can play upon it. But what need I thus
My well known body to anatomise
Among my houshold? From rumour's tongues,
They bring smooth comforts false, worse than true wrong

Shakespear's Second Part of K. Henry I

not some vain report, born without cause,
t envy or imagination draws
m private ends, to breed a publick fear,
muse the world with things that never were ?

Daniel's *Philotas.*

y that intend
do, are like deep waters that run quietly;
ving no face, of what they were, behind them.
s rumour is too common, and too loud
carry truth.

Beaumont and Fletcher's *Captain.*

gard not, as a straw, the world :
e from the tongues of men, doth injury
er than justice; and as conscience
y makes guilty persons, not report,
'shew we as clear as springs unto the world,
ur own knowledge doth not make us so,
t is small satisfaction to our selves):
and we ne'er so lep'rous to man's eye,
nnot hurt heart known integrity.

Nathaniel Field's *Amends for Ladies.*

ng'd by flying rumours, which like birds
ing at random, mute on any head.

Crown's *Ambitious Statesman.*

R E P R O O F.

ear sharp speeches to her. She's a Lady
ender of rebukes, that words are strokes,
. strokes death to her.

Shakespear's *Cymbeline.*

u turn'st mine eyes into my very soul,
there I see such black and grained spots,
vill not leave their tinct.

Shakespear's *Hamlet.*

ny here chance to behold himself,
him not dare to challenge me of wrong;
, if he shame to have his follies known,
t he should shame to act them. My strict hand
s made to seize on vice; and, with a gripe,

Squeeze

Squeeze out the humour of such spongy natures,
As lick up ev'ry idle vanity.
                Johnson's Every Man out of his Humou
You have heard
The fiction of the north-wind and the sun,
Both working on a traveller, and contending
Which had most pow'r to take his cloak from him:
Which, when the wind attempted, he roar'd out
Outragious blasts at him, to force it off,
Then wrapt it closer on : When the calm sun
(The wind once leaving) charg'd him with still bean
Quiet, and fervent, and therein was constant,
Which made him cast off both his cloak and coat:
Like whom should men do; if ye wish your wives
Should leave dislik'd things, seek it not with rage;
For that enrages: What ye give, ye have:
But use calm warnings, and kind manly means;
And that in wives most prostitute, will win
Not only sure amends, but make us wives,
Better than those that ne'er led faulty lives.
                Chapman's Revenge of Bussey D'amb

Prithee forgive me;
I did but chide in jest; the best loves use it
Sometimes, it sets an edge upon affection.
When we invite our best friends to a feast,
'Tis not all sweet meats that we set before them;
There's somewhat sharp and salt, both to whet appet
And make them taste their wine well: So methink
After a friendly, sharp, and savoury chiding,
A kiss tastes wond'rous well, and full o' th' grape.
                Middleton's Women beware Wom

As from water
Call on bitumen, so from these sharp checks
My flame encreateth.
                Nabbs's Hannibal and Sci

Do not with too severe
A harshness chide the error of his love;
Lest like a christal stream, which, unoppos'd

                                        R

with a smooth brow gently in it's course,
stop'd o'th' sudden, his calm nature riot
wilful fury, and persist
intended fancy?

Glapthorne's Albertus Wallenstein.

ve not in their wrath incensed men;
council comes clean out of season then:
hen his fury is appeas'd, and pass'd,
ill conceive his fault, and mend at last.
be is cool, and calm, then utter it;
an gives physick in the midst o'th' fit.

Randolph.

not let thee sleep, nor eat, nor drink;
will ring thee such a piece of chiding,
shalt confess the troubled sea more calm;
thunder with less violence cleaves the air:
avens, screech-owls, and the mandrakes voice
be thy constant musick.

Randolph's Jealous Lovers.

ot enough to strive against the act,
t to do't; we must reprove the fact
ters too: The sin being once made known:
, if not reprov'd, becomes our own :
must dissuade the vice, we scorn to follow.

Quarles.

ot just I should rebuke them for
harmony of mind; that were to shew
rage, and envious malice of the devil;
quarrels with the good, because they have
happiness, which he can ne'er enjoy.

Sir *W Davenant's Law against Lovers.*

REPUTATION.

purest treasure mortal times afford,
tless reputation; that away,
are but gilded loam, or painted clay.

Shakespear's King Richard II.

l name in man and woman,
e immediate jewel of their souls;

F 3

Who

Who steals my purse, steals trash ; 'tis something, nothing
'Twas mine, 'tis his ; and has been slave to thousands
But he that filches from me my good name,
Robs me of that, which not inriches him,
And makes me poor indeed.

Shakespear's Othello

───────────── Reputation
Thou awe of fools and great men ! thou that choak'd
Freest additions and mak'st mortals sweat
Blood and cold drops, in fear to loose, or hope
To gain thy never-certain, seldom-worthy gracings !

Marston's Sophonisba

Upon a time, reputation, love, and death,
Would travel o'er the world ; and 'twas concluded,
That they should part, and take three sev'ral ways:
Death told them, they should find him in great battle
Or cities plagu'd with plagues. Love gives them council
T'inquire for him 'mongst unambitious shepherds,
Where dowries were not talk'd of ; and sometimes
'Mongst quiet kindred, that had nothing left
By their dead parents. Stay, quoth reputation,
Do not forsake me ; for it is my nature,
If once I part from any man I meet,
I am never found again.

Webster's Dutchess of Malfy

The ulcerous reputation feels the poize
Of lightest wrongs ; as sores are vex'd with flies.

Middleton's Women beware Women

────────────If entreaty fail,
The force of reputation shall prevail.

Tourneur's Atheist's Tragedy

Thy credit wary keep, 'tis quickly gone ;
Being got by many actions, lost by one.

Randolph

This I'm sure of, that each man nat'rally
Addicts himself to make a choice of some
Way gaining a repute with others; in
Which, if he receive a check, there's nothing

C

more undervalue him ; he being
os'd to chufe that, in which he moſt excell'd.

The Hectors.

———————————— The reputation
irtuous actions pafs'd ; if not kept up
n accefs, and freſh fupply of new one,
t and foon forgotten ; and like palace ,
want of habitation and repair,
ilve to heaps of ruin.

Denham's Sophy.

rime fo bold, but would be underſtood
al, or at leaſt a feeming good :
fears not to do ill, yet fears the name,
free from conſcience, is a flave to fame.

Denham.

ıot neglect the candour of thy name ;
u ſhouldſt not ſtain thy cloaths, much lefs thy **fame:**
houfes men will build, repair, and trim,
keep them neat without, and fair within :
little they regard, if by foul ways
y blot their names, and flubber o'er their days :
men in life are odious, and ſhall be
eath a fcandal to poſterity.
read a righteous path ; a good report
es men live long, although their life is ſhort.

Watkins.

R E S E R V A T I O N.

hope and expectation of thy time
in'd, and the foul of ev'ry man
hetically does fore-think thy fall.
I fo laviſh of my prefence been,
ımmon-hackney'd in the eyes of men,
ıle and cheap to vulgar company ;
ion, that did help me to the crown,
ſtill kept loyal to poffeffion ;
left me in reputelefs baniſhment,
low of no mark, nor likelihood.
eing feldom feen, I could not ſtir.

F 4

But like a comet I was wonder'd at :
That men would tell their children, this is he.
Others would say, where ? Which is *Bolingbroke* ?
And then I stole all courtesy from heav'n,
And dress'd myself in such humility,
That I did pluck allegiance from men's hearts,
Loud shouts and salutations from their mouths,
Ev'n in the presence of the crowned king.
Thus did I keep my person fresh and new ;
My presence, like a robe pontifical,
Ne'er seen, but wonder'd at ; and so my state,
Seldom, but sumptuous, shewed like a feast,
And won, by rareness, such solemnity :
The skipping king, he ambled up and down
With shallow jesters, and rash bavin wits,
Soon kindled, and soon burnt ; carded his state ;
Mingled his royalty with carping fools ;
Had his great name profaned with their scorns ;
And gave his countenance against his name,
To laugh at gybing boys, and stand the push -
Of ev'ry beardless, vain comparative :
Grew a companion to the common streets,
Enfeoff'd himself by popularity :
That, being daily swallow'd by mens eyes,
They surfeited with honey ; and began
To loath the taste of sweetness ; whereof a little
More than a little, is by much too much.
So when he had occasion to be seen.
He was, but, as the cuckow is in *June*.
Heard, not regarded ; seen, but with such eyes,
As, sick and blunted with community,
Afford no extraordinary gaze ;
Such as is bent on sun-like majesty,
When it shines seldom in admiring eyes :
But rather drowz'd, and hung their eye lids down,
Slept in his face, and render'd such aspect,
As cloudy men use to their adversaries,
Being with his presence glutted, gorg'd, and full.

A

d in that very line, *Harry*, ſtandſt thou ;
thou haſt loſt thy princely privilege
h vile participation.   Not an eye,
is a-weary of thy common ſight,
mine, which hath deſir'd to ſee thee more ;
ch now doth, what I would not have it do,
e blind itſelf with fooliſh tenderneſs.

    Shakeſpear's Firſt Part of King Henry IV.

march'd before report : Where what he meant,
e never knew herſelf, till it was done ;
drifts and rumour ſeldom b'ing all one.

    Daniel on the *Death of the E. of Devonſhire.*

leem thoſe things our ſight doth moſt frequent,
e but mean, although moſt excellent :
trangers ſtill the ſtreets are ſwept and ſtrow'd ;
look on ſuch as daily come abroad :
gs much reſtrain'd, do make us much deſire them ;
beauties ſeldom ſeen, make us admire them.

    Drayton's Edward IV. to *Mrs. Shore.*

———Why then, being maſter
ch and ſo good parts, do you deſtroy them
ſelf-opinion ? or, like a rich miſer,
d up the treaſures you poſſeſs, imparting
o yourſelf nor others, the uſe of them ?
are to you, but like inchanted viands,
hich you ſeem to feed, yet pine with hunger.

    Beaumont and *Fletcher's Cuſtom of the Country.*

nat'ral greatneſs, never artful made,
o retir'd as if you ſought a ſhade ;
oy reſerv'dneſs would miſterious ſeem ;
rmal men retire to get eſteem.
ou would ſo be viſible and free.
th and valour ſtill ſhould publick be.
hate obſcureneſs and would ſtill be ſhown ;
grow more lov'd, as they become more known.

    Sir *W. Davenant* on the *Reſtauration.*

princes, that they may the rumour gain
inding buſ'neſs, mighty buſ'neſs ſeign ;

    F 5   And

And are lock'd up, to have it then suppos'd
They are more thoughtful when they are inclos'd:
But they from concourse privately remove,
Only to shun what they pretend to love.
Pow'r which itself does so reserv'dly keep
As if the being seen would make it cheap,
Should use the proper seasons for retreat:
For though decrepid age may think it meet
To hide stale objects from the people's sight;
Yet in a throne's new glory all delight:
All love young princes in their flourishing,
As all with joy, walk out to see the spring.
Sir W. Davenant on the Restauratio

RESOLUTION.

When resolution hath prepar'd the will;
It wants no helps to further any ill.
Mirror for Magistrat

Let come what will, I mean to bear it out,
And either live with glorious victory,
Or die with fame, renown'd for chivalry:
He is not worthy of the honey-comb,
That shuns the hives because the bees have stings.
That likes me best that is not got with ease,
Which thousand dangers do accompany:
For nothing can dismay our regal mind,
Which aims at nothing but a golden crown,
The only upshot of mine enterprizes.
Were they inchanted in grim *Pluto's* court,
And kept for treasure 'mong his hellish crew,
I'd either quell the triple *Cerberus*,
And all the army of his hateful hags,
Or roll the stone with wretched *Sisyphus.*
Shakespear's Locr

Experience teacheth us,
That resolution's a sole help at need:
And this, my lord, our honour teacheth us,
That we be bold in ev'ry enterprize:

T

fince there is no way, but fight or dye,
olute, my lord, for victory.
Shakefpear's Locrine.

————Why look you fad ?
at in act, as you have been in thought :
t the world fee fear, and fad diftruft
n the motion of a kingly eye :
ring as the time ; be fire with fire ;
ten the threat'ner, and out-face the brow
agging horror : So fhall inferior eyes,
orrow their behaviour from the great,
great by your example ; and put on
auntlefs fpirit of refolution.
, and glitter like the god of war,
he intendeth to become the field ;
boldnefs and afpiring confidence.
, fhall they feek the lion in his den,
ight him there ? And make him tremble there ?
et it not be faid ! Forage, and run
et difpleafure farther from the docrs ;
rapple with him, ere he come fo nigh.
Shakefpear's King John.

———— Tell fools of fools,
hofe effem'nate cowards that do dream
ofe fantaftick other worlds : There is
ich a thing in nature ; all the foul
an is refolution; which expires
from valiant men, till their laft breath ;
hen with it, like to a flame extinguifh'd,
ant of matter, it does not dye, but
r ceafes to live.
Chapman's Revenge for Honour.
efolution would fteel a coward
Beaumont and *Fletcher's Little French Lawyer.*
refolution ! I am proud to fee
et a graft upon a worm-wood tree ;
e juice is gall, but yet the fruit moft rare :
wreaks the tree, if that the fruit be fair ?
Heywood's Fair Maid of the Exchange.

She beheld the shepherd on his way,
Much like a bridegroom on his marriage-day ;
Increasing not his misery with fear :
Others for him, but he shed not a tear.
His knitting sinews did not tremble ought,
Nor to unusual palpitation brought
W. s or his heart, or liver ; nor his eye,
Nor tongue, nor colour shew'd a dread to dye.
His resolution keeping with his spirit,
Both worthy him that did them both inherit,
Held in subjection ev'ry thought of fear,
Scorning so base an executioner.

Brown's Pastorals

My resolution, grounded on his service,
'Ties more than formal contracts.

Habbington's Queen of Arragon

————————His resolution's like
A skillful horseman, and reason is the stirrup ;
Which though a sudden shock may make it loose,'
Yet does it meet it handsomely again.

Suckling's Aglaura

———————— Intice the trusty sun
From his ecliptick line, he shall obey
Your beck, and wander from his sphere, ere I
From my resolves.

Baron's Mirza

My resolution's firm, for all my shakings ;
They are but starts which sometimes nature makes ;
As wolves kept tame may, now and then,
Provok'd by appetite, or some displeasure,
Start into actions like their usual wildness,
Before they were reduc'd to an obedience :
So 'tis with me ; though I have brought my nature
To a tameness and submission ;
Yet, at the unwelcome prospect that it takes
Of my intended dissolution,
It starts within me ; and would fain break
Those severe fetters, virtue and reason ties them up with

Sir R. Howard's Surprisa

if your refolutions be like mine,
will yet give our forrows a brave end.
ce is for us, fo may fortune be :
a bright proof of her inconftancy.
if no god will lend us any aid,
us be gods, and fortune to ourfelves.

Crown's Darius.

R E T I R E M E N T.

wifdom, madam, of your private life,
re, with this wile you liv'd a widow'd wife,
the right ways you take unto the right,
conquer rumour, triumph over fpight ;
only fhunning, by your act, to do
ht that is ill, but the fufpicion too :
fo brave example, as he were
friend to virtue could be filent here.

Johnfon's Underwoods.

an of fp'rit beyond the reach of fear,
, difcontent with his neglected worth,
lects the light, and loves obfcure abodes :
he is young and haughty, apt to take
at advancement ; to bear ftate, and flourifh ;
is rife therefore fhall my bounties fhine :
e loaths the world fo much, nor loves to fcoff it ;
gold and grace will make him furfeit of it.

Chapman's Buffey D'ambois.

would believe thy metal could let floth --
and confume it ? If *Themiftocles*
liv'd obfcure thus in th'*Athenian* ftate,
res had made both him and it his flaves,
rave *Camillus* had lurk'd fo in *Rome*,
had not been five times dictator there,
four times triumph'd.   If *Epaminondas*,
liv'd twice twenty years obfcur'd in *Thebes*,
liv'd fo ftill, he had been ftill un-nam'd ;
paid his country nor himfelf their right :
putting forth his ftrength, he refcu'd both

From

From imminent ruin : and like burnifh'd fteel,
After long ufe he fhin'd

Chapman's Buffey D'ambois

'That, by their fubaltern minifters
   May be perform'd as well, and with more graces
For, to command it to be done, inferrs
   More glory than to do.   It doth embafe
'Th'opinion of a pow'r t'invulgar fo
'That facred prefence, which fhould never go,
Never be feen, but e'en as gods, below
Like to our *Perfian* king in glorious fhew ;
And who, as ftars affixed to their fphere,
May not defcend, to be, from what they are.

Daniel's Philotas

Court honours, and your fhadows of true joy,
'That fhine like ftars, but till a greater light
Drown your weak luftre ; I abjure your fight ;
Ev'n from my meditations, and my thoughts
I banifh your inticing vanities;
And clofely kept within my ftudy walls,
As from a cave of reft, henceforth I'll fee
And fmile, but never tafte your mifery.

Goffe's Raging Turk.

1. How like you this fair folitary life ?
2 As fhipwrack'd men the fhore, or prifners liberty.
I never thought a pleafure good in life to be,
Until I found it here.
1. This your content doth bring into my mind
'Thofe days that *Carens* liv'd upon the plain,
Unhappy courtier, yet a happy fwain.
Methinks I now do hear his well tun'd pipe
'That drew the cov'tous ear of lift'ning fhepherds.
'To hear him chant his paffed mifery

Dauborne's Poor Man's Comfort

'Thy father's poverty has made thee happy ;
For, though 'tis true, this folitary life
Suits not with youth and beauty, O my child !
Yet 'tis the fweeteft guardian to protect

Chaff

Chaſte names from court-aſperſions : There a lady
Tender and delicate in years and graces,
That doats upon the charms of eaſe and pleaſure,
Is ſhipwrack'd on the ſhore ; for 'tis much ſafer
To truſt the ocean in a leaking ſhip,
Than follow greatneſs in the wanton rites·
Of luxury and ſloth.

Beaumont and *Fletcher's Laws of Candy.*

Was man e'er bleſs'd with that exceſs of joy
Equal to ours, to us that feel no want
Of high court favours, life's licentiouſneſs :
Kings have their cares, and in their higheſt ſtate,
Want of free pleaſures crowns us ſortunate.

Richards's Meſſallina.

I'd rather like the violet grow
Unmark'd i'th' ſhaded vale,
Than on the hill thoſe terrors know
Are breath'd forth by an angry gale :
There is more pomp above, more ſweet below.

Habbington's Caſtara.

Yours is a virtue of inferior rate ;
  Here in the dark a pattern, where 'tis barr'd
From all your ſex that ſhould her imitate,
  And of that pomp which ſhould her foes reward :

Retir'd, as weak monaſticks fly from care ;
  Or devout cowards ſteal to forts, their cells,
From pleaſures, which the world's chief dangers are ;
  Her's 'paſſes yours, as valour fear excels.

Sir W. Davenant's Gondibert.

O happineſs of ſweet retir'd content !
To be at once ſecure and innocent.

Denham.

Though he in all the people's eyes ſeem'd great,
Yet greater he appear'd in his retreat.

Ibid.

Let us to private ſhades,
For darkneſs and diſhonour beſt agree

Crown's Regulus.

How mis'rable a thing is a great man !
Take noify vexing greatnefs they that pleafe,
Give me obfcure, and fafe, and filent eafe :
Acquaintance and commerce let me have none,
With any pow'rful thing, but time alone :
My reft let time be fearful to offend,
And creep by me, as by a flumb'ring friend :
Till with eafe glutted, to my grave I fteal,
As men to fleep, after a plenteous meal.

Crown's Thyfts.

R E V E N G E.

To be reveng'd of a woman, were a
Thing than love itfelf more womanifh.

Lilly's Endimion.

Now I might do it pat, now he is praying ;
And now I'll do't, —— and fo he goes to heav'n. ——
And fo am I reveng'd ? That would be fcann'd ;
A villain kills my father, and for that,
I, his fole fon, do this fame villain fend
To heav'n.——O this is hire and falary, not revenge.
He took my father grofly, full of bread,
With all his crimes broad-blown, as flufh as *May*;
And how his audit ftands, who knows, fave heav'n?
But in our circumftance and courfe of thought,
'Tis heavy with him.   Am I then reveng'd,
To take him in the purging of his foul,
When he is fit and feafon'd for his paffage ?
Up fword, and know thou a more horrid bent ;
When he is drunk, afleep, or in his rage,
Or in th' inceftuous pleafure of his bed ;
At gaming, fwearing, or about fome act
That has no relifh of falvation in't :
Then trip him, that his heels may kick at heav'n ;
And that his foul may be as damn'd and black
As hell, whereto it goes.

Shakefpear's Hamlet.

Horror hath her degrees : There is excefs
In all revenge, that may be done with lefs.

Lord Brooke's Alaham.

: falls heavy, that is rais'd by love.

Marston's Insatiate Countess.

—Oh mine's revenge !
o on that does dream,
a tyrant ever in extreme.

Ibid.

ikes a lion, must be sure strike home ;
ing at his life, he lose his own.

Dauborne's Poor Man's Comfort.

rest action of our humane life,
rning to revenge an injury ;
o forgives without a further strife,
dversary's heart to him doth tie :
a firmer conquest truly said,
the heart, than overthrow the head.
worthy enemy do find,
ield to worth, it must be nobly done :
f baser metal be his mind,
se revenge there is no honour won.
ould a worthy courage overthrow ?
o would wrestle with a worthless foe ?

our hearts are great, and cannot yield ;
se they cannot yield, it proves them poor :
earts are task'd beyond their pow'r ; but seld
weakest lion will the loudest roar.
school for certain doth this same allow,
eartedness doth sometimes teach to bow.

heart doth teach a virtuous scorn ;
corn to owe a duty over long :
n to be for benefits forborn ;
corn to lie, to scorn to do a wrong :
n to bear an injury in mind ;
n a free-born heart slave-like to bind.

or wrongs we needs revenge must have,
be our vengeance of the noblest kind :
his body from our fury save,
let our hate prevail against his mind ?

Wha

What can 'gainft him a greater vengeance be,
'Than make his foe more worthy far than he?
Lady Carew's Mariam.

All arm'd with malice, either lefs or more,
'To ftrike at him, who ftruck at all before.
Drayton's Barons Wars.

The boift'rous ocean when no winds oppofe,
Grows calm; revenge is loft, when 't hath no foes.
Goffe's Couragious Turk.

The beft revenge is to reform our crimes;
'Then time crowns forrows, forrows fweeten times.
Middleton and *Rowley's Spanish Gipfy.*

———————— ———— In this
You fati-fy your anger, and revenge:
Suppofe this, it will not
Repair your lofs; and there was never yet
But fhame, and fcandal in a victory,
When rebels unto reafon, paffions fought it.
'Then for revenge, by great fouls it was ever
Contemn'd, though offer'd, entertain'd by none
But cowards, bafe, and abject fpirits; ftrangers
'To moral honefty, and never yet
Acquainted with religion.
Maffinger's City Madam.

————— ———— How juft foever
Our reafons are to remedy our wrongs,
We're yet to leave them to their will and pow'r,
'That to that purpofe have authority.
Maffinger and *Field's Fatal Dowry*

Wife men fecure their fates; and execute
Invifibly, like that moft fubtil flame
'That burns the heart; yet leaves no path, or touch
Upon the fkin to follow or fufpect it.
Shirley's Traitor

A true *Italian* fpirit is a ball
Of wild-fire, hurting moft, when it feems fpent:
Great fhips on fmall rocks beating oft, are rent.
Sam. Rowley's Noble Spanifh Soldier
——Reveng

———— Revenge is able,
a flinty cowardice to strike
: of valour.

Nabbs's Hannibal and Scipio.

ft with courtesy a while confer ;
e proves its own executioner.

John Ford's Broken Heart.

m thy scorching den, thou soul of mischief !
od boils hotter than the poison'd flesh
cules cloath'd in the *Centaur's* shirt :
e revenge, till I become a hill
Olympus cloud-dividing top ;
might fall, and crush them into air.

Rawlins's Rebellion.

lifposition is for to requite
ry, before a benefit :
giving is a burden, and a pain ;
: is pleasing to us, as our gain.

Herrick.

e, impatient *Hubert* proudly sought,
:, which ev'n when just, the wise deride ;
aft wrongs we spend our time and thought,
scarce against the future can provide.

Sir *W. Davenant's Gondibert.*

•, weak womens valour, and in men,
uffian's cowardice, keep from thy breast :
lious palace is the serpent's den,
n cowards there, with secret slaughter feast.

e, is but a braver name for fear ;
Indian's furious fear, when they are fed
aliant foes ; whose hearts their teeth must tear,
: they boldly dare believe them dead.

Sir *W. Davenant's Gondibert.*

. poor, a low revenge, unworthy
ues, or my injuries ; and
my fame, so then my infamy,
olot out his ; and I, instead of his empire,

Shall

Shall only be the heir of all his curses.
No: I'll be still myself, and carry with me
My innocence to th'other world ; and leave
My fame to this : 'T will be a brave revenge,
To raise my mind to a conflancy fo high,
That may look down upon his threats : my patience
Shall mock his fury : Nor shall he be fo happy
To make me mis'rable : And my fuff'rings shall
Erect a prouder trophy to my name,
Than all my profp'rous actions.   Every pilot
Can fteer the ship in calms ; but he performs
The skillful part, can manage it in storms.
                                        Denham's Sophy.

There are affronts fo great,
And height'ned by fuch odious circumstances,
As do release us from the ufual forms
Of generous revenge ; and fets us free
To take it on any advantage,
                            Tuke's Adventures of Five Hours.
Who merits my revenge and hate, must prove
As brave and great, as he who gains my love.
                                        Crown's Juliana.
And what's fo defp'rate as an angry slave ;
When, by adventuring, he revenge may have?
                            Crown's Charles VIII. of France.

R E W A R D.

If either vice or virtue we abandon ;
We either are rewarded as we ferve,
Or elfe are plagued, as our deeds deferve.
                                        Mirror for Magistrates.
————————————Thou'rt fo far before,
That swiftest wing of recompence is slow,
To overtake thee.   Would thou'dst less deferv'd,
That the proportion both of thanks and payment
Might have been mine : Only I've left to fay,
More is thy due, than more than all can pay.
                                        Shakespear's Macbeth.

'Tis

if some men will do well for price ;

e virtuous, when reward's away.

Johnson's Catiline.

ow virtue, for reward, to day ;

w vice, if she give better pay :

so good, or bad, just at a price,

g else discerns the virtue or the vice.

Johnson's Epigrams.

great merit do upbraid, and call

: reward, or think the great too small.

 s love not to beholden ought ;

 makes their chiefest friends oft speed the worst:

 , by whom their fortunes have been wrought,

 m in mind of what they were at first ;

 ubtful faith, if once in question brought,

 ought they will offend, because they durst ;

 n in a fault, are never spar'd :   .

 er to revenge, than to reward.

Daniel's Civil War.

——————————— Honour pays

where kings neglect ; and he is valiant

hat dares forget to be rewarded.

Shirley's Young Admiral.

 a present worth acceptance ;

y came with them more than doubles

Jue : If vice blush not at rewards,

no shame for virtue to receive them.

Shirley's Example.

 e bestows rich largess on his men,

ame their minds ; that if they did not love

 r her own self, rewards should then

heir loves to her, and their dullness move.

is the great pillar of a state,

oth support as strongly as her fate.   -

A

A gen'rous spirit is not drawn, but led
 To stake a life, and hazard it in war:
Soldiers their blood will liberally shed,
 Where free rewards and lib'ral guerdons are.
Aurelian takes this council: To bestow
Gold on his men, and iron on his foe.

Alexn's Poem

Nor is it safe for subjects since,
Too much to oblige their prince,
With mighty service, that exceed
The power of his noblest meed:
For whom he cannot well reward,
He'll find occasion to discard.

Baron's Mi.

1. He who his country serves, with justice may
Challenge, nay force rewards; if none will pay.
It is a grief distracts a gen'rous mind,
When more to chance than merit is assign'd.
Merits more great than *Cæsar*, who can plead?
What he hath done for *Rome* respect should breed.
2. Who ever sav'd a town by his defence,
And did expect the town for recompence?
What though great *Cæsar* hath in battle stood,
For to maintain *Rome's* int'rest with his blood?
'Tis but a debt that's due: Let that suffice;
Must she herself, become her champion's prize?
1 But if such acts meet envy for return,
It kindles passion, and it makes us burn:
When senators repay such deeds with spight,
As our own carvers, we ourselves requite;
And then our publick power we reduce
To private ends, and to peculiar use.

Dover's Roman Gene

R U I N.

——————Fate will have thee pursue
Deeds, after which, no mischief can be new,

The ruin of thy country.——Thou wert built
For such a work, and born for no less guilt.

Johnson's Catiline.

It is decreed.   Nor shall thy fate, O *Rome*,
Resist my vow.   Tho' hills were set on hills,   .
And seas met seas to guard thee ; I would through :
I'd plough up rocks, steep as the *Alps*, in dust ;
And lave the *Tyrrhene* waters into clouds,
But I would reach thy head, thy head, proud city !

Ibid.

1. Repulse upon repulse ? An inmate consul ?
That I could reach the axle, where the pins are,
Which bolt this frame ; that I might pull 'em out,
And pluck all into chaos with myself.
2. What are we wishing now ?
1. Yes, my *Cethegus*,
Who would not fall with all the world about him ?
2. Not I, that would stand on it, when it falls ;
And force new nature out to make another.
These wishings taste of woman, not of *Roman.*
Let us seek other arms.
1. What should we do ?
2. Do, and not wish ; something that wishes take not :
So sudden, as the gods shall not prevent,
Nor scarce have time to fear.
It likes me better, that you are not consul.
I would not go through open doors, but break them ;
Swim to my ends through blood ; or build a bridge
Of carcasses ; make on upon the heads
Of men, struck down like piles ; to reach the lives
Of those remain and stand.   Then is't a prey,
When danger stops, and ruin makes the way.

Ibid.

Such are the judgments of the heav'nly pow'rs,
We others ruins work, and others ours.

Daniel's Philotas.

I do love these ancient ruins :
We never tread upon them, but we set

Our

Our foot upon some rev'rend history;
And questionless, here in this open court,
Which now lies naked to the injuries
Of stormy weather, some lie interr'd
Lov'd the church so well, and gave so largely to't,
They thought it should have canopy'd their bones
Till doomsday: But all things have their end;
Churches and cities, which have diseases like to men,
Must have like death that we have.

Webster's Dutchess of Malfy

—————————————————She but shews thee
The easy path to ruin, whose broad entrance
Painted with fallest pleasures, ends in a point
Of all the ends that attend on misery
Contracted into one.

Nabbs's Microcosm

—————————————— Destruction
O'ertakes as often those that fly, as those that
Boldly meet it.

Denham's Soph.

All things decay with time; the forest sees
The growth and downfal of her aged trees:
That timber tall, which threescore lustres stood
The proud dictator of the state like wood;
I mean the sov'reign of all plants, the oak,
Droops, dies, and falls without the cleaver's stroke.

Herrie

S A F E T Y.

NOUGHT's had, all's spent,
    Where our desire is got without content:
'Tis safer to be that which we destroy,
Than by destruction dwell in doubtful joy.

Shakespear's Macbet

B

en men think they moſt in ſafety ſtand ;
greateſt peril often is at hand.

Drayton's Barons Wars.

——This rule is certain ;
t purſues his ſafety from the ſchool
e, muſt learn to be madman, or fool.

John Ford's Lovers Melancholy.

aſeties had no counterpoiſe at all :
ales, this cannot riſe, unleſs that fall.

Aleyn's Henry VII.

iin yet apears not, and you think
: it lurks, you are ſafe :
t will be truly ſecure, muſt found
e on the deſtruction of all things
an impeach it.

Killegrew's Conspiracy.

——In that calm harbour,
ughts have been ſecur'd from ſtorm.
u may'ſt be much deceiv'd : The ſhip-wrack paſt,
lmeſt waters may conceal the fate,
l as the inſulting waves.

Sir *R. Howard's Blind Lady.*

hough the ſea be calm ? truſt to the ſhore ;
ave been drown'd, where late they danc'd before.

Herrick.

ippy were men, if they underſtood :
is no ſafety, but in being good.

Fountain's Rewards of Virtue.

S A T I R E.

es, each man, though untouch'd, complains
were hurt ; and hates ſuch biting ſtrains.

Johnſon's Poetaſter.

ires, ſince the moſt of mankind be
unavoided ſubject, feweſt ſee :
ne e'er took that pleaſure in ſin's ſenſe ;
hen they heard it tax'd, took more offence.

Johnſon on Dr. *Donne's Death.*

. III.　　　　G　　　　I'm

I'm one whose whip of steel can with a lash,
Imprint the characters of shame so deep,
Ev'n in the brazen forehead of proud sin,
That not eternity shall wear it out.
When I but frown'd in my *Lucilius'* brow,
Each conscious cheek grew red ; and a cold trembling
Freez'd the chill'd soul ; while ev'ry guilty breast
Stood fearful of dissection, as afraid
To be anat'miz'd by that skillful hand,
And have each artery, nerve, and vein of sin
By it laid open to the publick scorn.
I have untruss'd the proudest ; greatest tyrants
Have quak'd below my pow'rful whip, half dead
With expectation of the smarting jerk ;
Whose wound no salve can cure. Each blow doth leave
A lasting scar, that with a poison eats
Into the marrow of their fame, and lives ;
Th' eternal ulcer to their memories.

Randolph's Muses Looking-Glass.

So dost thou aim thy darts, which ev'n when
They kill the poisons, do but wake the men.
Thy thunders thus but purge ; and we endure
Thy lancings better than another's cure :
And justly too ; for th' age grows more unsound
From the fools balsam, than the wiseman's wound.

Cartwright.

Thy star was judgment only and right sense ;
Thyself being to thyself an influence :
Stout beauty is thy grace ; stern pleasures do
Present delights, but mingle horrors too :
Thy muse doth thus, like *Jove's* fierce girl appear,
With a fair hand, but grasping of a spear.

Ibid.

SECRECY, SECRETS.

My anticipation shall prevent your
Discovery ; and your secrecy to
The king and queen moult no feather.

Shakespear's Hamlet.
Why

Why have I blabb'd ? Who fhall be true to us,
When we are fo unfecret to ourfelves ?

Shakefpear's Troilus and Creffida.

'Tis no fin love's fruits to fteal ;
But the fweet thefts to reveal :
To be taken, to be feen ;
Thefe have crimes accounted been.

Johnfon's Volpone.

A fecret in his mouth,
Is like a wild bird put into a cage ;
Whofe door no fooner opens, but 'tis out.

Johnfon's Cafe is alter'd.

—————The open merry man
Moves like a fprightly river; and yet can
Keep fecret in his channels what he breeds,
'Bove all your ftanding waters choak'd with weeds.
They look at beft like cream-bowls, and you foon
Shall find their depth; they're founded with a fpoon.
They may fay grace, and for love's chaplains pafs ;
But the grave lover ever was an afs ;
Is fix'd upon one leg, and dares not come
Out with the other, for he's ftill at home :
Like the dull weary'd crane, that, come on land,
Doth while he keeps his watch, betray his ftand ;
Where he that knows, will, like a lap-wing fly,
Far from the neft, and fo himfelf belie
To others ; as he will deferve the truft
Due to that one that doth believe him juft.

Johnfon's Underwoods.

————————— Our grave counfellor
Well knows that great affairs will not be forg'd
But upon anvils that are lin'd with wool.
We muft afcend to our intention's top,
Like clouds, that be not feen, till they be up

Chapman's Second Part of Byron's Confpiracy

Intents ill carry'd are, that men may know ;
When things are done, let rumour freely go.

Lord *Brooke's Alaham.*

G 2   Sec

One should look well to whom his mind he leaves ;
In dang'rous times, when tales by walls are told,
Men make themselves unnecessar'ly slaves
Of those, to whom their secrets they unfold.

E. of Sterline's Julius Cæsar.

1. Canst thou conceal a secret ?
2. Yes, as long as it is a secret ; but
When two know it, how can it be a secret ?
And indeed with what justice can you
Expect secrecy in me, that cannot
Be private to yourself ?

Marston's Fawn.

———— It is an equal fault,
To tell one's secrets unto all, or none.

Webster's Dutchess of Malfy.

I'll conceal this secret from the world,
As warily as those that deal in poison,
Keep poison from their children.

Ibid.

Be well advis'd ; and think what danger 'tis
To receive a prince's secrets : They that do,
Had need have their breasts hoop'd with adamant,
To contain them : I pray thee yet be satisfy'd,
Examine thine own frailty, 'tis more easy
To tie knots than to unloose them : 'Tis a secret,
That, like a ling'ring poison, may chance lie
Spread in thy veins, and kill thee seven years hence.

Ibid.

Deep policy in us, makes fools of such :
Then must a slave die, when he knows too much.

Tourneur's Revenger's Tragedy.

For he that prates his secrets, his heart
Stands on the outside.

Ibid.

Secret ! I ne'er had that disease o' th 'mother,
I praise my father : Why are men made close,
But to keep thoughts in bell ? I grant you this ;
Tell but some women a secret over-night,

Your

: doctor may find it in the urinal

he morning.

Tourneur's Revenger's Tragedy.

hat knows great men's secrets, and proves slight;

t man ne'er lives to see his beard turn white.

Ibid.

f all court secrets come to light, what

become of the Farthingales think you

cover them? No, since ladies wear whale-bones,

/ have been swallow'd, and so may this.

W. Smith's Hector of Germany.

—He deserves small trust,

is not privy counsellor to himself.

John Ford's Broken Heart.

: so cover'd this advertisement,

none perceiv'd he saw, what he did see:

to the optick virtue in the eyes,

:n itself, yet all things else descries.

Aleyn's Henry VII.

mber that a prince's secrets

alm, conceal'd: But poison, if discover'd.

Massinger's Duke of Milan.

prentices though they are bound to keep

masters secrets, are not all privy

eir mistresses; that's a meer journeyman's

:.

Richard Brome's Mad Couple well match'd.

v, a broken oath is no such burthen

great secret is; besides the tickling

man has to in and out with it.   Oh,

tongue's itch is intolerable!

Richard Brome's Love-sick Court.

trust those secrets, whereon honour rests,

istody in mercenary breasts,

ive nobility: And though they pay

ly ransom, ne'er redeem't away.

Ibid.

Safe

Safe in thy breaft clofe lock up thy intents;
For he that knows thy purpofe, beft prevents.

Rand

I am ruin'd in her confeffion;
The man that trufts woman with a privacy,
And hopes for filence, he may as well expect it
At the fall of a bridge: A fecret with them,
Is like a viper; it will make way though
It eat through the bowels of them. 'Tis fo, that
Women thirft man's overthrow; that is a
Principle, as demonftrative as truth;
'Tis the only end they were made for: And
When they have infinuated themfelves
Into our councils, and gain'd the pow'r
Of our life, the fire is more merciful;
It burns within them, till it gets forth.

Marmion's Antiq

Guilty of folly I am, to truft a woman,
To keep for me, what for herfelf fhe cannot;
A fecret: That open fex! whofe fouls are
So loofe they cannot keep them in their breafts,
But they will fwim upon their lips.

Baron's M

———————— Thou hitteft
So juft upon my thoughts, thy tongue is tipt
Like nature's miracle, that draws the fteel
With unrefifted violence: I cannot keep
A fecret to myfelf, but thy prevailing
Rhetorick ravifhes and leaves my breaft
Like to an empty casket, that once was bleft
With keeping of a jewel, I durft not truft
The air with, 'twas fo precious.

Rawlins's Reb

Harken ye men that e'er fhall love like me;
I'll give you council *gratis*: If you be
Poffefs'd of what you like, let your fair friend
Lodge in your bofom: But no fecrets fend

To seek their lodging in a female breast;
For so much is abated of your rest.
The steed that comes to understand his strength,
Grows wild, and casts his manager at length:
And that tame lover who unlocks his heart
Unto his mistress, teaches her an art
To plague himself; shews her the secret way,
How she may tyrannize another day.

Bishop King.

The plot, wherewith I labour, can admit
No council, but a necessary faith
In the bold actor; whose subsistence binds him
To resolution and to secrecy:
All friendly trust is folly; ev'ry man
Hath one, to whom he will commit as much
As is to him committed: Our designs
When once they creep from our own private breasts,
Do in a moment through the city fly;
Who tells his secret, sells his liberty.

Freeman's Imperiale.

As winds, whose voilence out-does all art,
   Act all unseen; so we as secretly
These branches of that cedar Gondibert,
   Must force till his deep root in rising dye.

If we make noise, whilst our deep workings last,
   Such rumour through thick towns unheeded flies,
As winds through woods; and we, our great work past,
   Like winds will silence tongues, and 'scape from eyes.

Sir W. Davenant's Gondibert.

Search not to find what lies too deeply hid;
Nor to know things, whose knowledge is forbid.

Denham.

——————————— But if
This secrecy be a gallant's highest quality,
To please the females, curb'd by fear and honour;
May not these priests be held secure offenders,
Whom fear of death obliges to be silent?

G 4

Or,

Or, were there no such law, why, then
They're fav'rites of necessity, not choice,
Or prudence: Like to chief ministers of state,
Who dive so far into their masters secrets,
'Tis dang'rous to refuse to shew them more.

Fane's Love in the Dark.

I'm ruin'd, 'cause I know all their designs:
For now court-secrets are like fairies revels,
Or witches conventicles; men are spoil'd
With sudden blasts that either tell, or see them.

Crown's Ambitious Statesman.

S E N S E S.

But why do I the soul and sense divide,
 When sense is but a pow'r, which she extends;
Which b'ing in divers parts diversify'd,
 The divers forms of objects apprehends?

This pow'r spreads outward, but the root doth grow
 In th' inward soul, which only doth perceive;
For th' eyes and ears no more their objects know,
 Than glasses know what faces they receive.

For if we chance to fix our thoughts elsewhere,
 Though our eyes open be, we cannot see:
And if one pow'r did not both see and hear,
 Our sights and sounds would always double be.

Sir John Davies.

This pow'r's sense, which from abroad doth bring
 The colour taste, and touch, and scent, and sound,
The quantity and shape of ev'ry thing
 Within earth's centre, or heav'n's circle found.

This pow'r, in parts made fit, fit objects takes;
 Yet not the things, but forms of things receives:
As when a seal in wax impression make,
 The print therein, but not itself it leaves.

And though things sensible be numberless;
 But only five the senses organs be;
And in those five, all things their forms express,
 Which we can touch, taste, feel, or hear, or see

Ibid.

w does our palace now refemble great *Mahomet's*
dice ! How does it float in pleafures !
fmall-brain'd book-worms talk of fpeculations
empty notions floating in their underftandings
by our practice only will embrace
knowledge of our fenfes ; which they
ibute falfly unto beafts alone : But we
ing experienc'd its tranfcendent excellence,
bath'd us in the pleafing ftreams
ch flow from that fweet fountain of our fenfe ;
r deny, that brutes are capable of that
to be parak l'd felicity ; or if they are,
know not how to prize that excellent jewel :
here lies
effential diff'rence 'twixt them and us,
is my new philofophy; that men by often
ing and making ufe of it, rightly know
to prize it ; but brutes,
ugh that happinefs be in their poffeffion,
gnorant of the value :
know how t' improve the knowlege o' their fenfe,
inging and reducing it to practice :
the fenfe reprefents us lovely to them,
prefently embrace that object.

Unfortunate Ufurper.

S E R V A N T,   S E R V I C E.

good fervant does not all commands ;
nd, but to do juft ones.

Shakefpear's Cymbeline.

I but ferv'd my God with half the zeal
d my king ; he would not in mine age
left me naked to mine enemies.

Shakefpear's King Henry VIII.

——————————'Tis mad idolatry,
ake the fervice greater than the God ;
e will dotes, that is inclinable
at infectioufly itfelf affects,

G 5

Without

Without some image of th' affected merit.
Shakespear's Troilus and Cressida.

Petter to leave undone, than by our deed
Acquire too high a fame, when he, we serve's away.
Shakespear's Antony and Cleopatra.

———— "Tis the curse of service,
Preferment goes by letter and affection,
And not by old gradation ; where each second
Stead heir to the first.
Shakespear's Othello.

I follow him to serve my turn upon him.
We cannot all be masters, nor all masters
Cannot be truly follow'd.   You shall mark
Many a duteous and knee-crooking knave,
That, doting on his own obsequious bondage,
Wears out his time, much like his master's ass,
For nought, but provender ; and when he's old, ca-
        shier'd :
Whip me such honest knaves——others there are,
Who, trimm'd in form and visages of duty,
Keep yet their hearts attending on themselves ;
And, throwing but shews of service on their lords,
Well thrive by them ; and when they've lin'd their
        coats,
Do themselves homage : These folks have some soul,
And such a one do I profess myself.
Ibid.

There be some sports are painful, but their labour
Delight in them sets off : Some kinds of baseness
Are nobly undergone, and most poor matters
Point to rich ends.   This my mean task
Would be as heavy to me, as 'tis odious : But
The mistress which I serve, quickens what's dead,
And makes my labours, pleasures.
Shakespear's Tempest.

That such a slave as this should wear a sword,
Who wears no honesty ; such smiling rogues as these,
Like rats, oft bite the holy cords in twain,

Too

infitate t' unloose : Sooth ev'ry paffion,
the nature of their lords rebels ;
to fire ; fnow to their colder moods ;
affirm, and turn their halcion beaks
ry gale and vary of their mafters ;
ing nought, like dogs, but following.

Shakespear's King Lear.

s, thou art more honeft now, than wife,
oppreffing and betraying me,
ght'ft have fooner got another fervice :
y fo arrive at fecond mafters,
:ir firft lord's neck. But tell me true,
ft ever doubt, though ne'er fo fure,
kindnefs fubtle ; covetous,
g kindnefs, as rich men deal gifts,
g in return twenty for one ?
ny moft worthy mafter ; in whofe breaft
d fufpect, alas are plac'd too late ;
ld have fear'd falfe times, when you did feaft ;
ill comes, where an eftate is leaft.

Shakespear's Timon.

vices are, clock-like, to be fet,
d and forward, at their lord's command.

Johnfon's Cafe is alter'd.

!, in this divine difcipline, is
le, exceeding all the potentates
irth ; ftill waited on by mutes ; and all
nands fo executed : Yea ev'n in the war,
heard, and in his marches, moft
larges and directions giv'n by
l with filence : An exquifite art !
heartily afham'd and angry
es, that the princes of *Chriftendom,*
ffer a barbarian to tranfcend
fo high a point of felicity.

Johnfon's Silent Woman.

G 6

O more

O more than happy ten times were that king,
    Who were unhappy but a little space,
So that it did not utter ruin bring,
But made him prove a profitable thing !
    Who of his train did best deserve his grace
Then could, and would of these the best emb
Such vultures fled as follow but for prey,
    That faithful servants might possess their pl
All gallant minds it must with anguish sting,
Whilst wanting means, their virtue to display
    This is the grief which bursts a generous h
When favour comes by chance, not by des
                    E. of *Sterlin*

Then men are men, when they are all their
Not when, by others badges, but made know
                    E. of *Sterline's Juli*
——————————Oh fear a servant's tongue !
Like such as only for their gain do serve,
Within the vast capacity of place :
I know no vileness so most truly base :
Their lord's, their gain : And he that most w
With him they will not die, but they will live
Traytors and these are one : Such slaves once t
Whet swords to make thine own blood lick th
                    Marston's S
——————— 1. I'll double thy reward.
2, You are like to speed then :
For I confess what you will soon believe,
We serve them best, that are most apt to give.
        Beaumont and *Fletcher's Custom of the*
——————————— 1. Is all our train
Shrunk to this poor remainder ? 2. These are
Which have got little in your service, vow
To take your fortune : But your wiser bunting
Now they are sledg'd, are gone.
1. They have done wisely :
This puts me in mind of death ; physicians, t
With their hands full of money, use to give o'

patients.   2. Right, the fashion of the world !
decay'd fortunes, ev'ry flatt'rer shrinks;
afe to build, when the foundation sinks,

Webster's Dutchess of Malfy.

———— O the inconstant
ten ground of service ! You may see,
'n like him, that in a winter's night
a long slumber o'er a dying fire,
h to part from't : Yet parts thence more cold,
when he first sate down.

Ibid.

ocodile which lives in the river
hath a worm breeds i'th' teeth of it,
puts it to extreme anguish : A little
o bigger than a wren, is barber
n to this crocodile ; flies into
ws of it, picks out the worm, and brings
remedy.   The fish, glad of
ut ingrateful to her that did it ;
he bird may not talk largely of her
: for non-payment, closeth her chaps,
ng to swallow her, and so put
perpetual silence : But nature.
ng such ingratitude, hath arm'd this
th a quill, or prick on the head-top,
wounds the crocodile i' the mouth, forceth
er bloody prison, and away
e pretty tooth-picker from her cruel patient.
r application is, I have not rewarded
vice you have done me.

Webster's White Devil.

—As in virtuous actions,
dertaker finds a full reward,
;h conferr'd upon unthankful men :
r service done to so much sweetness,
er dangerous, and subject to
onstruction, in your favour finds
d, and glorious end.

Maſſinger's Duke of Milan.

———————————————————— Shall I then
For a foolish whipping leave to honour him
That holds the wheel of fortune ? No, that favours
Too much of th' ancient freedom : Since great men
Receive disgraces, and give thanks, poor knaves
Must have nor spleen, nor anger. Though I love
My limbs as well as any man, if you had now
A humour to kick me lame into an office,
Where I might sit in state and undo others,
Should not I be bound to kiss the foot that did it ?
Though it seem strange, there have been such things
     seen
In the memory of man.
                   Maffinger's Duke of Milan.

——— Equal nature fashion'd us
All in one mould : The bear serves not the bear ;
Nor the wolf, the wolf : 'Twas odds of strength in
     tyrants,
That pluck'd the first link from the golden chain
With which that thing of things bound in the world.
Why then, since we are taught by their examples,
To love our liberty, if not command ;
Should the strong serve the weak, the fair, deform'd
     ones ?
Or such as know the cause of things, pay tribute
To ignorant fools ? All's but the outward gloss
And politick form, that does distinguish us ?
                   Maffinger's Bondman.

———————————————— Happy those times,
When lords were stil'd *fathers* of families,
And not imperious *masters* ! when they number'd
Their *servants* almost equal with their *sons*,
Or one degree beneath them ! When their labours
Were cherish'd, and rewarded, and a *period*
Set to their suff'rings ! when they did not press
Their duties or their wills beyond the *pow'r*
And *strength* of their performance ! all things order'd
With such decorum, as wise law-makers,
                        From

From each well-govern'd private houfe deriv'd
The perfect model of a commonwealth !
Humanity then lodg'd in the hearts of *men*,
And thankful mafters carefully provided
For creatures wanting reafon : The noble horfe
That in his fiery youth from his wide noftrils
Neigh'd courage to his rider, and brake through
Groves of oppofed pikes, bearing his lord
Safe to triumphant victory ; old or wounded,
Was fet at liberty, and freed from fervice :
Th'*Athenian* mules that from the quarry drew
Marble, hew'd for the temples of the gods,
The great work ended, were difmifs'd, and fed
At the publick coft : Nay, faithful dogs have found
Their fepulchers ; but *man* to *man* more cruel,
Appoints no end to th' fuff'rings of his flave.
Since pride ftept in and riot, and overturn'd
This goodly frame of concord ; teaching mafters
To glory in the abufe of fuch, as are
Brought under their command ; who, grown unufeful,
Are lefs efteem'd than beafts : This *you have practic'd* ;
Practic'd *on us*, with rigour ; This hath forc'd us
To *fhake* our heavy yokes *off* ; and if redrefs
Of thefe juft grievances be not granted us,
We'll right *ourfelves*, and by ftrong hand defend
What we are now poffefs'd of.
Maffinger's Bondman.

By her example warn'd, let all great women
Hereafter throw pride and contempt on fuch
As truly ferve them ; fince a retribution
In lawful courtefies, is now ftil'd luft ;
And to be thankful to a fervant's merits,
Is grown a vice, not virtue.
Maffinger's Emperor of the Eaft.
——————————— 'Tis reported
There is a drink of forgetfulnefs, which once tafted,
Few mafters think of their fervants ; who, grown old,
Are

Are turn'd off like lame hounds and hunting horses,
To starve up on the commons.
Massinger's Bashful Lover.

I am not of that harsh and morose temper
As some great men are tax'd with ; who imagine
They part from the respect due to their honours,
If they use not such as follow them,
Without distinction of their births, like slaves.
I am not so condition'd : I can make
A fitting diff'rence between my foot boy,
And a gentleman, by want compell'd to serve me.
Massinger's New Way to pay Old Debts.

———————————— From the king
To the beggar, by gradation, all are servants ;
And you must grant the slavery is less
To study to please one, than many.
Well then, and first to you sir ; you complain
You serve one lord ; but your lord serves a thousand,
Besides his passions, that are his worst masters :
You must humour him, and he is bound to sooth
Ev'ry grim sir above him, if he frown :
For the least neglect, you fear to lose your place ;
But if, and with all slavish observation,
From the minion's self, to the groom of his close-stool,
He hourly seeks not favour, he is sure
To be eas'd of his office, though he bought it :
Nay more, that high disposer of all such
That are subordinate to him, serves, and fears
The fury of the many headed monster,
The giddy multitude ; and as a horse
Is still a horse, for all his golden trappings ;
So your men of purchas'd titles, at their best, are
But serving-men in rich liveries.
Massinger's Unnatural Combat.

———————————— If you punish
My hasty application of your favours,
You gave me the encouragement to be guilty :

anny to cherifh fervants,
fh their difobedience.

Shirley's Honoria and Mammon.

is noble, though the pop'lar blaft
', as giddy as thy youth,
'd thy name up to beftride a cloud,
fs in the chariot of the fun :
lod of trade, to lackey pride ;
your flave of expectation wait
ly hinges of your doors, or whiftle
cal conveyance to your bed-fports.

John Ford's Broken Heart.

vant's fervant's flaves, once relifh licence
opinion from a noble nature,
e upon them boldnefs to abufe
eft, and lord it o'er their fellows ;
y were exempt from that condition,

John Ford's Fancies chafte and noble.

iply do we fee fome fervice bought ?
it it is of fools, whofe ware is nought.

Aleyn's Crefcey.

are born to ferve, muft feek to pleafe.

Richard Brome's New Academy.

ty to ferve one lord : But he
iy ferves, ferves bafe fervility.

Herrick.

————When I may reveal
our fervant, I'll not do't in breath,
the adventure of my life or death.

Suckling's Sad One.

Cleander, as the lame
fupporting crutches ; that's no longer
hey need them ; when that they are able
alone, they caft them from them.

Tatham's Diftracted State.

it more from fervants than is juft ;
hem well, if they obferve their truft,

Nor

Nor them with cruelty, or pride invade;
Since God and nature them our brothers made:
If his offence be great, let that suffice;
If light, forgive; for no man's always wife,

Denba

Service beyond the gratitude of kings;
Like crimes, misfortune on the fubject brings.
    Crown's Firft Part of the Deftruction of Jerufal.

S I G H T.

Firft, the two eyes, which have the feeing pow'r,
  Stand as one watchman, fpy or centinel,
B'ing plac'd aloft, within the head's high tow'r;
  And though both fee, yet both but one thing tell;

Thefe mirrors take into their little fpace,
  The forms of moon and fun and ev'ry ftar,
Of ev'ry body, and of ev'ry place,
  Which with the world's wide arms embraced are;

Yet their beft object, and their nobleft ufe,
  Hereafter in another world will be,
When God in them fhall heav'nly light infufe,
  That face to face they may their maker fee.

Here are they guides, which do the body lead,
  Which elfe would ftumble in eternal night;
Here in this world they do much knowledge read,
  And are the cafements which admit moft light:

They are her fartheft reaching inftrument,
  Yet they no beams unto their objects fend;
But all their rays are from their objects fent,
  And in the eyes with pointed angels end.

If th' objects be far off, the rays do meet
  In a fharp point, and fo things feem but fmall;
If they be near, their rays do fpread and fleet,
  And make broad points, that things feem gr'
    withal.

Laft

Laftly, nine things to fight reqir'd are,
  The pow'r to fee, the light, the vifible thing,
Being not too fmall, too thin, too nigh, too far,
  Clear fpace and time, the form diftinct to bring.

Thus fee we how the foul doth ufe the eyes,
  As inftruments of her quick pow'r of fight ;
Hence doth th' arts optick, and fair painting rife ;
  Painting which doth all gentle minds delight.
Sir John Davies.

S I L E N C E.

————Silence fhall digeft
What folly hath fwallow'd, and wifdom wean
What fancy hath mourned.
Lilly's Sapho and Phao.

Out of this filence yet I pick'd a welcome :
And in the modefty of fearful duty
I read as much, as from the rattling tongue
Of fawcy and audacious eloquence.
Shakefpear's Midfummer-night's Dream.

Silence is the perfecteft herald of joy:
I were but little happy, if I could fay how much.
Shakefpear's Much ado about Nothing.

———————— Mean while, all reft
Seal'd up, and filent, as when rigid frofts
Have bound up brooks and rivers, forc'd wild beafts
Unto their caves, and birds into the woods,
Clowns to their houfes ; and the country fleeps :
That when the fudden thaw comes, we may break
Upon them like a deluge ; bearing down
Half <i>Rome</i> before us ; and invade the reft
With cries and noife, able to wake the urns
Of thofe are dead, and make their afhes fear.
The horrors that do ftrike the world, fhould come
Loud, and unlook'd for ; till they ftrike, be dumb.
Johnfon's Catiline.

Silence in woman, is like fpeech in man ;
Deny't who can.
Nor

Nor is't a tale,
That female vice fhould be a virtue male,
Or mafculine vice a female virtue be :
You fhall it fee,
Prov'd with increafe ;
I know to fpeak, and fhe to hold her peace.
Johnfon's Silent W'oma

Oh filence, thou doft fwallow pleafure right !
Words take away fome fenfe from our delight.
Marfton's Sophonisb

You know my wifhes, ever yours did meet :
If I be filent, 'tis no more but fear,
That I fhould fay too little when I fpeak.
Lady *Carew's Maria*

By utt'ring what thou know'ft, lefs glory's got,
Than by concealing, what thou knoweft not.
Brown's Paftora

Silence hath rhetorick ; and veils are beft
To portrait that, which cannot be exprefs'd.
Aleyn's Crefe

1. ———————————— In his looks
He carries guilt, whofe horror breeds this ftrange
And obftinate filence ; fhame and his confcience
Will not permit him to deny it.
2. 'Tis, alas,
His modeft, bafhful nature, and pure innocence,
That makes him filent : Think you that bright rofe
That buds within his cheeks, was planted there
By guilt or fhame? No, he has always been
So unacquainted with all arts of fin,
That but to be fufpefted, ftrikes him dumb,
With wonder and amazement.
Randolph's Amynt

This is a motion ftill, and foft ;
    So free from nofe or cry,
That *Jove* himfelf, who hears each thought,
    Knows not when we pafs by.
Killegrew's Confpira
Chan

us great a filence,
t tempeft ceafes, is the calm
s, no noife is heard ; as if the
blafts were breathlefs grown, and the feas
nd after fo much toil requir'd eafe.
Killegrew's Conspiracy.

S I N.

nfulnefs fo bold,
re like weeds ; they fprout fo faft
ie corpfe, as weeds the corn, at laft.
Mirror for Magiftrates.

ls procure us ftill,
good amongft much ill.
Brandon's Octavia.

—— From love of grace,
flatt'ring unction to your foul,
ur trefpafs, but my madnefs fpeaks :
kin and film the ulc'rous place ;
corruption, mining all within,
n ; confefs yourfelf to heav'n ;
t's paft, avoid what is to come ;
fpread the compoft on the weeds
em ranker.
Shakefpear's Hamlet.

Foul deeds will rife,
the earth o'erwhelm them, to men's eyes.
Shakefpear's Hamlet.

love of goodnefs hateth ill,
vn-worthy ftill,
hich for fin's penalty forbears ;
is, tho' he fears.
Johnfon's Epigrams.

fweet,
ill bent
pent ;
neet
nifhment.
Johnfon's Underwoods.
Alas,

Alas, that in the wane of our affections
We should supply it with a full dissembling
In which, each youngest maid is grown a m
Frailty is fruitful, one sin gets another.
Our loves like sparkles are, that brightest s
When they go out ; most vice shews most d
Chapman's Buss

Before, I was secure 'gainst death and hell ;
But now am subject to the heartless fear
Of ev'ry shadow, and of ev'ry breath,
And would change firmness with an aspen l
So confident a spotless conscience is ;
So weak a guilty.   O the dangerous siege
Sin lays about us ! And the tyranny
He exercises when he hath expugn'd,
Like to the horror of a winter's thunder,
Mix'd with a gushing storm ; that suffers no
To stir abroad on earth, but their own rages,
Is sin, when it hath gather'd head above us
No roof, no shelter can secure us so,
But he will drown our cheeks in fear or woe.

What tho' our sins go brave and better clad
They are, as those in rags, as base, as bad.
Daniel's Octavia

Bear witness yet ye good, and evil spirits,
Who in the air invisibly do dwell,
That these strange paths I walk of ugliness,
Are forc'd by threat'ning gulphs of treachery
Nourish'd by states, and times injurious :
Nor is it sin, which men for safety chuse ;
Nor hath it shame, which men are forc'd to
Lord Brooke'

God, that to pass, will have his justice come
Makes sin the thief, the hangman, and the d
Lord Brooke's Inquisition on Fame an
Pleasure and youth like smiling evils wooe us,
To taste new follies ; tasted, they undo us.
Middleton and Rowley's Spa

monſtrous days are theſe ?
ily to be vicious moſt men ſtudy,
it to be ugly ; ſtrive t' exceed,
other in the moſt deformed deed.

Middleton's Phœnix.

u ſo bitter ? 'Tis but want of uſe ;
nder modeſty is ſea-ſick a little,
not accuſtom'd to the breaking billow
man's wav'ring faith, blown up with temptations.
ut a qualm of honour ; 'twill away,
e bitter for the time, but laſts not.
ſtes at the firſt draught like wormwood water,
rank again, 'tis nectar ever after.

Middleton's Women beware Women.

i and their honours are like poor beginners ;
not ſin rich, there would be fewer ſinners.

Tourneur's Revenger's Tragedy.

—————————All men have ſins,
igh in their ſev'ral kinds, all end in this ;
ey get gold, they care not whoſe it is :
ing the court, uſe bears the city out,
rers their quirks, thus goes the world about.
at our villanies have but diff'rent ſhapes,
ffects all one, and poor men are but apes
mitate their betters : This is the diff'rence,
reat mens ſins muſt ſtill be humoured,
poor mens vices largely puniſhed.
privilege that great men have in evil,
is, they go unpuniſh'd to the devil.

Barry's Ram-Alley.

fearful building upon any ſin ;
miſchief enter'd, brings another in :
ſecond pulls a third, the third draws more,
they for all the reſt ſet ope the door :
cuſtom take away the judging ſenſe,
t to offend we think it no offence.
refore, my lord, kill miſchief while 'tis ſmall ;
y degrees, you may deſtroy it all.

Smith's Hector of Germany.

S I N

'Tis a bold cowardice, when men shall dare
To act the sin, and the suspicion fear.

Aleyn's Henry VII.

Another's sin, sometimes procures our shame:
It stains our body, or at least our name.

Quarles.

Three fatal sisters wait upon each sin;
First, fear and shame without, then guilt within.

Herrick.

What a strange glass they've shew'd me now myself in?
Our sins, like to our shadows
When our day is in it's glory, scarce appear'd:
Towards our evening how great and monstrous
They are? ————————

Suckling's Aglaura.

Tell me why heav'n first did suffer sin?
    Letting seed grow which it had never sown?
Why, when the soul's first fever did begin,
    Was it not cur'd, which now a plague is grown?

Why did not heav'n's prevention sin restrain?
    Or is not pow'rs permission a consent?
Which is in kings as much as to ordain;
    And ills ordain'd are free from punishment.

And since no crime could be ere laws were fram'd;
    Laws dearly taught us how to know offence:
Had laws not been, we never had been blam'd;
    For not to know we sin, is innocence.

Sin's childhood was not starv'd, but rather more
    Than finely fed; so sweet were pleasures made
That nourish it: For sweet is lust of pow'r,
And sweeter beauty, which hath pow'r betray'd.

Sin, which at fullest growth is childish still,
    Would but for pleasure's company decay;
As sickly children thrive that have their will,
    But quickly languish being kept from play.

Since

nce only pleasure breeds sin's appetite,
 Which still by pleasant objects is infus'd ;
nce 'tis provok'd to what it doth commit,
 And ills provok'd may plead to be excus'd ;

Vhy should our sins, which not a moment last,
 (For, to eternity compar'd, extent
Yf life, is, ere we name it, stopt and past)
 Receive a doom of endless punishment ?

If souls to hell's vast prison never come
 Committed for their crimes, but destin'd be,
Like bondmen born, whose prison is their home,
 And long ere they were bound could not be free ;

Then hard is destiny's dark law, whose text
 We are forbid to read, yet must obey ;
And reason with her useless eyes is vext,
 Which strive to guide her where they see no way.
 Sir *W. Davenant*'s *Philosopher to the Dying Christian.*
Who would be wicked ? When the very crime
Conceiv'd, torments our souls ; and at the time
When 'tis deliver'd, like an engine broke,
Destroys us with the force of our own stroke.
 Stapylton's *Step-Mother.*

——————————I perceive
In flesh or spirit we are sinners all,
But spiritual sins I think most dangerous :
Sins of the spirit will to age endure ;
But a flesh-wound, time seldom fails to cure.
 Crown's *Married Beau.*

——————————That sin
Becomes a virtue, that chastnes sin.
 Crown's *Thyestes.*

S I N C E R I T Y.
Men should be what they seem :
Or, those that be not, would they might seem none.
 Shakespear's *Othello.*
I cannot hide what I am : I must be
sad when I have cause, and smile at no man's

Jefts ; eat when I have ftomach, and wait for
No man's leifure ; fleep when I am drowfy,
And tend on no man's bufinefs ; laugh when I
Am merry, and claw no man in his humour.
Shakefpear's Much ado about Nothing.

His nature is too noble for the world :
He would not flatter *Neptune* for his trident,
Or *Jove* for's power to thunder : His heart's his mouth:
What his breaft forges that his tongue muft vent ;
And, being angry, does forget that ever
He heard the name of death.
Shakefpear's Coriolanus.

While others fifh with craft for great opinion,
I, with great truth, catch mere fimplicity.
While fome, with cunning, gild their copper crowns,
With truth and plainnefs, I do wear mine bare.
Fear not my truth ; the moral of my wit
Is plain and true ; there's all the reach of it.
Shakefpear's Troilus and Creffida.

His words are bonds, his oaths are oracles ;
His love fincere, his thoughts immaculate ;
His tears pure meffengers fent from his heart ;
His heart as far from fraud, as heav'n from earth.
Shakefpear's Two Gentlemen of Verona.

What is it troublefome to be belov'd ?
How is it then, *Charinus*, to be loath'd !
If I had done like *Chloris*, fcorn'd your fuit,
And fpurn'd your paffion in difdainful fort,
I had been woo'd, and fought, and highly priz'd ;
But having n'other art to win thy love,
Save by difcov'ring mine, I am defpis'd ;
As if you would not have the thing you fought,
Unlefs you knew it were not to be got :
And now becaufe I lie here at thy feet,
The humble booty of thy conqu'ring eyes,
And lay my heart all open in thy fight,
And tell thee I am thine, and tell thee right ;
And do not fute my looks, nor cloath my words

In

colours than my thoughts do wear,
thee right in all, thou fcorneft me
hou didſt not love finceriy.
lid cryſtal more apparently
the colour it contain'd within,
ave theſe eyes, theſe tears, this tongue of mine
'd my heart, and told how much I'm thine.

Daniel's Arcadia.

earts do think, the tongues were made to fhew.

E. of Sterline's Crœfus.

neſs feize you——we pronounce
robbery, murder, treafon; which
muft needs be far more loathſome
in act which is fo natural, juſt,
ceſſary, as that of procreation:
ll have an hypocritical, veſtal
fpeak that, with cloſe teeth publickly,
fhe will receive with open mouth
ly. For my own part, I confider
without apparel; without difguifing
om or complement; I give thoughts
and words truth, and truth boldneſs. She whoſe
freeneſs makes it her virtue, to
vhat fhe thinks, will make it her neceſſity
ik what is good.

Marſton's Courtezan.

t cloath my thoughts, and juſt defence
an abject phrafe, but 'twill appear
if not above my low condition.
no bombaſt language, ſtol'n from ſuch,
:e nobility from prodigious terms
arers underſtand not; I bring with me
lth to boaſt of; neither can I number
ain fortune's favours, with my merits:
iot force affection, or prefume
fure her difcretion, that looks on me
:ak man, and not her fancy's idol.

Maſſinger's Bondman.

H 2

Her

Her words are trusty heralds to her mind.
John Ford's Love's Sacrifice.

Wealth shall not now be made the price of blood,
   Nor to be rich be reck'ned an offence;
Though it be valu'd less than to be good,
   And merit be preferr'd to innocence:
Men shall not most be priz'd who most appear,
Nor known for what they have, but what they are.
Sir *Thomas Higgons on the Restoration.*

Men that are hearty and sincere, come late
With promises, and early with their deeds.
Sir *W. Davenant's Platonick Lovers.*

——————— Innocence below, enjoys
Security, and quiet sleeps; murder's not heard of,
Treachery in a stranger there; they enjoy
Their friends and lovers, without ravishment;
They are all equal, ev'ry one's a prince,
And rules himself: They speak not with their eyes,
Or brows, but with the tongue, and that too dwells
In the heart.
Sicily and Naples.

God weighs the heart; whom we can never move
By outward actions, without inward love.
Watkins.

S I N G L E   L I F E.

Wrong not thy fair youth, nor the world deprive
   Of these rare parts which nature hath thee lent,
'Twere pity thou by niggardice should'st thrive,
   Whose wealth by waxing craveth to be spent;
   For which, thou of the wisest shall be shent:
Like to some rich churl hoarding up his pelf,
Both to wrong others, and to starve himself.
Drayton's Legend of Mutilda.

——————— A wife! Oh fetters
To man's bless'd liberty! All this world's a prison,
Heav'n the high wall about it, sin the gaoler;
But th' iron shackles weighing down our heels,
Are only women; those light angels turn us

To

ſhly devils.   I the ſex admire,
ver will ſit near their wanton fire.

Dekker's Wonder of a Kingdom.

ipon this ſingle life I forego it.
ad how *Daphne*, for her peeviſh flight
e a fruitleſs bay-tree : *Syrinx* turn'd
: pale empty reed : *Anaxarete*
·ozen into marble : Whereas thoſe
i marry'd, or prov'd kind unto their friends,
oy a gracious influence, tranſhap'd
ie olive, pomgranet, mulberry ;
e flow'rs, precious ſtones, or eminent ſtars.

Webſter's Dutcheſs of Malfy.

man never marry, nor have children ;
takes that from him ? Only the bare name
ing a father, or the weak delight
: the little wanton ride a cock-horſe
a painted ſtick, or hear him chatter
. taught ſtarling.

Ibid.

i free wanton jennet in the meadows,
about, and neigh ; take hedge and ditch,
n my neighbours paſtures, pick my choice
their fair maned mares ; but marry'd once,
i is ſtak'd, or pounded, and cannot
beyond his own hedge.

Maſſinger and *Field's* Fatal Dowry.

——————A batchelor
hrive by obſervation on a little ;
le life's no burthen : but to draw
:es is chargeable, and will require
ble maintenance.

John Ford's Fancys chaſte and noble.

more, like you, might pow'rfully confute
ppoſers of prieſts marriage, by the fruit :
ſince 'tis known for all their ſtrait vow'd life,
like the ſex in any ſtile but wiſe ;

H 3

'Cauſe

'Cause then to change their cloister for that state
Which keeps men chaste by vows legitimate:
Nor shame to father their relations,
Or, under nephews names, disguise their sons.

Bishop *King*.

S M E L L.

Next, in the nostrils doth she use the smell,
  As God the breath of life in them did give;
So makes he now this pow'r in them to dwell,
  To judge all airs, whereby we breath and live.

This sense is also mistress of an art,
  Which to soft people sweet perfumes doth sell;
Though this dear art doth little good impart,
  Since they smell best, that do of nothing smell;

And yet good scents do purify the brain,
  Awake the fancy, and the wits refine:
Hence old devotion, incense did ordain,
  To make mens sp'rits more apt for thoughts divine.

Sir *John Davies*.

——————————For thy smell,
Sabæa, shall be translated where thou goest,
And strew they path with spices.   Panthers skins
Shall be thy couch, and amber pave the floor
Where thy foot treads.   This breath's perfume enough
To create a *Phænix*.

Nabbs's Microcosmus.

S O R R O W.

—— Great grief will not be told,
  And can more easily be thought than said.
Right so, quoth he, but he, that never would,
  Could never: Will to might gives greatest aid.
  But grief, quoth she, does greater grow display'd;
If then it finds not help, it breeds despair.
  Despair breeds not, quoth he, where faith is stay'd.
No faith so fast, quoth she, but flesh does 'pair.
Flesh may empair, quoth he, but reason can repair.

Spenser's Fairy Queen.

We

He oft finds med'cine, who his grief imparts ;
But double griefs afflict concealing hearts.
Spenser's Fairy Queen.

—— She bad him tellen plain
The further process of her hidden grief :
The lesser pangs can bear, who hath endur'd the chief.
Ibid.

My heart is as an anvil unto sorrow,
Which beats upon it like the *Cyclops* hammers,
And with the noise turns up my giddy brain,
And makes me frantick.
Marloe's Edward II.

Our pleasures, posting guests, make but small stay,
   And never once look back when they are gone :
Where griefs bide long, and leave such scores to pay,
   As make us bankrupt ere we think thereon.
Brandon's Octavia.

One fire burns out another's burning ;
One pain is lessen'd by another's anguish ;
Turn giddy, and be help'd by backward turning ;
One desp'rate grief cure with another's languish :
Take thou some new infection to the eye,
And the rank poison of the old will dye.
Shakespear's Romeo and Juliet.

1. My *Dionysia*, shall we rest us here,
And by relating tales of others griefs,
See if 'twill teach us to forget our own ?
2. That were to blow at fire in hope to quench it ;
For who digs hill, because they do aspire,
Throws down one mountain to cast up a higher.
O my distress'd lord, ev'n such our griefs are !
Here they're but felt, and seen, with mischiefs eyes,
But like to groves, being topt, they higher rise.
Shakespear's Pericles.

———— For my particular grief
s of so flood-gate and o'er-bearing nature,

H 4   That

That it ingluts and swallows other sorrows,
And yet is still itself.

Shakespear's Othello.

He bears the sentence well, that nothing bears
But the free comfort which from thence he hears;
But he bears both the sentence, and the sorrow,
That, to pay grief, must of poor patience borrow.

Ibid.

Great lords, wise men ne'er sit and wail their loss,
But chearly seek how to redress their harms.
What though the mast be now blown over-board,
The cable broke, the holding anchor lost,
And half our sailors swallow'd in the flood?
Yet lives our pilot still. Is't meet that he
Should leave the helm, and, like a fearful lad,
With tear full eyes add water to the sea;
And give more strength to that which hath too much?
While in his moan, the ship splits on the rock,
Which industry and courage might have sav'd?

Shakespear's Third Part of **King Henry** VI.

Griefs of mine own lie heavy in my breast;
Which thou wilt propagate, to have them prest
With more of thine: this love, that thou hast shewn,
Doth add more grief to too much of mine own.

Shakespear's Romeo and Juliet.

Oh, who can hold a fire in his hand,
By thinking on the frosty *Caucasus?*
Or cloy the hungry edge of appetite,
By bare imagination of a feast?
Or wallow naked in *December's* snow,
By thinking on fantastick summer's heat?
Oh, no! the apprehension of the good,
Gives but the greater feeling to the worse;
Fell sorrow's tooth doth never rankle more
Than when it bites, but lanceth not the fore.

Shakespear's King Richard II.

1. You yield too much unto your griefs, and fate,
Which never hurts, but when we say it hurts us
2. O peace, *Tibullus,* your philosophy   *lends*

Lends you too rough a hand to search my wounds.
Speak they of griefs, that know to sigh and grieve;
The free and unconstrained spirit feels
No weight of my oppression.
Johnson's Poetaster.

Griefs that found so loud, prove always light;
True sorrow evermore keeps out of sight.
Chapman's Widow's Tears.

It is some ease our sorrows to reveal,
    If they to whom we shall impart our woes,
Seem but to feel a part of what we feel,
    And meet us with a sigh but at the close.
Daniel's Cleopatra.

What news brings't thou, can *Egypt* yet yield more
    Of sorrow than it hath ? What can it add
To the already overflowing store
    Of sad affliction, matter yet more sad ?
Is there behind yet something of distress
 ·Unseen, unknown ? Tell if that greater misery
There be, that we wail not that which is less.
    Tell us what so it be, and tell at first ;
    For sorrow ever longs to hear her worst.
Ibid.

Amaz'd he stands, nor voice nor body stirs ;
Words had no passage, tears no issue found ;
For sorrow shut up words, wrath kept in tears ;
Confus'd effects each other do confound :
Opprefs'd with grief, his passions had no bound.
Striving to tell his woes, words would not come ;
For light cares speak, when mighty griefs are dumb.
Daniel's Rosamund.

My coming but increas'd grief's starving store;
    For 'till that passion of itself expire,
All kind of comfort but augments it more :
    Like drops of oil thrown on a mighty fire.
E. of S....line's Craesus.

H 5 Shall

Shall forrow, through the waves of woes to fail,
   Have ftill your tears for feas, your fighs for winds?
To mifery what do bafe 'plaints avail?
   A courfe more high becomes heroick minds:

None are o'ercome, fave only thofe who yield.
   From froward fortune though fome blows be born,
Let virtue ferve adverfity for fhield:
   No greater grief to grief, than th' enemy's fcorn.
               E. of *Sterline's Julius Cæfar.*

—————————————— I drink
So deep of grief, that he muft only think,
Not dare to fpeak, that would exprefs my woe:
Small rivers murmur, deep gulfs filent flow.
               Marfton's Sophonisba.

——————Long time he tofs'd his thoughts;
And as you fee a fnow-ball being rowl'd
At firft a handful, yet long bowl'd about,
It fenfibly acquires a mighty globe:
So his cold grief through agitation grows,
And more he thinks, the more of grief he knows.
                 Ibid.

Language, thou art too narrow, and too weak
To eafe us now; great forrows cannot fpeak.
If we could figh our accents, and weep words,
Grief wears and leffens, that tears breath affords:
Sad hearts, the lefs they feem, the more they are;
So guiltieft men ftand muteft at the bar:
Not that they know not, feel not their eftate,
But extreme fenfe hath made them defp'rate.
               Dr. *Donne.*

As doth the yearly augur of the fpring,
In depth of woe, thus I my forrows fing;
My tunes with fighs yet ever mix'd among,
A doleful burthen to a heavy fong:
Words iffue forth, to find my grief fome way;
Tears overtake them, and do bid them ftay:
                 'Thus

n us whilſt one ſtrives to keep the other back,
th once too forward, ſoon are both too ſlack.

Drayton's Queen Iſabel to Richard II.

hings of ſmall moment we can ſcarcely hold,
ut griefs that touch the heart, are hardly told.

Drayton's Barons Wars.

————————Oh, be of comfort !
Make patience a noble fortitude,
And think not how unkindly we are us'd :
Man, like to caſſia, is prov'd beſt being bruis'd.
My heart's turn'd to a heavy lump of lead,
With which I found my danger.

Webſter's Dutcheſs of Malfy.

I ſuffer now for what hath former been :
Sorrow is held the eldeſt ſon of ſin.

Ibid.

Paſt ſorrows, let us mod'rately lament them ;
For thoſe to come, ſeek wiſely to prevent them.

Ibid.

Unkindneſs do thy office ; poor heart break :
Thoſe are the killing griefs which dare not ſpeak.

Webſter's White Devil.

Be of comfort ! and your heavy ſorrow
Part equally among us ; ſtorms divided,
Abate their force, and with leſs rage are guided.

Heywood's Woman kill'd with Kindneſs.

———————— Woe will break ;
'Tis not the greateſt grief, that moſt do ſpeak.

Goffe's Oreſtes.

Great ſorrows have no leiſure to complain :
Leaſt ills vent forth, great griefs within remain,

Goffe's Raging Turk.

There's no way to make ſorrow light
But in the noble bearing ; be content ;
Blows giv'n from heav'n are our due puniſhment :
All ſhipwrecks are not drownings ; you ſee buildings
Made fairer from their ruins.

Will. Rowley's New Wonder.

H 6   He

He doubles grief, that comments on a woe.

Return from Parnassus.

'Times have their changes, sorrow makes men wise;
'I he sun himself must set as well as rise.

John Ford's Perkin Warbeck.

Souls sunk in sorrows, never are without them;
They change fresh airs, but bear their griefs about them.

John Ford's Broken Heart.

Sorrow doth hate
To have a mate;
True grief is still alone.

Brown's Pastorals.

Oh do not hide thy sorrows, shew them brief;
He oft finds aid that doth disclose his grief.
If thou would'st it continue, thou dost wrong;
No man can sorrow very much, and long.
——————————— But had he been here
He had been flint had he not spent a tear.
For still that man the perfecter is known,
Who others sorrows feels, more than his own.

Ibid.

What I have lost, kind shepherds, all you know;
And to recount it were to dwell in woe:
To shew my passion in a funeral song,
And with my sorrow draw your sighs along;
Words, then well plac'd might challenge somewhat due,
And not the cause alone, win tears from you.
This to prevent, I set orations by;
For passion seldom loves formality.
What profits it a pris'ner at the bar,
To have his judgment spoken regular?
Or in the prison hear it often read,
When he at first knew what was forfeited?
Our griefs in others tears, like plates in water,
Seem more in quantity.   To be relator
Of my mishaps speaks weakness, and that I
Have in myself no pow'r of remedy.

Ibid
1. Pray

ray do not conceal
t's your difturbance. By communicating,
ll leffen fomething of the fuffering,
1aking me partaker.
. fhall add to't.
fhall be like two neighbour-buildings, when
ame proceeding from the one hath feiz'd
: other's roof, it makes the burning greater.
:nd, let me fuffer, be thou free.

Nabbs's *Unfortunate Mother.*

—— Be advis'd how you
refs your trouble! Grief while it is dumb
th fret within : But when we give our thoughts
ticulate found, we muft diftinguifh hearers.

Shirley's *Love's Cruelty.*

/ griefs fhall lead me this way,
d my love a happy harbour find;
efe tears the ocean, and my fighs the wind.

Sharp's *Noble Stranger.*

—— He, fad heart, being robb'd
'all his comfort, having loft the beauty
hich gave him life and motion, feeing *Claius*
joy thofe lips, whofe cherries were the food
1at nurs'd his foul, fpent all his time in forrow,
melancholy fighs and difcontents :
ok'd like a wither'd tree o'ergrown with mofs;
s eyes were ever dropping ificles.

Randolph's *Amyntas.*

————————There is no joy,
t either paft, or fleeting; and poor man
ows up but to the experience of grief;
d then is truly paft minority,
hen he is paft all happinefs.

Gomerfall's *Lodowick Sforza.*

) vex, when mifchiefs are quite paft and gone,
the next way to bring more mifchiefs on.

Nevile's *Poor Scholar.*

To

To grieve at this, were in thefe fenfelefs times
To become monftrous; and to feel no grief,
Were to be fenfelefs with the times themfelves.
Jones's Atrofta.

I need no mufe to give my paffion vent;
He brews his tears, that ftudies to lament.
Cleveland.

——————————————The remedy to woe,
Is to leave what of force we muft forego.
Merry Devil of Edmonton.

I muft confefs, when I did part from you,
I cou'd not force an artificial dew
Upon my cheeks; nor with a gilded phrafe
Exprefs how many hundred fev'ral ways
My heart was tortur'd; nor with arms acrofs,
In difcontented garbs fet forth my lofs:
Such loud expreffions many times do come
From lighteft hearts; great griefs are always dumb:
The fhallow rivers roar, the deep are ftill.
Numbers of painted words may fhew much fkill,
But little anguifh; and a cloudy face
Is oft put on, to ferve both time and place:
The blazing wood may to the eye feem great,
But 'tis the fire rak'd up, that has the heat,
And keeps it long; True forrow's like to wine,
That which is good, does never need a fign.
Suckling.

Like the camelion's colours that decay
But feemingly to give new colours way;
So our falfe griefs, had not themfelves outworn,
But ftep'd afide, to vary in return.
Sir *William Davenant's Journey into Worcefterfhire.*
——————All we gain
By grief, is but the licence to complain.
Sir *William Davenant's Elegy on B. Hafelrick.*
How beautiful is forrow, when tis dreft
By virgin innocence? it makes
Felicity in others feem deform'd.
Sir *William Davenant's Love and Honour.*

t both your griefs I'll chide, as ignorance;
Call you unthankful : for your great griefs shew
he heav'n has never us'd you to mischance,
Yet rudely you repine to feel it now.

your contextures be so weak and nice,
  Weep that this stormy world you ever knew :
ou are not in those calms of paradise,
  Where slender flow'rs as safe as cedars grew.
                Sir *William Davenant*'s *Gondibert.*

rief's conflict, gave these hairs their silver shine ;
  Torn ensigns which victorious age adorn :
'outh is a dress too garish and too fine,
  To be in foul tempestuous weather worn.

rief's want of use, does dang'rous weakness make ;
  But we by use of burdens are made strong :
nd in our practis'd age, can calmly take
  Those sorrows, which like fevers, vex the young.
                      Ibid.

onsider sorrows, how they are aright :
rief, if 't be great, 'tis short ; if long, 'tis light.
                    Herrick.

or still jmparted councils do encrease ;
nd grief divided to a friend, grows less.
           Sir *Robert Howard*'s *Blind Lady.*

Why shouldst thou grieve ?——
rief seldom join'd with blooming youth is seen ;
an sorrow be, where knowledge scarce has been ?
          Sir *Robert Howard*'s *Indian Queen.*

he sharpest drugs are of the healthiest operation :
t from a cloudy morn, ensues a glorious day.
        Gilbert Swinhoe's *Unhappy Fair Irene.*

r grief conceal'd, like hidden fire, consumes ;
hich, flaming out, would call in help to quench it.
              Denham's *Sophy.*

o vent my sorrows yields me no relief ;
e grieves but little, that can tell his grief.
               Thomas Ford.
                Believe

Believe that forrow trueft is, which lies   ?
Deep in the breaft, not floating in the eyes.

                                        Bifhop King.

Sorrows fpeak loud without a tongue;
And my perplexed thoughts forbear
To breath your felves in any ear:
'Tis fcarce a true or manly grief
Which gads abroad to find relief.

                                        Id.

Know henceforth that grief's vital part
Confifts in nature, not in art:
And verfes that are ftudied,
Mourn for themfelves, not for the dead.

                                        Bifhop Corbet.

That grief does far all other griefs tranfcend,
Which greater grows, when trufted to a friend:
Friendfhip in noble hearts would never reign,
If friendfhip's duty fhould be friendfhip's pain.

                        E. of Orrery's Henry V.

Grief fpeaks there loudeft, where the mourner's dumb.

                                        Orgula.

Grief's like a river which does filent creep,
And makes but little noife, if it be deep.

                        Dover's Roman Generals.

You hunt our griefs, as they were hard to find,
And ftudy arts how to perplex yourfelf.

                                        Crown's Regulus.

1 Can human forrows be delights to the gods?
2. Our forrows are not, but our troubles may;
A great man vanquifhing his deftiny,
Is a great fpectacle worthy of the gods.

                                        Crown's Darius.

S O U L.

For how may we to other things attain,
    When none of us his own foul underftands?
For which the devil mocks our curious brain,
    When, *know thy felf*, his oracles commands.

                                        For

y fhould we the bufy foul believe,
m boldly fhe concludes of that and this;
f herfelf fhe can no judgment give,
how, nor whence, nor where, nor what fhe is?

igs without, which round about we fee,
eek to know, and have therewith to do:
t whereby we reafon, live and be
ain ourfelves, we ftrangers are thereto.

k to know the moving of each fphere,
the ftrange caufe o' th' ebbs and floods of *Nile*;
that clock, which in our breafts we bear,
fubtile motions we forget the while.

t acquaint ourfelves with ev'ry zone,
pafs the tropicks, and behold each pole;
we come home, are to ourfelves unknown,
unacquainted ftill with our own foul.

Sir *John Davies*.

ie fable of the lady fair,
ch for her luft was turn'd into a cow;
thirfty, to a ftream fhe did repair,
faw herfelf transform'd fhe knew not how;

fhe ftartles, then fhe ftands amaz'd;
ft with terror fhe from thence doth fly,
aths the wat'ry glafs wherein fhe gaz'd,
fhuns it ftill, altho' for thirft fhe die:

man's foul, which did God's image bear,
was at firft fair, good, and fpotlefs pure;
ith her fins, her beauties blotted were,
a of all fights, her own fight leaft endure.

n at firft reflection fhe efpies
ftrange chimeras, and fuch monfters there,
ys, fuch anticks, and fuch vanities,
he retires, and fhrinks for fhame and fear.

Ibid.

One

One thinks the foul is air; another, fire;
    Another, blood diffus'd about the heart;
Another faith, the elements conſpire,
    And to her eſſence each doth give a part.

Muſicians think, our ſouls are harmonies;
    Phyſicians hold, that they complexions be;
Epicures make them ſwarms of atomies,
    Which do by chance into our bodies flee.

Some think one gen'ral ſoul fills ev'ry brain,
    As the bright ſun ſheds light in ev'ry ſtar;
And others think the name of ſoul is vain,
    And that we only well mix'd bodies are.

In judgment of her ſubſtance thus they vary,
    And vary thus in judgment of her ſeat;
For ſome her chair up to the brain doth carry,
    Some ſink it down into the ſtomach's heat.

Some place it in the root of life, the heart;
    Some in the liver, fountain of the veins:
Some ſay, ſhe's all in all, and all in ev'ry part;
    Some ſay, ſhe's not contain'd, but all contains.

Thus theſe great clerks their little wiſdom ſhew,
    While with their doctrines they at hazard play;
Toſſing their light opinions to and fro,
    To mock the lewd, as learn'd in this as they.
                        Sir *John Davis.*

To judge herſelf, ſhe muſt herſelf tranſcend,
    As greater circles comprehend the leſs:
But ſhe wants pow'r, her own pow'rs to extend,
    As fetter'd men cannot their ſtrength expreſs.
                            Ibid.

The workman on his ſtuff his ſkill doth ſhew,
    And yet the ſtuff gives not the man his ſkill:
Kings their affairs do by their ſervants know,
    But order them by their own royal will:

                                .So,

;h this cunning miftrefs, and this queen,
as her inftruments, the fenfes ufe,
all things that are felt, heard, or feen;
herfelf doth only judge and chufe:

prudent emperor, that reigns
'eign title, over fundry lands,
ι mean affairs, his fubjects pains,
their eyes, and writeth by their hands;

of weight and confequence indeed,
 doth in his chamber them debate;
his counfellors he doth exceed,
n judgment, as he doth in ftate.

Sir *John Davies.*

In man there is a nature found,
he fenfes, and above them far;
noft men b'ing in fenfual pleafures drown'd,
; their fouls but in their fenfes are.

nought but fenfe, then only they
lave found minds, which have their fenfes found;
n grows, when fenfes do decay,
ly moft in quickeft fenfe is found.

nought but fenfe, each living wight
we call brute, would be more fharp than we;
fenfes apprehenfive might,
ire clear and excellent degree.

Ibid.

e but the body's quality,
'ould fhe be with it fick, maim'd and blind;
rceive, where thefe privations be,
thy, perfect and fharp-fighted mind.

Ibid.

an at once two forms admit,
the one the other do deface;
foul ten thoufand forms do fit,
ne intrudes into her neighbour's place.

Ibid.

But

But how shall we this union well express?
  Nought ties the soul, her subtilty is such;
She moves the body, which she doth possess,
  Yet no part toucheth, but by virtue's touch.

Then dwells she not therein as in a tent,
  Nor as a pilot in his ship doth sit;
Nor as the spider in his web is pent;
  Nor as the wax retains the print in it;

Nor as a vessel water doth contain;
  Nor as one liquor in another shed;
Nor as the heat doth in the fire remain;
  Nor as a voice throughout the air is spread:

But as the fair and chearful morning light,
  Doth here and there her silver beams impart,
And in an instant doth herself unite
  To the transparent air, in all, and ev'ry part:
Still resting whole, when blows the air divide;
  Abiding pure, when th' air is most corrupted;
Throughout the air her beams dispersing wide,
  And when the air is toss'd, not interrupted:

So doth the piercing soul the body fill,
  B'ing all in all, and all in part diffus'd,
Indivisible, incorruptible still;
  Not forc'd, encounter'd, troubled, or confus'd.

And as the sun above, the light doth bring,
  Though we behold it in the air below;
So from th' eternal light the soul doth spring,
  Though in the body she her pow'rs do shew.
                              Sir *John Davies.*

But high perfection to the soul it brings
  T' encounter things most excellent and high;
For when she views the best and greatest things,
  They do not hurt, but rather clear the eye.
                                        Ibid.

                                        Our

Our bodies, ev'ry footstep that they make,
  March towards death, until at laſt they dye :
Whether we work, or play, or ſleep, or wake,
  Our life doth paſs, and with time's wings doth fly :

But to the ſoul, time doth perfection give, ‑
  And adds freſh luſtre to her beauty ſtill,
And makes her in eternal youth to live ;
  Like her which nectar to the gods doth fill.

The more ſhe lives, the more ſhe feeds on truth ;
  The more ſhe feeds, her ſtrength doth more increaſe ;
And what is ſtrength but an effect of youth,
  Which if time nurſe, how can it ever ceaſe ?
                              Sir *John Davies.*

As a cunning prince that uſeth ſpies,
  If they return no news, doth nothing know ;
But if they make advertiſement of lies,
  The prince's councils all awry do go :

Ev'n ſo the ſoul to ſuch a body knit,
  Whoſe inward ſenſes undiſpoſed be ;
And to receive the forms of things unfit,
  Where nothing is brought in, can nothing ſee.
                              Ibid.

Yet ſay theſe men, if all her organs die,
  Then hath the ſoul no pow'r her pow'rs to uſe :
So, in a ſort, her pow'rs extinct do lie,
  When unto act ſhe cannot them reduce.

And if her pow'rs be dead, then what is ſhe ?
  For ſince from ev'ry thing ſome pow'rs do ſpring,
And from thoſe pow'rs, ſome acts proceeding be ;
  Then kill both act and pow'r, and kill the thing.

Doubtleſs the body's death, when once it dies,
  The inſtruments of ſenſe and life doth kill ;
So that ſhe cannot uſe thoſe faculties,
  Although their root reſt in her ſubſtance ſtill.

                              But,

But as, the body living, wit and will
  Can judge and chuse, without the body's aid ;
Though on such objects they are working still,
  . As through the body's organs are convey'd :

So, when the body serves her turn no more,
  And all her senses are extinct and gone ;
She can discourse of what she learn'd before,
  In heav'nly contemplations, all alone :

So, if one man well on the lute doth play,
  And in good horsemanship, have learning skill ;
Though both his lute and horse we take away,
  Doth he not keep his former learning still ?

He keeps it, doubtless, and can use it too ;
  And doth both th' other skills in pow'r retain ;
And can of both the proper actions do,
  If with his lute or horse he meet again :

So though the instruments, by which we live,
  And view the world, the body's death do kill ;
Yet with the body they shall all survive,
  And all their wonted offices fulfil.

But how, till then, shall she herself employ ?
  Her spies are dead, which brought home news before:
What she hath got, and keeps, she may enjoy ;
  But she hath means to understand no more.

Then what do these poor souls, which nothing get ?
  Or what do those which get, and cannot keep ?
Like buckets bottomless, which all out let ;
  Those souls, for want of exercise, must sleep.

See how man's soul against itself doth strive !
  Why should we not have other means to know ?
As children, while within the womb they live,
  Feed by the navel : Here they feed not so.

Thes

ildren, if they had fome ufe of fenfe,
hould by chance their mother's talking hear,
n fhort time they fhall come forth from thence,"
l fear their birth, more than our death we fear:

ould cry out, " if we this place fhall leave,
en fhall we break our tender navel-ftrings:
fhall we then our nourifhment receive,
:e our fweet food no other conduit brings?"

man fhould to thefe babes reply,
at into this fair world they fhall be brought,
e they fhall view the earth, the fea, the sky,
e glorious fun, and all that God hath wrought:

there ten thoufand dainties they fhall meet,
ch by their mouths they fhall with pleafure take;
h fhall be cordial too, as well as fweet;
d of their little limbs, tall bodies make:"

rld they'd think a fable; ev'n as we
ink the ftory of the golden age:
me fenfual fpirits 'mongft us be,
h hold the world to come, a feigned ftage:

l thefe infants after find all true,
nothing then thereof they could conceive:
as they are born, the world they view,
with their mouths, the nurfes milk receive:

the foul is born, for death is nought
e foul's birth, and fo we fhould it call,
ufand things fhe fees beyond her thought;
n an unknown manner, knows them all.

xth fhe fee by fpectacles no more,
ears not by report of double fpies;
in inftants doth all things explore,
ach thing's prefent, and before her lies.

Sir John Davies.

Think

Think of her worth, and think that God did mean
   This worthy mind should worthy things embrace:
Blot not her beauties with thy thoughts unclean,
   Nor her dishonour with thy passion base.
                          Sir *John Davies.*

That our souls, in reason, are immortal,
Their natural and proper objects prove;
Which immortality and knowledge are.
For to that object, ever is referr'd
The nature of the soul; in which the acts
Of her high faculties are still employ'd:
And that true object must her pow'rs obtain,
To which they are in nature's aim directed.
Since 'twere absurd, to have her see an object,
Which possibly she never can aspire.
                 Chapman's Cæsar and Pompey.

I was a scholar: Seven useful springs
Did I deflow'r in quotations,
Of cross'd opinions 'bout the soul of man;
The more I learn'd, the more I learn'd to doubt;
Knowledge and wit, faith's foes, turn faith about.
Nay, mark; *Delight*, my spaniel, slept; whilst I paus'd
     leaves,
Toss'd o'er the dunces, por'd on the old print
Of titled words; and still my spaniel slept.——
Whilst I wasted lamp oil, bated my flesh,
Shrunk up my veins; and still my spaniel slept.——
And still I held converse with *Zabarell*,
Aquinas, Scotus, and the musty saw
Of antick *Donate*; still my spaniel slept.——
Still on went I, first, *an sit anima?*
Then, and it were mortal? O hold, hold,——
At that, they are at brain-buffets, fell by the ears
Amain, pell mell together; still my spaniel slept.——
Then, whether 'twere corporeal, local, fix'd,
Ex traduce? but, whether't had free-will
Or no?——the philosophers?
Stood banding factions, all so strongly propt,

I

I stagger'd ; knew not which was firmer part,
But thought, quoted, read, obferv'd, and pryed,
Stuff'd noting-books, and still my fpaniel flept.——
At length he wak'd, and yawn'd ; and by yon sky,
For aught I know, he knew as much as I.
Marfton's What you will.

Let man's foul be a fphere ; and then in this
Th' intelligence that moves, devotion is :
And as the other fpheres, by being grown
Subject to foreign motion, lofe their own ;
And being by others hurry'd ev'ry day,
Scarce in a year their nat'ral form obey :
Pleafure or bufinefs fo our fouls admit
For their firft mover, and are whirl'd by it.
Dr. *Donne.*

For bodies fhall from death redeemed be,
Souls but preferv'd, born naturally free ;
As men t' our prifons now, fouls t' us are fent,
Which learn vice there, and come in innocent.
Ibid.

Who is there fure he hath a foul, unlefs
It fee, and judge, and follow worthinefs,
And by deeds praife it ? He who doth not this,
May lodge an inmate foul, but 'tis not his.
Ibid.

The foul her liking eas'ly can efpy
   By fympathy, to her by heav'n affign'd
Through her clear windows, the well-feeing eye ;
   Which doth convey the image to the mind,
Without advifement ; and can apprehend,
That, whofe true caufe man's knowledge doth tranfcend.
Drayton's Pierce Gaveston.

That learned father which fo firmly proves
   The foul of man immortal and divine,
   And doth the fev'ral offices define ;
Anima, Gives her that name, as fhe the body moves ; !

Amor, Then is she love embracing charity;
 Animus, Moving a will in us, it is the mind,
  Mens, Retaining knowledge, still the same in kind
Memoria, An intellectual, it is memory;

Ratio, in judging, reason only is her name:
 Sensus, in speedy apprehension it is sense;
  Conscientia, in right or wrong they call her conscience;
Spiritus, the spirit, when it to God-ward doth enflame;
These of the soul the sev'ral functions be.

Drayton's Idea.

———— Didst thou never see
A lark in a cage? Such is the soul in
The body: This world is like her little
Turf of grass, and the heav'n o'er our heads, like
Her looking glass; only gives us a mis'rable
Knowledge of the small compass of our prison.

Webster's Dutchess of Malfy.

1. That souls immortal are, I eas'ly grant:
Their future state distinguish'd, joy, or pain,
According to the merits of this life.
But then I rather think, being free from prison,
And bodily contagion, they subsist
In places fit for immaterial spirits:
Are not transfus'd from men to beasts, from beasts
To men again: Wheel'd round about by change.
2. And were it not more cruel, to turn out
Poor naked souls, stripp'd of warm flesh; like landlords,
Bidding them wander? Than forsooth imagine
Some unknown cave or coast, or where all the myriads
Of souls deceas'd are slipt, and thrust together.
Nay, reason rather says, as at one moment,
Some dye, and some are born; so may their ghosts
Without more cost, serve the succeeding age:
For sure they don't wear, to be cast aside,
But enter strait, less, or more noble bodies,
According to desert of former deeds;
The valiant into lions; coward minds

Into

Into weak hares ; th' ambitious into eagles
Soaring aloft ; but the perverfe and peevifh
Are next indenizon'd into wrinkled apes :
Each vice and virtue wearing fev'ral fhapes.
1. So, you debafe the Gods moft lively image,
The human foul, and rank it with mere brutes,
Whofe life of reafon void, end with their fenfe.

True Trojans.

Every foul's alike, a mufical inftrument,
The faculties in all men equal ftrings,
Well, or ill handled, and thofe fweet or harfh.

Maffinger's Very Woman.

Philofophers who have fo anxious been,
 Inquiring where the foul doth chief refide,
Within the heart or brain ? If they had feen
 How weapons were by all the foldiers ply'd,
The queftion then had been no longer fcann'd ;
They had defin'd the feat t'ave been the hand.

Aleyn's Henry VII.

How formlefs is the form of man, the foul !
How various ftill, how diff'rent from itfelf !
How falfly call'd queen of this little world !
When fhe's a flave, and fubject not alone,
Unto the body's temp'rature, but all
The ftorms of fortune.

May's Cleopatra.

Man's foul immortal is ; whilft here they live,
The pureft minds for perfect knowledge ftrive ;
Which is the knowledge of that glorious God,
From whom all life proceeds : In this abode
Of flefh, the foul can never reach fo high ;
So reafon tells us : If the foul then dye,
When from the body's bonds fhe takes her flight,
Her unfulfill'd defire is fruftrate quite,
And fo beftow'd in vain ? It follows then,
The beft defires unto the beft of men,
The great creator did in vain difpenfe ;
Or elfe the foul muft live when gone from hence :

I 2   And

... live after the body fall,
... that it should dye at all?
Since ... compounded as the body is,
... of ever fighting contraries,
But are ... Like itself: and may
By ... alone for aye.
And though we ... that God, who did create,
... again annihilate
The ... and nothing in that sense can be,
... the ...:
... which in their nature do agree
... shall ne'er dissolved be,
... their wished end attain,
... immortal by themselves remain.

... quoth he, divine philosopher:
... of true knowledge here
... dreams? Who, more than beasts, should we
... to live of piety,
... should virtue be
... true beauty,
... place are? Virtue here
... beautie appear.
... rather? Nor is the
... we do not see,
... from the ...
... name, or fortune's slave.
... that souls do live,
What ... the other world will give:
... living ... God's depart ... hence,
... will put a difference.
... that while they lived here,
By pious ... contemplation were
... the body, that with true
... heavenly beauties view,
... they from hence are fled
... and knowledge perfected.
... the heav'ns shall they for ever be,
... with heav'n they made affinity.

Ll

But thofe dark fouls which drowned in the flefh,
Did never dream of future happinefs ;
That, while they lived here, believ'd, or lov'd
Nothing but what the bodies tafte approv'd ;
When they depart from hence, fhall fear the fight
Of heav'n, nor dare t' approach that glorious light ;
But wander ftill in difmal darknefs, near
Their bodies, whom alone they loved here.
Thofe fad, and ghaftly vifions, which to fight
Of frighted people do appear by night,
About the tombs and graves, whete dead men lie,
Are fuch dark fouls condemn'd t'accompany
Their bodies there ; which fouls, becaufe they be
Grofs and corporeal, men do therefore fee.

May's Continuation of Lucan.

Ill purchas'd life, indeed ; whofe ranfom craves
A fadder price, than price of bloodfhed faves.
Go, learn, bad woman, what it is, how foul,
By gaining of a life to fave a foul?
The price of one foul doth exceed as far
A life here, as the fun in light a ftar.
Here though we live fome threefcore years or more ;
Yet we muft die at laft, and quit the fcore
We owe to nature : But the foul once dying,
Dies ever, ever ; no repurifying ;
No earneft fighs or groans, no interceffion,
No cares, no pennance, no too late confeffion
Can move the ear of juftice, if it doom
A foul paft cure to an infernal tomb.

The Queen, or, *The Excellency of her Sex.*

——————— 'Tis true, that the fouls
Of all men are alike ; of the fame fubftance.
By the fame maker into all infus'd ;
But yet the fev'ral matters which they work on,
How different they are, I need not tell you :
And as thefe outward organs give our fouls
Or more, or lefs room, as they are contriv'd
To fhew their luftre ; fo again comes fortune,

    And

And darkens them to whom the gods have giv'n
A soul divine, and body capable
Of that divinity and excellence.

Rutter's Shepherd's Holiday.

'Though life, since finite, has no ill excuse
    For being but in finite objects learn'd ;
Ye sure the soul was made for little use,
    Unless it be in infinites concern'd.

Sir *W. Davenant's Philosopher to the Christian.*

Our souls but like unhappy strangers come
    From heav'n, their country, to this world's bad coast;
They land, then strait are backward bound for home,
    And many are in storms of passion lost !

They long with danger sail through life's vext seas,
    In bodies, as in vessels full of leaks ;
Walking in veins, their narrow galleries,
    Shorter than walks of seamen on their decks.

Ibid.

Man's soul in a perpetual motion flows,
And to no outward cause that motion owes ;
And therefore that no end can overtake,
Because our minds cannot themselves forsake.
And since the matter of our soul is pure,
And simple, which no mixture can endure
Of parts, which not among themselves agree,
Therefore it never can divided be :
And nature shews, without philosophy,
What cannot be divided, cannot die.

Denham.

That soul, which gave me life, was seen by none ;
Yet by the actions i' design'd, was known :
And though its flight no mortal eye shall see,
Yet know, for ever it the same shall be.
That soul, which can immortal glory give,
To her own virtues must for ever live.

Ibid.

Sure

ure some mens souls are given 'em for plagues,
My soul to me, is all the plagues of *Eyypt*.
My thoughts are frogs, and flies, and lice, and locusts.
Crown's Ambitious Statesman.

S P R I N G.

Whence is it that the air so sudden clears,
And all things in a moment turn so mild ?
Whose breath or beams, have got proud earth with child,
Of all the treasure that great nature's worth,
And makes her ev'ry minute to bring forth ?
How comes it winter is so quite forc'd hence,
And lock'd up under ground ? That ev'ry sense
Hath sev'ral objects ? Trees have got their heads,
The fields their coats ? That now the shining meads
To boast the paunse, lily, and the rose :
And ev'ry flow'r doth laugh as *Zephyr* blows ?
The seas are now more even than the land :
The rivers run as smoothed by his hand ;
Only their heads are crisped by his stroke.
How plays the yearling, with his brow scarce broke,
Now in the open grass ? And frisking lambs
Make wanton salts about their dry-suck'd dams,
Who to repair their bags do rob the fields.
How is't each bough a sev'ral musick yields ?
The lusty throstle, early nightingale,
Accord in tune, tho' vary in their tale :
The chirping swallow call'd forth by the sun,
And crested lark doth his division run :
The yellow bees the air with murmur fill,
The finches carol, and the turtles bill.
Johnson's Masques.

The wanton spring lies dallying with the earth,
And pours fresh blood in her decayed veins.
Look how the new-sapp'd branches are in child
With tender infants ! How the sun draws out,
And shapes their moisture into thousand forms

Of fprouting buds ! All things that fhew or breath,
Are now inftaur'd !

Marfton's What you will.

Now had the fun rode through his winter ftage,
   And lighted at the lufty ram : The earth
With herbs, as *Æfon*, did renew her age,
   And was impregnate with a num'rous birth :
Flora to ope her wardrobe did begin,
As 'twere to deck her at her lying in.

The conftellation of the winged fteed
   Rifing with *Sol*, attempereth the air
To the radical humour ; and doth breed
   Blood in the fprouting veins, and fp'rits repair ;
Soldiers in fpring double their fervice can ;
A man in winter is but half a man.

The fpeckled fnake when he hath new put on
   His annual coat, with feeming triple tongue,
Calls for the fight ; and basked in the fun,
   Is able er to give, or pay a wrong :
But when th' earth lies like one great ball of fnow,
Alas, poor fnake, what mifchief can it do !

Aleyn's Poictiers.

Now that the winter's gone, the earth hath loft
Her fnow white robes, and now no more the froft
Candies the grafs, or cafts an icy cream
Upon the filver lake, or cryftal ftream ;
But the warm fun thaws the benumbed earth,
And makes it tender ; gives a facred birth
To the dead fwallow ; wakes in hollow tree
The drowfy cuckow, and the humble bee :
Now do a choir of chirping minftrels bring
In triumph to the world, the youthful fpring.
The valleys, hills, and woods, in rich array,
Welcome the coming of the long'd for *May*.
Now all things fmile.

Carew.

The

The ox which lately did for shelter fly
Into the stall, doth now securely lie
In open fields; and love no more is made
By the fire side, but in the cooler shade.

Carew.

What a verdent weed the spring arrays
Fresh *Tellus* in! how *Flora* decks the fields
With all her tapestry! And the choristers
Of ev'ry grove chaunt carols! Mirth is come
To visit mortals. Ev'ry thing is blith,
Jocund and jovial.

Randolph's Jealous Lovers.

S T A T E S M E N.

There can no king imagine aught so bad,
But shall find some that will perform it glad:
For sickness seldom doth so swiftly breed,
As humours ill do grow the grief to feed.

G. Ferrers in the Mirror for Magistrates.

When wilful princes carelessly despise
To hear th' oppressed people's heavy cries,
Nor will correct their polling thieves; then God
Doth make those thieves, the reckless princes rod.

Mirror for Magistrates

At what a divers price, do divers men
Act the same things! another might have had
Perhaps the hurdle, or at least the ax,
For what I have this coronet, robes, and wax.
There is a fate, that flies with tow'ring spirits
Home to the mark, and never checks at conscience.
Poor plodding priests, and preaching fryars may make
Their hollow pulpits, and the empty isles
Of churches ring with that round word: but we
That draw the subtile and more piercing air,
In that sublimed region of a court,
Know all is good, we make so; and go on,
Secur'd by the prosperity of our crimes.

Johnson's Mortimer.

Forbear

——————Forbear, you things,
That stand upon the pinnacles of state,
Tob ait your slipp'ry height; when you do fall,
You'd sh yourselves in pieces, ne'er to rise:
And he that lend, you pity, is not wise.
Johnson's Sejanus.

I will not ask, why *Cæsar* bids do this:
But joy, that he bids me.   It i the bliss
Of courts, to be employ'd; no matter how;
A prince' power makes all his actions virtue.
We, whom he works by, are dumb instruments,
To do, but not enquire: his great intents
Are to be serv'd, not search'd: Yet, as that bow
I. most in hand, whose owner best doth know
T' affect his aims; so let that statesman's hope
Most use, most price, can hit his prince's scope.
Nor must he look at what, or whom to strike,
But loose at all; each mark must be alike:
Were it to plot against the same, the life
Of one, with whom I twinn'd: remove a wife
From my warm side, as lov'd as is the air;
Practice away each parent; draw mine heir
In compass, though but one; work all my kin
To swift perdition; leave no untrain'd engine,
For friendship, or for innocence; nay, make
The gods all guilty: I would undertake
This, being impos'd me, both with gain and ease:
The way to rise, is to obey and please.
He that will thrive in state, he must neglect
The trodden paths that truth and right respect;
And prove new, wilder ways: for virtue there,
Is not that narrow thing, she is elsewhere;
Mens fortune there, is virtue; reason their will;
Their licence, law; and their observance skill.
Occasion is their foil; conscience their stain;
Profit their lustre, and what else is vain.
If then it be the lust of *Cæsar's* pow'r
T' have rais'd *Sejanus* up, and in an hour

O'ertum

O'erturn him, tumbling down from height of all ;
We are his ready engine, and his fall
May be our rife : it is no uncouth thing,
To see fresh buildings from old ruins spring.

Johnson's *Sejanus.*

He must be the organ we must work by now ;
Though none less apt for trust : need doth allow
What choice would not.   I have heard, that aconite
B'ing timely taken, hath a healing might
Against the scorpion's stroke ; the proof we'll give :
That while too poisons wrestle we may live.   -
He hath a sp'rit too working to be us'd
But to th' encounter of his like : excus'd
Are wiser sov'reigns then, that raise one ill
Against another, and both safely kill.

Ibid.

————————As a city dame
Brought by her jealous husband, to the court,
Some elder courtiers entertaining him,
While others snatch a favour from his wife ;
One starts from this door, from that nook another
With gifts and junkets, and with printed phrase
Steal her employments ; shifting place by place
Still as her husband comes : so duke *Byron*
Was woo'd, and worship'd in the arch-duke's court :
And as the assistance that your majesty
Join'd in commission with him, or myself,
Or any other doubted eye appear'd,
He ever vanish'd : and as such a dame
As we compar'd with him before, being won
To break faith to her husband, lose her fame,
Stain both their progenies, and coming fresh
From underneath the burden of her shame,
Visits her husband with as chast a brow,
As temperate, and confirm'd behaviour,
As she came quitted from confession : ·
So from his 'scapes, would he present a presence,
The practice of his state adultery

And guile, that should a graceful bosom strike,
Drown'd in the set lake of a hopeless cheek.

Chapman's First Part of Byron's Conspiracy.

Than so we do, who are enthrall'd to kings;
Whatever they will, just or unlawful things.

Daniel's Philotas.

For they, who speak but privately to kings,
Do seldom speak the best and finest things.

Ibid.

'Tis still the fate of those that are
  By nature or their fortunes eminent;
Who either carry'd in conceit too far,
  Do work their own, or others discontent,
Or else are deemed fit to be suppress'd:
  Not for they are, but that they may be ill.
Since states have ever had far more unrest
  By sp'rits of worth, than men of meaner skill;
And find, that those do always better prove,
  Who are equal to employment, not above.
For self-opinion would be seen more wise,
  Than present councils, customs, orders, laws:
And to the end to have them otherwise,
  The commonwealth into combustion draws,
As if ordain'd t'embroil the world with wit,
As well as goodness, to dishonour it.

Ibid.

See how these great men cloath their private hate
  In those fair colours of the publick good!
And to effect their ends, pretend the state;
  As if the state by their affections stood:
And arm'd with pow'r and princes jealousies,
  Will put the least conceit of discontent
Into the greatest rank of treacheries;
  That no one action shall seem innocent:
Yea, valour, honour, beauty shall be made
  As accessaries unto ends unjust:
And e'en the service of the state must lade
  The needfull'st undertakings with distrust.

Ibid.

Who sees not, that sees aught, woe worth the while,
 The easy way, that greatness hath to fall!
Environ'd with deceit, hemm'd in with guile;
 Sooth'd up in flatt'ry, fawned on of all;
Within his own, living as in exile;
 Hears but with others ears, or not at all;
And ev'n is made a prey unto a few,
Who lock up grace, that would to other shew.

And who, as let in lease, do farm the crown,
 And 'joy the use of majesty and might;
Whilst we hold but the shadow of our own,
 Pleas'd with vain shews, and dally'd with delight:
They, as huge unproportion'd mountains grown,
 Between our land and us, shadowing our light,
Bereave the rest of joy, and us of love;
And keep down all, to keep themselves above.

Which wounds, with grief, poor unrespected zeal,
 When grace holds no proportion in the parts;
When distribution in the common-weal
 Of charge and honour, due to great deserts,
Is stopt; when others greedy hands must deal
 The benefit that majesty imparts;
What good we meant, comes gleaned home but light;
Whilst we are robb'd of praise, they of their right.

       Daniel's Civil War.

Nor is it so much princes weaknesses,
 As the corruption of their ministers,
Whereby the commonwealth receives distress?
 For they attending their particulars,
Make imperfections their advantages,
 To be themselves both kings and counsellors:
And sure this commonwealth can never take
Hurt by weak kings, but such as we do make.

         Ibid.

And it is just, that they who make a prey
 Of princes favours, in the end again
Be made a prey to princes; and repay
 The spoils of misery with greater gain:

Whose sacrifices ever do allay
The wrath of men conceiv'd in their disdain :.
For that their hatred persecuteth still
More than ill princes, those that make them ill.

                        Daniel's Panegyrick to the King.

But on the stage of state when one must stand
    A publick actor plac'd in all mens sight ;
And swaying pow'r with an imperious hand
    Doth ho'd the balance both of wrong and right:
Then, he for ev'ry action that is his,
    The censure of a thousand tongues must have ; .
Not only damn'd for doing things amiss,
    But for not doing all, that all men crave.

                        E. of *Sterline's Alexandrean Tragedy.*

But where the better rules the greater part,
And reason only is the prince's art ;
There as in margents of great volum'd books,
The little notes, whereon the reader looks,
Oft aid his over-pressed memory
Unto the author's sense, where he would be :
So do true counsellours assist good kings,
And help their greatness on, with little things.

                        Lord Brooke's Mustapha.

For they must flatter good and evil too,
That under princes all alone will do.

                        Lord Brooke's Alaham.

Why thus should statesmen do, .
That cleave thro' knots of craggy policies,
Use men like wedges, one strike out another ;
'Till by degrees, the tough and knurly trunk
Be riv'd in sunder ?

                        Marston's Second Part of Antonio and Mellida.
——————What if I got him !
He's but a shallow old fellow ; and to build
On the greatest, wisest statesman, in a design
Of this high daring, is most dangerous:

                                        We

We see the tops of tall trees, not their heart;
To find that found or rotten, there's the art.

Dekker's Match me in London.

Then daily begg'd I great monopolies,
  Taking the lands belonging to the crown;
Transporting all the best commodities
  Useful to *England*, needed of her own:
And basely sold all offices, till then
The due reward of well deserving men.

And being inconsiderately proud,
  Held all things vile that suited not my vein;
Nothing might pass, but that which I allow'd,
  A great opinion to my wit to gain:
Giving vile terms and nick names of disgrace,
To men of great birth, and of greater place.

Drayton's Pierce Gaveston.

Our honest actions, and the light that breaks
Like morning from our service, chaste and blushing,
Is that that pulls a prince back; then he sees,
And not till then, truly repents his errors,
When subjects crystal souls are glasses to him.

Beaumont and Fletcher's Valentinian.

now perceive the great thieves eat the less,
And the huge leviathans of villany
sup up the merits, nay the men and all
That do them service, and spout them out again
into the air, as thin and unregarded
As drops of water that are lost i'th' ocean.

Beaumont and Fletcher's False One.

An honest statesman to a prince,
Is like a cedar planted by a spring;
The spring baths the tree's root, the grateful tree
Rewards it with the shadow.

Webster's Dutchess of Malfy.

The tricks of state-moles that work under princes,
Are at the best, but like the viper's young;
That howsoe'er prodigious and hurtful
To many open and secure passengers;

Yet

Yet do they never live, without the death
Of him, that firſt gave motion to their breath.
Maſon's Mulcaſſes.

A ſtate villain muſt be like the wind,
That flies unſeen ; yet lifts an ocean
Into a mountain's height, that on the ſands
Whole navys may be ſplit in their deſcent.
Ibid.

————We, like inferior lights
Take life from your reflection ; for like ſtars
Unto the ſun, are counſellors to kings :
He feeds their orbs with fire, and their ſhine
Contend to make his glory more divine.
Day's Humour out of Breath.

Hard things are compaſs'd oft by eaſy means ;
And judgment, being a gift deriv'd from heav'n,
Though ſometimes lodg'd i'th' hearts of worldly men
That ne'er conſider from whom they receive it,
Forſakes ſuch as abuſe the giver of it :
Which is the reaſon, that the politick,
And cunning ſtateſman, that believes he fathoms
The councils of all kingdoms on the earth,
Is by ſimplicity over-reach'd.
Maſſinger's new Way to pay old Debts.

This bile of fate wears purple tiſſue,
Is high fed, proud, ſo is his lordſhip's horſe ;
And bears as rich capariſons. I know,
This elephant carries on his back not only
Tow'rs, caſtles, but the pond'rous republick ;
And never ſtoops for't : with his ſtrong breath'd trunk
Snuffs others titles, lordſhips, offices,
Wealth, bribes, and lives, under his rav'nous jaws.
Maſſinger and *Field's Fatal Dowry.*

You have not as good patriots ſhou'd do, ſtudy'd
The publick good, but your particular ends ;
Factious among yourſelves ; preferring ſuch
To offices and honours, as ne'er read
The elements of ſaving policy ;
But

But deeply skill'd in all the principles
That usher to destruction :
Your senate-house which us'd not to admit
A man, however popular, to stand
At the helm of government, whose youth was not
Made glorious by action ; whose experience
Crown'd with gray hairs, gave warrant to her counsels
Hand, and receiv'd with rev'rence ; is now fill'd
With green heads that determine of the state
Over their cups, or when their sated lusts
Afford them leisure ; or supply'd by those
Who rising from base arts and sordid thrift,
Are eminent for wealth, not for their wisdom :
Which is the reason, that to hold a place
In council, which was once esteem'd an honour,
And a reward for virtue, hath quite lost
Lustre, and reputation, and is made
A mercenary purchase.

Massinger's Bondman.

————————————There is
A statesman, that can side with e'ery faction,
And yet most subtly can untwist himself,
When he hath wrought the business up to danger :
He lives within a labyrinth, some think
He deals with the devil, and he looks like one,
With a more holyday face.

Shirley's Court Secret.

Oh he that's active in a state, has more
Chain'd to him by the pow'r and strength of office,
Than genuine respect ; and 'tis not worth
Or person, but the fortunes of a statesman
That sometimes men adore.

Shirley's Royal Master.

Statesmen, like virgins, first should give denial;
Experience and opportunity make the trial.

Shirley's Bird in a Cage.

Let dull patricians boast their airy titles,
And count me base, whilst I commend their lives,

And

And for the furtherance of my high intents,
Make noblest men my hated instruments.

May's Agrippina.

Wise counsellors shine nearest to the king,
Upon this lower orb ; as in the sky,
Sol constantly is nearest *Mercury.*

Aleyn's Henry VII.

——————————'The fox refus'd
To have the flies remov'd, which suck'd him first ;
He knew that fresh ones would torment him worst.

Ibid.

And as the lower orbs are wheel'd about,
Wrapt by the motions of the orbs above ;
So were inferior agents soon found out,
Which mov'd and turn'd, when he began to move :
For 'tis observ'd, that princes sooner get
Men for their humour, than their honour fit.

Bid.

Men sweat at helm, as much as at the oar.

Randolph's Muses Looking-glass.

Three tedious winters have I waited here,
Like patient chymists blowing still the coals,
And still expecting, when the blessed hour
Wou'd come, shou'd make me master of
The court elixir pow'r ; for that turns all.

Suckling's Aglaura.

He has inverted all the rule of state,
Confounded policy ;
There is some reason why a subject
Should suffer for the errors of his prince ;
But why a prince shou'd bear
The faults of's ministers, none, none at all.

Suckling's Goblins.

I am a rogue if I do not think
I was design'd for the helm of state :
I am so full of nimble stratagems,
That I should have order'd affairs, and
Carry'd it against the stream of a faction.

With

much eafe, as a skipper
.ver againft the wind.

Suckling's *Goblins.*

res his prince in what is judg'd unjuft ;
vn law, ferves not his pow'r, but luft.

Baron.

r's and the courtier's mafter-peice,
ftatefman's, diffimulation is ;
rour and fure friendfhip to pretend
 whofe throat he'll cut, to gain his end :
ft he do, will rife ; and then it's beft
: moft love, when he intends it leaft.

Baron's *Mirza.*

ace's favour turns to a difeafe
ir ambitious greedinefs he feeds,
oes furfeit with his love : and ftill
l'cine for that ficknefs we apply
ipon falve, not to ourfelves but him,
, the fword, which made the wound : and this
l'cine is our feeming induftry,
th falfe cares refembling falfe alarms,
of dangers warn when none are near ;
tors wake, we, with our undifturb'd
r, fleep fafely, and at eafe ;
content ourfelves, the world difpleafe.

Sir *W. Davenant*'s *Unfortunate Lovers.*

-The world would ftill
:ly round, but for you ftate-cripples,
ke it halt with your politick ftop3
iuch caution.

Sir *W. Davenant*'s *Law againft Lovers.*

ft not, whilft fo young and guiltlefs too,
gs mean feldom what their ftatefmen do ;
afure not the compafs of a crown
e head that wears it, but their own :
ring peace, becaufe they ftewards are,
account, to that wild fpender war.

Sir *W. Davenant*'s *Siege of Rhodes.*

The

The righteous ſtate-phyſicians that attend
On ſickly kings, preſcribing unto us,
As nature to the hungry diſeaſe of tygers
And of wolves; when to preſerve their lives
They feed on all the weak ſubmitting herd.
But how accurs'd would ſubjects be, were we
Not born with far more virtue, than we're taught?

Sir W. Davenant's Fair Favourite

He was her father's counſellor; a man
Created in the dark: he walks inviſibly,
He dwells in labyrinths, and loves ſilence:
But when he talks, his language carries more
Promiſcuous ſenſe, than ancient oracles:
So various in his ſhapes, that oft he is
Diſguis'd from his own knowledge.   An error
Much incident to human politicks,
Who ſtrive to know others more than themſelves.

Sir W. Davenant's Albovine, K. of Lombardy

Th' ambitious ſtateſman not himſelf admires
For what he hath, but what his pride deſires;
Doth inwardly confeſs, he covets ſway,
Becauſe he is too haughty to obey:
Who yield to him, do not their reaſon pleaſe,
But hope, their patience may procure them eaſe;
How proudly glorious doth he then appear,
Whom even the proud envy, th' humble fear.

Sir W. Davenant to Henry Jarmin

Thus the court wheel goes round like fortune's ball;
One ſtateſman riſing on another's fall.

Richard Brome's Queen's Exchange

He was not of that ſtrain of counſellors,
That like a tuft of ruſhes in a brook,
Bends ev'ry way the current turns itſelf,
Yielding to ev'ry puff of appetite
That comes from majeſty, but with true zeal
He faithfully declared all.

Brewer's Love-ſick King

1. T

name I muſt remember, and with horror ;
ave dy'd for doing,
y had dy'd for, if they had not done :
e king's command, and I was only
ppy miniſter.
uch a miniſter as wind to fire,
ls an accidental fierceneſs to
l fury.
ere the king's command, 'twas firſt thy malice
ded that command, and then obey'd it.
if you have refolv'd it, truth and reaſon
and idle arguments :
e pity thee the unhappy inſtrument
e's wills, whoſe anger is our fate ;
their love's more fatal than their hate.

Denham's Sophy.

—My Lords,
you now to prey upon your ſelves :
levours the reſt, in time may be
er, more o'ergrown than e'er I was.
ou are low and poor, you are all friends,
ne fair pretence together join ;
v'ry one conceals his own deſign.
country's cauſe, until full grown
ſought pow'r ; then it proves your own.
ou ſeem good, your crimes are not the leſs ;
re all new creations by ſucceſs.

Sir *Robert Howard's Great Favourite.*

ights muſt not be judg'd by theſe baſe ſlaves,
ng upon my fortune, not on me ;
truments, like flatter'd princes,
ver hear but of proſperity.
an ſingly ſtand on its own truſt ;
ons muſt depend on truth of others :
es of victory on mean mens valours ;
n upon baſe and wretched Inſtruments ;
nens love, more treacherous than all.

I'll

I'll find a conqueft, in a fafe retreat,
And though they rife, I'll fink to be as great.
Sir *Robert Howard's Great Favou*

He that feeks fafety in a ftatefman's pity,
May as well run a fhip upon fharp rocks,
And hope a harbour.

D'ye think that ftatefmens kindneffes proceed
From any principles but their own need ?
When they're afraid, they're wondrous good and fi
But when they're fafe, they have no memory.
Sir *Robert Howard's Veftal Vir*

A ftatefman all but int'reft may forget,
And only ought in his own ftrength to truft :
'Tis not a ftatefman's virtue to be juft.
E. of *Orrery's Henry*

But fear in ftatefmen is the higheft crime.
Thofe who to empire's upper ftations climb,
Are not fo ufeful in their being wife,
As they may huitful be by cowardice :
For they, fearing to act, what they fhould do ;
Make with themfelves the valiant ufelefs too.
E. of *Orrery's Muftal*

Ah ! had I ftudy'd but as much to gain
Heav'n, as this world, I had not fweat in vain :
Inftead of horrors that purfue me now,
Immortal crowns had waited for my brow ;
But my amazing miferies now are
Beyond the aid of penitence and pray'r :
To my own idols I too long did bow,
To put that fawning cheat on heaven now ;
For he hath my religion underftood
To be but craft, and my devotion blood.
My heav'n was to afcend the papal throne,
Where to fave others fouls, I've loft my own.
And now, alas ! 'twere' folly to deny
Myfelf the pleafure to defpair and die.

N

great men learn by my wretched fate,
o ftake their fouls at games of ftate;
ugh a while perhaps they feem to win;
find at laft, there is no cheat like fin.

Crown's Juliana.

ı religious to be damn'dly wicked;
all villany by holy fhews,
ıt for piety on fools impofe:
ll faiths, that fo there may be none,
ıke religion throw religion down.
:em loyal, the more rogue to be;
n the king by's own authority:
ing men from tyranny to fave,
ıe foolifh cred'lous world enflave.

Crown's Ambitious Statefman.

S U C C E S S.

m call it mifchief————
t's paft, and profper'd, 'twill be virtue.
e petty crimes are punifh'd; great rewarded.
ıft you think of peril, fince attempts
with danger, ftill do end in glory;
hen need fpurs, defpair will be call'd wifdom.
ght the care of men or fame to fright you;
y that win, do feldom receive fhame
ory, howe'er it be atchiev'd;
ngeance leaft. For who befieg'd with wants,
ftop at death, or any thing beyond it?
there was never any great thing yet
l, but by violence or fraud:
that fticks for folly of a confcience,
:h it, is a good religious fool.

Johnfon's Catiline.

———————— Good fuccefs
ıore fatal far than bad; one winning
ım a flatt'ring die, tempting a gamefter
:ard his whole fortunes.

Chapman's Revenge for Honour.

Shews

Shews to aspire just objects, are laid on
With cost, with labour, and with form enough;
Which only makes our best acts brook the light,
And their ends had, we think we have their right:
So worst works are made good, with good success;
And so for kings, pay subjects carcasses.

   Chapman's First Part of Byron's Conspira;

And tho' the fortune of some age consents
 Unto a thousand errors grossly wrought;
Which flourish'd over with their fair events,
 Have pass'd for current, and good courses thought
The least whereof, in other times, again
 Most dang'rous inconveniencies have brought:

Whilst to the time, not to mens wits, pertain
 The good successes of ill manag'd deeds:
Tho' th' ignorant deceiv'd with colours vain,
 Miss of the causes whence this luck proceeds.
Foreign defects giving home-faults the way,
 Make ev'n that weakness sometimes well succeed.

       Daniel's Musophil

What suit of grace hath virtue to put on,
 If vice shall wear as good, and do as well?
If wrong, if craft, if indiscretion,
 Act as fair parts, with ends as laudable?

Which all this mighty volume of events,
 The world, th' universal map of deeds,
Strongly controuls; and proves from all descents,
 That the directest courses best succeeds;
When craft (wrapt still in many cumberments)
 With all her cunning thrives not, tho' it speeds.

For should not grave and learn'd experience,
 That looks with th' eyes of all the world beside,
And with all ages holds intelligence,
 Go safer than deceit without a guide?
Which in the by-paths of her diffidence,
 Crossing the ways of right, still runs more wide.

        Prosp

rous ſucceſs gives blackeſt actions glory ;
neans are unremembred in moſt ſtory.

Marſton's Sophoniſba.

ſ, like Lethe, to the ſouls in bliſs,
ſ men forget things paſt, and crowns our ſins
name of valour. Be we impious,
lus Felix ſtiles us virtuous ?

Maſon's Mulcaſſes.

ſs muſt follow thoſe attempts that riſe
a juſt cauſe, and crown the enterprize.

Nabbs's Hannibal and Scipio.

out endeavour untill perfected
: ſucceſs, and that is fortune's only ;
: ſhares little in it.

Ibid.

—— So they thrive,
a fate in ſpight of ſtorms hath kept alive.

John Ford's Lover's Melancholy.

;s that in th' period proſp'rouſly ſucceed ;
gh croſs'd before, are acted well indeed.

Glapthorne's Hollander.

;s once well begun,
alf perform'd ; the managing an act
cloſe and hidden practice, 'mongſt the wiſe
olitick people, brings aſſur'd ſucceſs :
open ways the heavy ſnail does take,
. untrod paths beſt pleaſe the ſubtle ſnake.

Glapthorne's Albertus Wallenſtein.

of reward, or one victorious field,
irm ground for any one to build.
ll ſucceſs cloath him with diſcontent,
oallanceth the cauſe by the event.

Lady Alimony.

——Proud ſucceſs admits no probe
tice to correct or ſquare the fate,
oears down all as illegitimate :
hatſoe'er it liſts to overthrow,
er finds it, or elſe makes it ſo.

Cleveland.

z. III..   K   My

My intent's good, () let it so succeed,
And be auspicious still to each good deed.
Shropham's Flirt.

—————————(), success
In a rare paint! that which succeeds is good:
When the same action, if it fails, is naught.
Baron's Mirza.

All are not ill plots, that do sometimes fail:
Nor those false vows, which oft times don't prevail.
Herald.

In tracing human glory, we shall find
The cruel more successful, than the kind.
Sir W. Davenant's Siege of Rhodes

If we but prosper now, not we on late,
But she on us, shall for direction wait.
Sir Robert Howard's Great Favourite

1 If all things by success are understood,
Men that make war, grow wicked to be good:
But let you vow, those that were overcome,
And he that conquer'd, both should share one doom!
There's no excuse, for one of these must be
Not your devotion, but your cruelty.
2 To that rash stranger, sir, we nothing owe:
What he had rais'd, he strove to overthrow:
That duty lost, which should our actions guide:
Courage proves guilt, when merits swell to pride.
Sir Robert Howard's Indian Queen

As all those sins which for a crown are done,
Heav'n does absolve, when heav'n does put it on:
So all those crimes, which are perform'd in love,
Do lose that name when we successful prove.
E. of Orrery's Black Prince

That's villany, that by its ill succeeds
Betrays a man, and into ruin throws:
When once it gains a crown, it virtue grows.
Crown's Second Part of Henry VI

It is success makes innocence a sin:
And there is nothing but a sword between:

th' end be glorious, glorious is the way;
ey always have the caufe, who have the day.
Crown's Darius.

T A S T I N G.

T H E body's life with meats and air is fed;
   Therefore the foul does ufe the tafting pow'r
eins, which through the tongue and pallate fpread,
iftinguifh ev'ry relifh, fweet and fow'r.

is the body's nurfe; but fince man's wit
und th' art of cook'ry to delight his fenfe,
bodies are confum'd and kill'd with it,
han with the fword, famine, or peftilence.
Sir John Davies.

————Would'ft delight thy tafte?
Samian peacocks, and Ambracian kids,
of <i>Numidia</i>, pheafants, phenicopters,
fian lampreys, eels of Benacus,
les of <i>Locrine</i>, <i>Eleufinian</i> plaice
fill thy difh, and thoufand changes more.
Nabbs's Microcofmus.

T A X E S.

hy tribute? why fhould we pay tribute? If
r can hide the fun from us with a
cet, or put the moon in his pocket,
vill pay him tribute for light; elfe, fir,
ore tribute.
u muft know,
he injurious <i>Romans</i> did extort
tribute from us, we were free. <i>Cæfar</i>'s ambition,
h fwell'd fo much, that it did almoft ftretch
fides o'th' world, againft all colour, here
ut the yoke on us; which to fhake off,
nes a warlike people, which we reckon
lves to be, to do.
Shakefpear's Cymbeline.

K 2
Our

Our trade is tax, comprifing men, and things;
And draw not they mankind's wealth under kings?
Soothing the Tyrant, till by his excefs,
Want makes the majefty of thrones grow lefs;
By taxing peoples vice at fuch a rate,
As to fill up a fieve, exhaufts the ftate:
Laftly, fo fhuffling trade, law, doctrine, will,
As no foul fhall find peace in good or ill:
Both being traps alike us'd, to entice
The weak, and humble, into prejudice.

Lord Brooke's Muftapha.

——————————————Projector, I treat firft
Of you and your difciples; you roar out
All is the king's; his will's above his laws:
And that fit tributes are too gentle yokes
For his poor fubjects; whifp'ring in his ear,
If he would have them fear, no man fhould dare
To bring a fallad from his country garden,
Without the paying gabell; kill a hen
Without excife: and that if he defire
To have his children, or his fervants wear
Their heads upon their fhoulders, you affirm,
In policy, 'tis fit the owners fhould
Pay for them by the poll: or if the prince want
A prefent fum, he may command a city's
Impoffibilities; and for non performance
Compel it to fubmit to any fine
His officers fhall impofe.   Is this the way
To make our emperor happy? can the groans
Of his fubjects yield him mufick? muft his threfholds
Be wafh'd with widows and wrong'd orphans tears,
Or his power grow contemptible?

Maffinger's Emperor of the Eaft

Study fome monopoly
May fweep the kingdom at a flake; defpife
A project will not bring in half the city:
Find out a way to forfeit all the charters;
Have an exchequer of your own, and keep

The princes round about in penſion :
Theſe are becoming buſineſſes, and ſpeak
An active ſtateſman.

Shirley's Conſtant Maid.

In things a moderation keep ;
Kings ought to ſhear, not skin their ſheep.

Herrick.

The law takes meaſure of us all for cloaths,
Diets us all, and in the ſight of all,
To keep us from all private leagues with wealth.

Crown's Regulas.

T E M P E R A N C E.

——————— His moſt truſty guide,
Who ſuffer'd not his wandring feet to ſlide :
But when ſtrong paſſion, or weak fleſhlineſs
  Would from the right way ſeek to draw him wide,
He would through temperance and ſtedfaſtneſs,
Teach him the weak to ſtrengthen, and the ſtrong
    ſuppreſs.

Spenſer's Fairy Queen

Tho' I look old, yet I am ſtrong and luſty ;
For in my youth I never did apply
Hot and rebellious liquors in my blood ;
Nor did I with unbaſhful forehead woo
The means of weakneſs and debility :
Therefore my age is as a luſty winter,
Froſty, but kindly.

Shakeſpear's As you like it.

Rewards will only crown
The end of a well proſecuted good.
Philoſophy, religious ſolitude
And labour wait on temperance ; in theſe
Deſire is bounded : they inſtruct the mind's
And body's actions.

Nabbs's Microcoſmus.

—————————————Temperance,
She's the Physician that doth moderate
Desire with reason bridling appetite.

Nabbs's Microcosm

Yonder's her cave; whose plain yet decent roof
Shines not with ivory or plates of gold:
No *Tyrian* purples cover her low couch,
Nor are the carv'd supporters, artists work,
Bought at the wealth of provinces; she feeds not
On costly viands in her gluttony,
Wasting the spoils of conquests: from a rock
That weeps a running crystal she doth fill
Her shell-cup, and drinks sparingly.

1. Canst thou be content
With my poor diet too? 2. Oh wondrous well!
'Twas such a diet which that happy age
That poets stile the golden, first did use.
1. And such a diet to our chests will bring
The golden age again. 2 Beside the gain
That flows upon us, health and liberty
Attend on these bare meals; if all were blest
With such a temperance, what man would fawn,
Or to his belly sell his liberty?
There would be then no slaves, no scycophants
At great mens tables. If the base *Sarmentus,*
Or the vile *Galba* had been thus content,
They had not born the scoffs of *Cæsar's* board.
He whose cheap thirst the springs and brooks can quer
How many cares is he exempted from?
He's not indebted to the merchants toil;
Nor fear that pyrates force, or storms should rob h
Of rich *Canarye,* or sweet *Candyan* wines:
He smells, nor seeks no feasts; but in his own
True strength contracted lives, and there enjoys
A greater freedom than the *Parthian* king.
Besides, pure chearful health ever attends it;
Which made the former ages live so long.

th riotous banquets, ficknesses came in,
en death 'gan mufter all his difmal band
pale difeafes; fuch as poets feign
:p centinel before the gates of hell,
l bad them wait about the glutton's tables;
om they, like venom'd pills, in fweetest wines
:eived fwallow down, and haften on
at moft they would efchew, untimely death.
from our tables here, no painful furfeits,
fed difeafes grow, to ftrangle nature,
l fuffocate the active brain ; no fevers,
apoplexies, palfies or catarrhs
here ; where nature not entic'd at all
h fuch a dang'rous bait as pleafant cates,
tes in no more than fhe can govern well.

May's Old Couple.

np'rate in what does needy life preferve,
s thofe whofe bodies wait upon their minds ;
ft as thofe minds which not their bodies ferve ;
eady as pilots wak'd with fudden winds.

Sir W. Davenant's Gondibert.

who the rules of temperance neglects,
n a good caufe may produce vile effects.

Tuke's Adventures of Five Hours.

T E M P T A T I O N.

ave your honour.
'rom thee ; ev'n from thy virtue.
it's this ? what's this ? is this her fault, or mine ?
tempter, or the tempted, who fins moft ?
fhe ; nor doth fhe tempt ; but it is I,
t lying by the violet in the fun,
is the carrion does, not as the flow'r,
upt with virtuous feafon. Can it be,
t modefty, may more betray our fenfe,
n woman's lightnefs ? having wafte ground enough,
l we defire to raze the fanctuary,
pitch our evils there ? oh fie, fie, fie !
it doft thou ? or what art thou, <i>Angelo</i> ?

K 4.

Doft

Doſt thou deſire her fouly, for thoſe things
'That make her good ? oh, let her brother live !
'Thieves for their robb'ry have authority,
When judges ſteal themſelves.   What ? do I love her,
That I deſire to hear her ſpeak again ?
And feaſt upon her eyes ? what is't I dream on ?
Oh cunning enemy, that to catch a ſaint,
With ſaints doſt bait thy hook ! moſt dangerous
Is that temptation that doth goad us on
To ſin, in loving virtue : never could the ſtrumpet,
With all her double vigour, art and nature,
Once ſtir my temper ; but this virtuous maid
Subdues me quite : ever till now,
When men were fond, I ſmil'd ; and wonder'd how,
Shakeſpear's Meaſure for Meaſure.

This is woman. who well knows her ſtrength,
And trims her beauty forth in bluſhing pride,
To draw, as doth the wanton morning ſun
The eyes of men to gaze : but mark their natures,
And from their cradles you ſhall ſee them take
Delight in making babies, deviſing chriſt'nings,
Bidding of goſſips, calling to up-ſittings,
And then to feſtivals, and ſolemn churchings ;
In imitation of the wanton ends,
Their riper years will aim at.   But go further,
And look upon the very mother of miſchief,
Who as her daughters ripen, and do bud
Their youthful ſpring. ſtraight ſhe inſtructs them how
To ſet a gloſs on beauty, add a luſtre
To the defect of nature ; how to uſe
The myſtery of painting, curling, powd'ring,
And with ſtrange perriwiggs, pin knots, borderings,
To deck them up like to a vintner's buſh.
For men to gaze at on a midſummer-night.
This done, they are inſtructed by like art,
How to give entertainment and keep diſtance
With all their tutors, friend, and favourites ;
When to deny, and when to feed their hopes ;

draw on, and then again put off;
n and fmile; to weep and laugh outright,
breath, and all to train poor man
ruin: nay, by art they know
form all their gefture; how to add
mole on ev'ry wanton cheek;
e a grateful dimple when fhe laughs:
her teeth be bad, to lifp and fimper,
, to hide that imperfection:
fe once learn'd, what wants the tempter now,
; the ftouteft champion of men?
re, grave judges, let me thus conclude,
npts not woman, woman doth him delude.

Swetnam the Woman Hater.

aft virtue to fecure all; I am confident
tions will fhake thy innocence
e, than waves, that climb a rock, which foon
heir weaknefs; and difcover thee,
ear and more impregnable.

Shirley's Hide-Park.

frail thing is man! it is not worth
ry to be chaft, while we deny
nd converfe with women: He is good,
ares the tempter, yet corrects his blood.

Shirley's Lady of Pleafure.

, tho' late, yet at the laft begin
the leaft temptation to a fin;
to be tempted be no fin, untill
th' alluring object gives his will.

Herrick.

o will run fo near the brink of fin,
gly pufh'd, is fure to tumble in.

Crown's Married Beau.

T I M E.

t which might by fecret means hath wrought,
t of time to open fhew is brought.

Mirror for Magiftrates.

The

The time is out of joint; oh cursed spight !
That ever I was born to set it right.
Shakespear's **Hamlet.**

For he is but a bastard t the time,
That doth not smack of observation.
Shakespear's **King John.**

Time travels in divers paces, with divers persons ;
I'll tell you who time ambles withal, who time
Trots withal, who time gallops withal,
And who he stands still withal.
2. Prithee whom doth he trot withal ?
1. Marry, he trots hard with a young **maid,** between
The contract of her marriage, and the day
it is solemniz'd : if the interim
be but a se'nnight, time's pace is so hard,
That it seems the length of seven years.
2 Who ambles time withal ?
1. With a priest that lacks *Latin,*
And with a rich man that hath not the gout ;
For th' one sleeps easily, 'cause he cannot study ;
And th' other lives merrily, 'cause he feels no pain :
The one lacking the burthen of lean and
Wasteful learning ; the other knowing no
burthen of heavy tedious penury
Whom doth he gallop withal ?
1 With a thief to the gallows .
For though he goes as softly as foot can fall,
He thinks himself too soon there.
2 Whom stays it still withal ?
1 With the lawyers in the vacation : for they sleep
Between term and term, and then they perceive
Not how time moves.
Shakespear's As you like it.

It is an argument the times are fore
When virtue cannot safely be advanc'd,
Nor vice reprov'd.
Johnson's **Sejanus.**

Altho' the cause seem'd right, and title strong,
The time of doing it, yet makes it wrong.
Daniel's Civil W

ıs time, unto the good unjuſt ;
ıow may weak poſterity ſuppoſe
· have their merit from the duſt,
nſt them thy partiality that knows ﬀ
report, O who ſhall ever truſt !
mphant arches building unto thoſe
l the longeſt memory to have,
ʼere the moſt unworthy of a grave !

Drayton in the *Mirror for Magiſtrates*

il at *Jove*, and ſigh for *Saturn*'s time,
to the preſent, ages paſt prefer ;
urden would the gods with ev'ry crime,
damn the heav'ns, where only earth doth err.

E. of *Sterline*'s *Julius Cæſar*.

yet am not to deſtroy ſucceſſion,
vice of other kingdoms, give him time :
ɩes without me, can make no progreſſion ;
ıe alone, ev'n truth doth fall or climb :
ſtant petty webs, without me ſpun,
·ly ended be, as they begun.

Lord *Brooke*'s *Muſtapha*.

er of heaven am I, but God, none greater ;
like my parents, life and death of action,
of ill ſucceſs to ev'ry creature,
ſe pride againſt my periods make a faction :
ıe who go along, riſe while they be ;
ʒ of mine reſpects eternity.

Ibid.

the truth to light, detect the ill ;
ıative greatneſs ſcorneth bounded ways ;
ly pow'r, a few days ruin will ;
worth it ſelf falls, till I liſt to raiſe.
rth is mine ; of earthly things the care
to men, that like them, earthy are.

Ibid.

ath ſeveral falls,
ıft up joys, feaſts put down funerals.

Tourneur's *Revenger's Tragedy*.

K 6   Old

Old time will end our ſtory ;
But no time, if we end well, will end our glory.
                    Beaumont and *Fletcher's Sea Voyag*

He cuts the green tufts off th' enamel'd plain,
And with his ſcythe hath many a ſummer ſhorn
The plow'd lands lab'ring with a crop of corn :
Who from the cloud clipt mountains by his ſtroke
Fells down the lofty pine, the cedar, oak :
He opes the flood gates, as occaſion is,
Sometimes on that man's land, ſometimes on this.
He had a being, ere there was a birth ;
And ſhall not ceaſe, untill the ſea and earth :
And what they both contain, ſhall ceaſe to be ;
Nothing confines him but eternity.
By him the names of good men ever live,
Which ſhort liv'd men unto oblivion give :
And in forgetfulneſs he lets him fall,
That is no other man than natural :
'Tis he alone that rightly can diſcover,
Who is the true, and who the feigned lover.
                    Brown's Paſtora

Time is the moth of nature, devours all beauty.
                    Shirly's Humorous Courti

The ancient times what is the beſt do ſhew ;
The modern teach what is moſt fit to do.
                    Alyn's Poiſit

Time flows from infants, and of theſe, each one
Should be eſteem'd, as if it were alone :
The ſhorteſt ſpace, which we ſo highly prize
When it is coming, and before our eyes,
Let it but ſlide into th' eternal main,
No realms, no worlds can purchaſe it again :
Remembrance only makes the footſteps laſt,
When winged time, which fixt the prints is paſt.
                    Sir *John Beaun*

Weep no more for what is paſt ;
For time in motion makes ſuch haſte

le hath no leisure to descry
those errors, which he passeth by.

Sir W. Davenant's Cruel Brother.

—————— Time lays his hand
In pyramids of brass, and ruins quite
What all the fond artificers did think
immortal workmanship; he sends his worms
To books, to old records, and they devour
Th' inscriptions.   He loves ingratitude,
For he destroy'd the memory of man.

Ibid.

Our time consumes like smoke, and posts away;
Nor can we treasure up a month or day.
The sand within the transitory glass
Doth hast, and so our silent minutes pass.
Consider how the ling'ring hour-glass sends
and after sand, untill the stock it spends.
Year after year we do consume away,
Untill our debt to nature we do pay.
Old age is full of grief; the life of man,
If we consider, is but like a span
stretch'd from a swollen hand : the more extent
t is by strength, the more the pains augment :
Desire not to live long, but to live well ;
How long we live, not years, but actions tell.

Watkyns.

T I T L E S.

How does he feel his title
Hang loose about him, like a giant's robe
Upon a dwarfish thief.

Shakespear's Macbeth.

Thou wert the first, mad'st merit know her strength,
nd those that lack'd it, to suspect at length,
'Twas not entail'd on titles; that some word
Might be found out as good, and not my lord.
That nature no such diff'rence had imprest
In men, but ev'ry bravest was the best :
That blood not minds, but minds did blood adorn,
And to live great, was better, than great born.

Thefe were thy knowing arts : which who doth now
Virtuoufly practice, muft at leaft allow
Them in, if not, from thee ; or muft commit
A defp'rate folœcifm in truth and wit

Johnfon's Epigrams.

Man is a name of honour for a king ;
Additions take away from each chief thing.

Chapman's Buffy D'ambois.

Where titles prefume to thruft before fit
Means to fecond them, wealth and refpect
Often grow fullen, and will not follow.

Chapman Johnfon and Marfton's Eaftward Ho.

What tho' he hath no title ? He hath might :
That makes a title, where there is no right.

Daniel's Civil War.

He that above the ftate of man will ftrain
  His ftile, and will not be that which we are ;
Not only us contemns, but doth difdain
  The gods themfelves, with whom he would compaff.

Ibid.

After me, let none whom greatnefs throwds,
  Truft tumid titles, nor oftentive fhews,
Sails fwol'n with winds ; whilft emulating clouds,
  That which puffs up, oft at the laft o'erthrows.

E. of Sterline's Crœfus.

All tranfitory titles I deteft,
A virtuous life I mean to boaft alone ;
Our births our fires, our virtues be our own.

Drayton's Legend of Matilda.

That height and god-like purity of mind
  Refteth not ftill, where titles moft adorn,
With any, nor peculiarly confin'd
  To names, and to be limitted doth fcorn :
Man doth the moft degenerate from kind ;
  Richeft and pooreft both alike are born ;
And to be always pertinently good,
Follows not ftill the greatnefs of our blood.

Drayton in the *Mirror for Magiftrates.*
———'Thefe

—————————These are lords
That have bought titles.   Men may merchandize
Wares, ay, and traffick all commodities
From sea to sea, ay, and from shore to shore :
But in my thoughts, of all things that are sold ;
Tis pity honour should be bought for gold ;
It eats off all desert.

> *Heywood's Royal King.*

We all are soldiers, and all venture lives :
And where there is no diff'rence in mens worths,
Titles are jests.

> *Beaumont* and *Fletcher's King or no King.*

I look down upon him
With such contempt and scorn, as on my slave ;
He's a name only, and all good in him
He must derive from his great grandsire's ashes :
For had not their victorious acts bequeath'd
His titles to him, and wrote on his forehead,
This is a lord——he had liv'd unobserv'd
By any man of mark, and dy'd as one
Amongst the common rout.

> *Beaumont* and *Fletcher's Custom of the Country.*

—————————How dejectedly
The baser spirit of our present time
Hath cast itself below the ancient worth
Of our fore-fathers ! from whose noble deeds
Ignobly we derive our pedigrees.

> *Tourneur's Atheist's Tragedy.*

Are you in love with title ?
will have a herald, whose continual practice ?
all in pedigree, come a wooing to you,
or an antiquary in old buskins.

> *Webster's Devil's Law Case.*

Am I not emperor ? men call me so :
A rev'rend title, empty attributes,
And a long page of words follow my name,
But no substantial true prerogative.

> *Goffe's Raging Turk.*

——————— If that titles
Or the adorned name of queen could take me,
Here would I fix mine eyes and look no farther:
But these are baits to take a mean born lady,
Not her that boldly may call *Cæsar* father:
In that, I can bring honour unto any,
But from no king that lives, receive addition
To raise desert and virtue by my fortune;
Though in a low estate 'twere greater glory,
Than to mix greatness with a prince, that owes
No worth but that name only.
              Massinger and *Dekker's Virgin Martyr.*

——————Poor windy titles
Of dignity and offices, that puff up
The bubble pride, 'till it swell big, and burst:
What are they but brave nothings? toys, call'd honour,
Make them on whom they are bestow'd, no better
Than glorious slaves, the servants of the vulgar.
             Randolph's Muses Looking-Glass.

———————Brush off
This honour'd dust that soils your company;
This thing, whom nature carelesly obtruded
Upon the world, to teach, that pride and folly
Makes titular greatness the envy but
Of fools, the wise man's pity.
             Hallington's Queen of Arragon.

————————I'll d invest
Myself of all; additions can but swell
Our pride, not virtue up; my ancestors
Have left me rich enough in title to
Your friendship.
                Sicily and Naples.

1. Thy blood runs high; there's not one purple stream
Cas'd in these azure veins, but is deriv'd
From the spring of princely ancestry; and thou art
The wealthy storehouse of their fortunes too.
2. 'Las! what are these, but what the owner makes them
Of themselves nothing, only as we use them,

                               Ar

are good or bad, a blessing or a curse:
. But then their virtues, by a thrifty providence,
are all sum'd up in thy blest self, and make thee
A happiness, which if enjoy'd, must be
bestow'd by gift, because above all purchase.

Sicily and Naples.

Had my birth but been
As free from height as from ambition,
I might have slept under a silent roof,
And eat securely of a country feast ;
Bound to no ceremonious paths of state,
Nor forc'd to torture mine affections,
Or chain them till they starve, to some deform'd
Remedy of love ; and change our lives content
For a bare title : that forsooth must come
To edge a line of words, and make our names swell
To fill th' ambitious thirst of greedy age.

Jones's Adrasta.

No future titles swell'd him ; in his sight,
The worthy man seem'd greater than the knight :
True honour he to merit chain'd, and found
Desert the title gives, kings but the sound.

Llewellin.

To pow'r, adoption makes thy title good ;
   Preferring worth, as birth gives princes place ;
And virtue's claim exceeds the right of blood,
   As soul's extraction does the body's race.

Sir *W. Davenant's Gondibert.*

learned to admire goodness ; that
gives the distinction to men ; without
This, I behold them but as pictures, which
Are flourish'd with a pencil, to supply
The absence of inward worth, their titles
like landskips gracing them only far off.

Sir *W. Davenant's Siege.*

Princes may easily pay their debts, when
They enforce their creditors to buy titles
And places too, at their own rates.

Sir *W. Davenant's Albovine.*

——————Honours, mighty fir,
When they meet fortunes, are fupports to thrones;
But join'd to poverty, are the fhakers of it:
And wafting crowns fink with fuch deep confumptions.

Sir Robert Howard's Great Favourite.

A fool indeed, has great need of a title.
It teaches men to call him count and duke,
And to forget his proper name of fool.

Crown's Ambitious Statefman.

1. Have you no titles and diftinctions there?
2. Only what merit makes, we mind not blood,
Nor a vain title floating on that ftream;
Only great actions there beget great founds.
Your high fprung blood in *Sparta* will be loft;
I mean all your precedency of birth:
You muft give place to aged matrons there,
Whofe greateft riches are their filver hair.

Crown's Regulus.

Oh! we with fpecious names ourfelves deceive,
And folid joys for empty titles leave.

Crown's Second Part of the Deftruction of Jerufalem.
T R A V E L.

1. Have you been a traveller?
2. My lord, I have added to my knowledge the *Low
Countrys,*
France, Spain, Germany and *Italy*;
And tho' fmall gain of profit I did find,
Yet it did pleafe my eye, content my mind.
1. What do you think of the feveral *States*,
And princes courts as you have travell'd?
2. My lord, no court with *England* may compare,
Neither for ftate, nor civil government:
Luft dwells in *France*, in *Italy*, and *Spain*,
From the poor peafant, to the prince's train;
In *Germany*, and *Holland*, riot ferves;
And he that moft can drink, moft he deferves:
England! I praife not, for I here was born,
But that fhe laughs the others unto fcorn.

Shakefpear's Cromwell.

traveller ! by my faith, you have great
great reason to be sad : I fear you have
sold your own lands, to see other mens ;
then, to have seen much, and to have nothing,
is to have rich eyes, and poor hands.
. Yes, I have gain'd my experience. r. And your
experience
Makes you sad : I had rather have a fool
To make me merry, than experience
To make me sad, and travel for it too.
Farewell, *Monfieur* traveller ; look you lisp,
and wear strange suites : difable all the benefits
Of your own country, be out of love with your
Nativity, and almost chide God for
Making you that countenance you are ;
Or I'll scarce think you have swam in a gondola.

Shakespear's As you like it.

. Some few particulars I have set down,
Only for this meridian ; fit to be known
Of your crude traveller.
First, for your garb, it must be grave and serious,
Very reserv'd and lockt ; not tell a secret
On any terms, not to your father ; scarce
A fable, but with caution ; make sure choice
Both of your company and difcourse ; beware
You never speak a truth—2. How! 1. Not to strangers?
For those be they you must converse with most :
Others I would not know fir, but at diftance,
So as I still might be a faver in 'em :
You shall have tricks else paft upon you hourly :
And then for your religion, profefs none,
But wonder at the diverfity of them all ;
And for your part, proteft, were there no other
But fimply the laws o'th' land, you could content you.

Johnfon's Volpone.

Sir, to a wife man all the world's his foil :
It is not *Italy*, nor *France*, nor *Europe*,
That must bound me, if my fates call me forth.

Yet.

Yet, I protest, it is no salt desire
Of seeing countries, shifting a religion,
Nor any disaffection to the state
Where I was bred, and unto which I owe
My dearest plots, hath brought me out ; much less
That idle, antick, stale, grey-headed project
Of knowing mens minds and manners, with *Ulysses*
But a peculiar humour of my wive's,
Laid for this height of *Venice*, to observe,
To quote, to learn the language, and so forth——
I hope you travel sir, with licence ?——
Johnson's Volpone.

——These same travellers,
That can live any where, make jests of any thing,
And call so far from home, for nothing else,
But to learn how they may cast off their friends.
Chapman's Monsieur d'Olive.

This is that *Colax*, that from foreign lands,
Hath brought home that infection, that undoes
His country's goodness, and impoisons all :
His being abroad would mar us quite at home.
'Tis strange to see, that by his going out,
He hath outgone that native honesty,
Which here the breeding of his country gave.
Daniel's Arcadia.

Some travel hence, t' enrich their minds with skill,
Leave here then good, and bring home others ill ;
Which seem to like all countries but their own,
Affecting most, where they the least are known,
Their leg, then thigh, then back, their neck, their head
As they had been in sev'ral countries bred :
In their attire, their gesture, and their gait,
Found in each one, in all *italionate* ;
So well in all deformity in fashion,
Borrowing a limb of ev'ry sev'ral nation ;
And nothing more than *England* hold in scorn,
So live as strangers where as they were born.

B

thy return in this I do not read,
u art a perfect gentleman indeed.

Drayton's Lady Geraldine to the E. of *Surrey.*

rayels beſt, that knows when to return.

Middleton's Phœnix.

have thought good and meet by the conſent
theſe our nobles, to move you toward travel,
better to approve you to yourſelf,
give you apter power, foundation :
ſee affections actually preſented
by thoſe men that own them, yield more profit,
more content, than ſingly to read of them,
e love or fear, make writers partial :
good and free example which you find
ther countries, match it with your own ;
ill to ſhame the ill ; which will in time,
y inſtruct you how to ſet in frame,
ingdom all in pieces.

Ibid.

is is a traveller, ſir ; knows men and
nners, and has plow'd up the ſea ſo far
l both the poles have knock'd ; has ſeen the ſun
ke coach, and can diſtinguiſh the colour
his horſes, and their kinds, and had a
ders Mare leap'd there.

Beaumont and *Fletcher's Scornful Lady.*

avell'd he ſhould be, but through himſelf exactly ;
'tis fairer to know manners well, than countries.

Beaumont and *Fletcher's Wild Gooſe Chace.*

u ſhall find his travel has not ſtop'd him
you ſuppoſe, nor alter'd any freedom,
made him far more clear and excellent :
drains the groſſneſs of the underſtanding,
d renders active and induſtrious ſpirits:
that knows mens manners, muſt of neceſſity
ſt know his own, and mend thoſe by example :
s a dull thing to travel like a mill-horſe,
ll in the place he was born in, round and blinded.

Living

Living at home is like it : pure and strong spirits
That like the fire still covet to fly upward,
And to give fire as take it, cas'd up, and mew'd here
I mean at home, like lusty mettled horses,
Only ty'd up in stables to please their masters,
Beat out their fiery lives in their own litters.
        Beaumont and *Fletcher's Queen of Corinth*

1. How have thy travels
Disburthen'd thee abroad of discontents ?
2. Such cure as sick men find in changing beds,
I found in change of airs; the fancy flatter'd
My hopes with ease, as theirs do, but the grief
Is still the same.
        John Ford's Lover's Melancholy

1. I'll freely speak as I have found :
In *Spain* you lose experience; 'tis a climate
Too hot to nourish arts ; the nation proud,
And in their pride unsociable ; the court
More pliable to glorify it self
Than do a stranger grace : if you intend
To traffick like a merchant, 'twere a place
Might better much your trade ; but as for me
I soon took surfeit of it.
2. What for *France* ?
1. *France* I more praise and love ; you are, my lord,
Yourself for horsemanship much fam'd, and there
You shall have many proofs to shew your skill ;
The *French* are passing courtly, ripe of wit,
Kind, but extreme dissemblers.   You shall have
A *Frenchman* ducking lower than your knee,
At th' instant mocking ev'n your very shoe-tyes:
To give the country due, it is on earth
A paradise ; and if you can neglect
Your own appropriaments, but praising that
In others, wherein you excel yourself,
You shall be much belov'd there.
2 *England* ?
1 I'll tell you what I found there ; men as neat,

ourtly as the *French,* but in condition
e oppofite : put the cafe that you my lord
ld be more rare on horfeback than you are,
ere, as there are many, one excell'd
in your art, as much as you do others,
will the *Englifh* think, their own is nothing
ipar'd with you, a ftranger ; in their habits
y are not more fantaftick, than uncertain :
iort, their fare, abundance, manhood, beauty,
nation can difparage but it felf.

John Ford's Love's Sacrifice.

y fir, do gallants travel ?
wer that queftion ; but that at their return
h wonder to the hearers, to difcourfe of
: garb and difference in foreign females.
he lufty girl of *France,* the fober *German,*
: plump *Dutch* froe, the ftately dame of *Spain,*
: *Roman* libertine, and fpriteful *Tufcan,*
: merry *Greek, Venetian* courtezan,
: *Englifh* fair complexion, that learns fomething
n every nation, and will flie at all.

Maffinger's Guardian.

irken ye gallants that will crofs the feas,
are induftrious for a new difeafe ;
ou would needs be gadding, and defpife
foreign toys, our home bred rarities,
e this example with you ; if you go,
vel not from religion. Why, although
never touch at *Rome,* or elfe perchance
fcarce fee *Spain,* and glean but part of *France,*
may be weary, think your travel great.

Gomerfall.

it angle of the earth muft be my grave?
fea and fun have bounds, and know their courfe,
fons of men have none :
itlefs he wanders the foreign defarts,
begets more wonders every hour.

Knave in Grain.
———You

——————You have begun,
Taught travell'd youth, what 'tis it should have done?
For't has indeed too strong a custom been,
To carry out more wit, than we bring in.

Suckling.

What need I travel, since I may
More choicer wonders here survey?
What need I *Tyre* for purple seek;
When I may find it in a cheek?
Or sack the eastern shores; there lies
More precious diamonds in her eyes?
What need I dig *Peru* for ore,
When ev'ry hair of hers yields more?
Or toil for gums in *India*,
Since she can breath more rich than they?
Or ransack *Africk*, there will be
On either hand more ivory?
But look within, all virtues that
Each nation would appropriate,
And with the glory of them rest,
And in this map at large exprest;
That, who would travel, here might know
The little world in folio.

Cleveland.

He foreign countries knew, but they were known
Not for themselves, but to advance his own:
As merchants trade i'th' *Indies*, not live there,
Traffick abroad, but land their prizes here.

Lluellin.

By's travels, he could make the sun appear,
A young and unexperienc'd traveller.
Sir *William Davenant on Colonel Goring.*
Misguided travellers that rove,
Oft find their way by going somewhat back.
Sir *William Davenant's Gondibert.*

Thefe

fir, faid he, we heedlefly pafs by
Great towns, like birds that from the country come
t to be fcar'd, and on to forefts fly ;
Let's be no travell'd fools, but rooft at home.

ee, reply'd his friend, you nothing lack
Of what is painful, curious, and difcreet
travellers ; elfe would you not look back,
So often, to obferve this houfe and ftreet :

rawing your city map with coafter's care,
Not only marking where foft channels run,
ut where the fhelves and rocks, and dangers are;
To teach weak ftrangers what they ought to fhun.
Sir W. Davenant's Gondibert.

hou art a right traveller ;
n old acquaintance in every town
broad, and a new ftranger ftill at home.
Sir W. Davenant's Fair Favourite.

lan is a ftranger to himfelf, and knows
lothing fo naturally as his woes ;
e loves to travel countries, and confer
he fides of Heav'n's vaft diameter ;
elights to fit in <i>Nile</i>, or <i>Thetis</i> lap,
:fore he hath fail'd over his own map;
' which means he returns, his travel fpent,
:fs knowing of himfelf than when he went.
'ho knowledge hunt, kept under foreign locks,
ay bring home wit to hold a paradox ;
:t be fools ftill. Therefore might I advife,
vould inform the foul before the eyes :
ake man into his proper opticks look,
id fo become the ftudent and the book.
Bifhop King.

l travellers thefe heavy judgments hear,
handfome hoftefs makes a reck'ning dear.
Ibid.

. . . .

. . . .

. . . .

. . . .

. . . .

. . . .

. . . . *King IV.*

. . . .

. . . .

. . . .

. . . .

. . . .

. . . .

. . . .

. . . .

. . . .

. . . .

With pardons, duties, and with terms being fetch'd
. . . . gentle . . . . of piety:
But he that temper'd thee, bad thee stand up;
Gave thee no instance why thou should'st do treason,
Un'ess to dub thee with the name of traitor.
                              Shakespear's King Henry V.

Smo . . .   ater, where the brook is deep;
                new he harbours treason.
                                          The

barks not, when he would steal the lamb.
Shakespear's Second Part of King Henry VI.

tands up 'gainst traitors, and their ends,
d a double guard of law, and friends :
/ in such an envious state,
ier will accuse the magistrate,
: delinquent ; and will rather grieve
on is not acted, than believe.

Johnson's Catiline.

————If they be ill men,
mighty ones ; and we must so provide,
ile we take one head from this foul Hydra,
ing not twenty more.

Ibid.

————Should we take,
a swarm of Traytors, only him,
: and fears might seem a while reliev'd ;
iain peril would bide still inclos'd
the veins and bowels of the state :
n bodies labouring with fevers,
:y are tost with heat, if they do take
er, seem for that short space much eas'd,
vard are ten times more afflicted.

Ibid.

nisters men must for practice use !
th' ambitious, needy, desperate,
ind wretched, ev'n the dregs of mankind,
:s and women ! still it must be so ;
e their proper place, and in their rooms
the best : grooms fittest kindle fires. ;
ry burdens, butchers are for slaughters,
ries, butlers, cooks, for poison ;
ir me.

Ibid.

oughts they brake not into deeds ;
s the cause, not will : the mind's free act
i, still is judg'd as th' outward fact

Chapman's Second Part of Byron's Conspiracy.

    Treason

Treason hath blister'd heels ; dishonest things
Have bitter rivers, though delicious springs.
                    Chapman's Second Part of Byron's Conspiracy.
For treason taken ere the birth, doth come
Abortive, and her womb is made the tomb.
                                        Daniel's Philotas.

Treason affords a priviledge to none ;
Who like offends, hath punishment all one.
                                                    Ibid.

What need have *Alexander* so to strive,
    By all these shews of form, to find this man
Guilty of treason, when he doth contrive
    To have him so adjudg'd ? do what he can,
He must not be acquit, tho' he be clear :
'Th' offender, not the offence, is punish'd here.
And what avails the fore-condemn'd to speak ?
However strong his cause, his state is weak.
2. Ah, but it satisfies the world ; and we
Think that well done, which done by law we see :
1. And yet your law serves but your private ends,
And to the compass of your pow'r extends.
                                                    Ibid.

When darts invisible do fly,
A slave may kill a lion in the eye.
                        Dekker's Match me in London.
Treason, like spiders weaving nets for flie ,
By her foul work is found, and in it dies.
                                Webster's White Devil.
However you are tainted, be no traytor ;
Time may outwear the first, the last lives ever.
                    Beaumont and *Fletcher's Valentinian.*
Foreign attempts against a state and kingdom,
Are seldom without some great friends at home.
                        John Ford's Perkin Warbeck.

——————————Were my breast
Transparent, and my thoughts to be discern'd,
Not one spot shall be found to taint the candour
Of my allegiance.   And I must be bold

                                                    To

'o tell you, fir, for he that knows no guilt
'an know no fear, 'tis tyranny t' o'ercharge
'n honeſt man, and ſuch till now I've liv'd,
'nd ſuch my lord will die.

Maſſinger's Great Duke of Florence.

——————Take heed,
Treaſon's a race that muſt be run with ſpeed.

Goffe's Raging Turk.

'his treaſon is a kind of a quotidian,
: leaves a man no interval.

Shirley's Court Secret.

Ie's ſafe in the king's boſom, who keeps warm
'ſerpent, till he find a time to gnaw
'ut his preſerver.

Shirley's Polititian.

'I have ſome faction; the people love me,
'hey gain'd to us, we'll fall upon the court.
'Unleſs *Demetrius* yield himſelf, he bleeds.
'Who dares call treaſon ſin, when it ſucceeds?

Shirley's Coronation.

he ſeeds of treaſon choak up as they ſpring;
e acts the crime, that gives it cheriſhing.

Herrick.

——————Treaſons are acted,
' ſoon as thought; though they are ne'er believ'd,
'ntil they come to act.

Denham's Sophy.

'r active treaſon muſt be doing ſtill,
'ſt ſhe unlearn her art of doing ill.

Lluellin.

'here's no ſuſpicion of my treaſon. Nothing
'o holy villany! am I a ſaint, or not?
'he ſaint and devil differ in men ſo little.
'hoſe open bare-fac'd mortals look as ſimply
's naked dogs, or new-ſhorn ſheep, expos'd
'o th' injuries and ſcorn of all mankind;
'hile I, like viſiting angels, kill unſeen.

L 3

Here I lie round, and close as sleeping serpents:
He that treads on me, feels, before he sees me
Fane's Sacrifice.

Victorious princes, traitors do disdain,
Though by their treason they do profit gain.
Fane's Love in the Dark.

If I had us'd this fool to sin, I might
Have lodg'd my treason in his brawny head,
As safe as perkin in an axle's hoof.
Green's Ambitious Statesman.

And could the traitors find no fitter time,
But this, the more to aggravate their crime?
When heav'n abandons a declining king,
Rebellion then grows a religious thing:
Though on heav'n's party they devoutly fight,
To whom all kings must bow their sovereign rights
And this with vulgar heads succeeds so well,
Sometimes seems heav'n's commission to rebel.
Crown's Charles the VIIIth of France.

T R U T H

Foul is the task, though ne'er so quaint the skill,
That conceals truth to lessen any ill.
Mir. for Magistrates.

Thy truth o'ermastur'd by thy fortune,
And thou art judg'd unfaithful, because thou
Art unhappy
Lee's Endimion.

The test of truth is our secret hearts,
Not in the tongue, which falshood oft imparts
Branden's Octavia.

What! gone without a word?
Ay, so true love should do: it cannot speak:
For truth hath better deed, than words, to grace it
Shakespear's Two Gentlemen of Verona.

The truth you speak, doth lack some gentleness,
And time to speak it in: you rub the sore,
When you should bring the plaister
Shakespear's Tempest
Thin

bove all, to thine own felf be true ;
: muft follow, as the night the day,
canft not then be falfe to any man.

Shakefpear's Hamlet.

ignity of truth, is loft
much protefting.

Johnfon's Catiline.

her head fhe wears a crown of ftars,
gh which her orient hair waves to her waifte,
ich, believing mortals hold her faft,
i thofe golden cords are carry'd even,
ith her breath fhe blows them up to heaven.
ars a robe enchas'd with eagles eyes,
nify her fight in myfteries ;
each fhoulder fits a milk-white dove,
her feet do wily ferpents move :
acious arms do reach from eaft to weft,
ou may fee her heart fhine through her breaft :
ght hand holds a fun with burning rays,
ft a curious bunch of golden keys ;
vhich heav'n's gates fhe locketh, and difplays :
al mirror hanging at her breaft,
ch mens confciences are fearch'd, and dreft :
coach-wheels hypocrify lies rack'd,
uint-ey'd flander, with vain glory back'd ;
ight eyes burn to duft ; in which fhines fate :
el ufhers her triumphant gait ;
with her fingers fan of ftars fhe twifts,
th them beats back error, clad in mifts :
unity behind her fhines ;
re, and water, earth and air combines.
ice is like a trumpet, loud and fhrill ;
bids all founds in earth, and heav'n be ftill.

Johnfon's Mafques.

————Thy impartial words
brave faulcons that dare trufs a fowl
greater than themfelves ; flatt'rers are kites,

That

That check at sparrows : thou shall be my eagle,
And bear my thunder underneath thy wings :
Truth's words like jewels, hang in th' ears of kings.
Chapman's Bussy D'ambois.

Truth's pace is all upright, found ev'ry where;
And like a die, sets ever on a square.
Chapman's Widow's Tears.

Though love be past, yet truth should still remain;
I virtuous parts ev'n in my foes applaud :
A gallant mind doth greater glory gain,
To dye with honour, than to live by fraud.
E. of Sterline's Alexandrean Tragedy.

The truth, to suffer force of tyranny,
From his enforced father's jealousy :
Who utters this, is to his prince a traytor :
Who keeps this, guilty is : his life is ruth,
And dying lives, ever denying truth.
Thus hath the fancy law of pow'r ordain'd,
That who betrays it most, is most esteem'd :
Who faith it is betray'd, is traytor deem'd.
Lord Brooke's Mustapha.

Who measures hopes, and losses by the truth,
Goes ever naked in this world of might.
Lord Brooke's Alaham.

He is an adorer of chaste truth,
And speaks religiously of ev'ry man :
He will not trust obscure traditions,
Or faith implicit, but concludes of things
Within his own clear knowledge : what he says,
You may believe, and pawn your soul upon't.
Shirley's Example.

Time's daughter will appear, although she blush
To shew her nakedness.
Nabb's Unfortunate Mother.

'Twixt truth and error, there's this diff'rence known,
Error is fruitful, truth is only one.
Howk.

'True

hmself and others ; with whom both
alike, a promise and an oath.

Cartwright.

' too oft like friendship shews,
vho speak plain truth, we think our foes.

Denham.

time may shine, and virtue sigh ;
like heav'n's sun plainly doth reveal,
ge or crown, what darkness did conceal.

Davenport's *City-Nightcap.*

————Oh truth,
, whilst tenant in a noble breast,
of crystal in an iv'ry chest !

Davenport's *King John and Matilda.*

ot seen by judgments prepossest,
than light by eyes with rheum opprest.

Fane's *Sacrifice.*

T Y R A N T S.

s of kings with sycophants do swarm ;
o want no instruments of harm.

Mirror for Magistrates.

th tyrants down to death amain ;
' yet, nor shall be, cruel deed
/arded with as cruel meed.

Mirror for Magistrates.

: supple knees, fleak'd brows, but hearts of gall :
ness shall be wash'd off with blood ;
vim safest in a crystal flood.

Marloe's *Lust's Dominion.*

n tyrannous ; and tyrants fears ·
ot, but grow faster than their years.

Shakespear's *Pericles.*

d *Cæsar* be a tyrant then ?
! I know he w. u'd not be a wolf,
: fees the *Romans* are but sheep ;
u lien, were not *Romans* hinds.

Shakespear's *Julius Cæsar.*

——————————————Tyrants arts,
Are to give flatt'rers grace ; accusers, pow'r ;
That those may seem to kill, whom they devour.

Johnson's Sejanus.

Woe be to that state,
Where treach'ry guards, and ruin makes men great!

Chapman's Revenge of Bussy D'ambois.

Th' aspirer once attain'd unto the top,
Cuts off those means by which himself got up :

And with a harder hand, and straighter rein,
    Doth curb that looseness he did find before ;
Doubting th' occasion like might serve again :
    His own example makes him fear the more.

Daniel's Civil War.

Of Tyrants ev'n the wrong revenge affords ;
All fear but theirs, and they fear all mens swords.

E. of *Sterline's Julius Cæsar.*

The people who by force subdu'd remain,
    May pity those by whom opprest they rest ;
They but one tyrant have, whereas there reign
    A thousand tyrants, in one tyrant's breast.

Ibid.

Thus tyranny, their brood whose courage fails,
    Doth force the parent in despair to fall ;
To fight a dastard ; proud when it prevails,
    But yet, as fear'd of all, doth still fear all :
And tyrants no security can find,
For ev'ry shadow frights a guilty mind.

E. of *Sterline's Cræsus.*

Tyrants! why swell you thus against your makers?
Is rais'd equality so soon grown wild ?
    Dare you deprive your people of succession,
Which thrones, and scepters, on their freedoms build?
    Have fear, or love, in greatness no impression ?
Since people who did raise you to the crown,
Are ladders standing still to let you down.

Lord *Brooke's Mustapha.*

Even

ants covet to uphold their fame;
ing evil deeds, but evil name.
> Lord *Brooke's Muſtapha.*

lful is that pow'r that all may do;
, that all men fear, are fearful too.
> *Ibid.*

uld be tyrants, tyrants would be gods;
ey become our ſcourges, we their rods.
> Lord *Brooke of Wars.*

: the tree, that ſerveth for a ſhade,
: big-grown body doth bear off the wind,
: his waſtful branches do invade
iew-ſprung plants, and them in priſon bind;
: a tyrant to his weaker made,
s a vile devourer of his kind,
their hands at his large root to hew,
: greatneſs hind'reth others that would grow.
> *Drayton's Barons Wars.*

————————Alas,
a man ſequeſter'd from the world,
private perſon, is preferr'd,
y allows of in a king!
: juſt, or thankful, makes kings guilty;
h, though prais'd, is puniſh'd, that ſupports
good fate forſakes. Join with the gods,
the man they favour, leave the wretched;
s are not more diſtant from the earth,
:ofit is from honeſty; all the pow'r,
ive, and greatneſs of a prince,
if he deſcend once but to ſteer
:ſe, as what's right guides him: let him leave
pter, that ſtrives only to be good,
ngdoms are maintain'd, by force and blood.
> *Beaumont* and *Fletcher's Falſe One.*

ot thy blade unſheath'd; a tyrant's heart
own ſword a ſcabbard ſhould impart.
> *True Trojans.*

L 6   ———A

To know the heads of danger ; where 'tis fit
To bend, to break, provoke, or suffer it :
All this is valour !

Johnson's Underwoods.

1. What is true valour ?
2. It is the greatest virtue, and the safety
Of all mankind ; the object of it's danger.
A certain mean 'twixt fear and confidence ;
No inconsid'rate rashness, or vain appetite
Of false encounting formidable things,
But a true science of distinguishing
What's good or evil.   It springs out of reason,
And tends to perfect honesty, the scope
Is always honour, and the publick good :
It is no valour for a private cause.
1. No, not for reputation ?
2. That's man's idol,
Set up 'gainst God, the maker of all laws,
Who hath commanded us we should not kill.
And yet we say, we must for reputation.
What honest man can either fear his own,
Or else will hurt another's reputation ?
Fear, to do base unworthy things, is valour ;
If they be done to us, to suffer them,
Is valour too.   The office of a man
That's truly valiant, is considerable
Three ways ; the first is in respect of matter,
Which still is danger ; in respect of form,
Wherein he must preserve his dignity ;
And in the end, which must be ever lawful.
1. But men, when they are heated, and in passion,
Cannot consider.   2. Then it is not valour.
I never thought an angry person valiant :
Virtue is never aided by a vice.
What need is there of anger, and of tumult,
When reason can do the same things, or more ?
1. O yes, 'tis profitable, and of use,
It makes us fierce, and fit to undertake.
2. Why, so will drink make us both bold and rash,

y if you will; do thefe make men valiant?
poor helps, and virtue needs them not.
s valianter by being angry,
at could not valiant be without:
comes not in the aid of virtue,
ftead of it.   1. He holds the right.
is an odious kind of remedy,
ur health to a difeafe.

Johnfon's New Inn.

angry valiant?
does that differ from true valour?

fficient, or that which makes it:
xceeds from paffion, not from judgment:
e beafts have it, wicked perfons: there
in the fubject; in the form,
'd rafhly, and with violence;
the end, where it refpects not truth,
k honefty, but meer revenge.
fident, and undertaking valour,
m the true, two other ways; as being
our own faculties, skill, or ftrength,
the right, or confcience of the caufe,
ks it: then in the end, which is the
and not the honour.
e ignorant valour,
ows not why it undertakes, but doth it
: the infamy meerly?————
vorft of all:
our lies in th' eyes of the lookers on,
ll'd valour with a witnefs.   2. Right.
things true valour's exercis'd about,
rty, reftraint, captivity,
nt, lofs of children, long difeafe:
is death.   Here valour is beheld;
feen; about thefe, it is prefent,
al things, which but require our confidence:
t to thofe, we muft object ourfelves,

Only

Only for honesty: if any other
Respect be mixt, we quite put out her light.
And as all knowledge, when it is remov'd,
Or separate from justice, is call'd craft,
Rather than wisdom: so a mind affecting,
Or undertaking dangers for ambition,
Or any self-pretext, not for the publick,
Deserves the name of daring, not of valour;
And over-daring is as great a vice,
As over fearing.   2 Yes, and often greater.
1. But as it is not the meer punishment,
But cause, that makes a martyr; so it is not
Fighting or dying, but the manner of it
Renders a man himself.   A valiant man
Ought not to undergo, or tempt a danger,
But worthily, and by selected ways,
He undertakes with reason, not by chance.
His valour is the salt t' his other virtues,
They're all unseason'd without it: The waiting-maid
Or the concomitants of it, are his patience,
His magnanimity, his confidence,
His constancy, security, and quiet:
He can assure himself against all rumour;
Despair of nothing; laughs at contumelies;
As knowing himself advanced in a height
Where injury cannot reach him, nor aspersion
Touch him with soyle!
Johnson's New In

He is shot-free, in battle is not hurt,
Not he that is not hit, so he is valiant,
That yields not unto wrongs, not he that scapes them.
Johnson's New In

And thus we see, where valour most doth vaunt,
What 'tis to make a coward valiant.
Chapman's Revenge of Bussy D'ambois

It seems the conduct of the language
Hath kill'd thy courage with a host of fears.
L. of Surlow's Darius
———The

Then ſhines valour,
ration from her fix'd ſphere draws,
omes burniſh'd with a righteous cauſe.
　　　　　 Middleton and *Rowley*'s *Fair Quarrel.*

valour hath this gift aſſign'd,
1 may dye, yet deeds ſtill reſt in mind.
　　　　　　　　 Goffe's *Couragious Turk.*

it will : in midſt of horrors noiſe,
:ling flames, when all is loſt, we'll dye
pons in our hands, and victory ſcorn :
one that dye ſo poor, as they were born.
　　　　　　　　　　 True Trojans.

ld have thought, had *Mars* his actions ſeen,
he tranſumpt, this the pattern been.
　　　　　　　　 Aleyn's *Henry* VII.

noſe lets which did his valour ſtay ;
ive ſelf-motions, take the dams away.
　　　　　　　　 Aleyn's *Poictiers.*

my fancy ſees great *Edward* riſe
is enthuſiaſt ; his actions were
f valour, and deep extaſies
1 above himſelf : for drawing here
; from their matter, 'paſſed more
than he ſurpaſs'd the world before.

ſtage of *Aquitain* did play
art, which none beſide can perſonate :
ourſe, or found, or made a way,
ollrates as infallible as fate :
eath's harbinger his paſſage made,
death lodged, where he lodg'd his blade.
　　　　　　　　　　　 Ibid.

──Thus noble cauſes
to the ſpirits of full men :
ometimes ſeeming valour may ariſe
luſt, or wine, from hateful cowardice.
　　　　　　　　 Nabbs's *Covent-Garden.*
　　　　　　　　　　　 Who

Who may do moft, does leaft: the braveft will
Shew mercy there, where they have pow'r to kill.

Herri

When fortune, honour, life, and all's in doubt,
Bravely to dare, is bravely to get out.

Suckling's Aglau

In envy of thy hopes they hither came,
And envy, men in war, ambition name,
Ambition, valour: but 'tis valour's fhame,
When envy feeds it more than noble fame.

Sir *W. Davenant's Madaga*

Moft to himfelf, his valour fatal was,
Whofe glories oft to others dreadful are ;
So comets, though fuppos'd deftruction's caufe,
But wafte themfelves to make their gazers fear.

Sir *W. Davenant's Gondib*

His courage, like to powder, careflefly
Laid up, is in continual danger
Of ev'ry accidental fpark that may
Inkindle it to ruin.

Sir *W. Davenant's Diftr*

That courage which the vain for valour take,
Who proudly danger feek for glory's fake,
Is impudence; and what they rafhly do,
Has no excufe, but that 'tis madnefs too:
Yet, when confin'd, it reaches valour's name,
Which feeks fair virtue, and is met by fame:
It weighs the caufe, ere it attempts the fact,
And bravely dares forbear, as well as act :
It would reclaim much rather than fubdue ;
And would the chacer, not the chac'd purfue :
Would rather hide fuccefs, than feek applaufe,
And though of ftrength feem'd, yet trufts the caufe
And all the aid of ftrength it meafures too,
Not by the acts it did, or ftill can do,
But paffively, by what it well endures :
This noble valour is, and this is yours.

Sir *W. Davenant* to the E. of *Orr*

ght us, all affaults, all ills to bear,
fly from danger, but from fear.

Lluellin.

in great diftrefs, can only aid,
of what fhould help, will be afraid.

Sir *Robert Howard's Veftal Virgin.*

rs a manlike foul, or valiant breaft,
not dangers to difturb his reft :
prodigal on ev'ry caufe
t, to fpend his ftrength, but when the laws
religion, or his country's good
affiftance, freely fpills his blood.
way our lives denotes a fear ;
ows not off that life he cannot bear ?
Caffius fcarce deferv'd a room
and virtue groan'd to raife their tomb :
t more juftly praife to *Otho* lend,
d a woman, like a man did end.

Dancer.

n fcorn death, but yet they value life ;
heir lives are ufeful to the world.

Crown's Darius.

ntemn thy felf ; he who will have
r women love him, muft be brave.

n's Second Part of the Deftruction of Jerufalem.

V E R T U E

e and greatnefs, vertue feldom dwells;
rs pride, pride all good grace expells.

Mirror for Magiftrates.

the fteps, that happily do end
rfe, begun in vertue's painful race ;
gin that fteep hill to afcend, -
rtue dwells ; but few do find fuch grace
faint, ere they attain that place.

Ibid.

elf turns vice, b'ing mifapply'd ;
fometime by action's dignify'd.

Shakefpear's Romeo and Juliet.
Forgive

Forgive me this my virtue;
For, in the fatness of these pursy times,
Vertue it self of vice must pardon beg,
Yea, courb, and woee, for leave to do it good.
Shakespear's Hamlet.

——————————Vertues forces
Shew ever noblest in conspicuous courses.
Johnson's Sejanus.

Happen what there can, I will be just;
My fortune may forsake me, not my vertue:
That shall go with me, and before me still,
And glad me doing well, though I hear ill.
Johnson's Catiline.

Heroick vertue sinks not under length
Of years, or ages, but is still the same,
While he preserves, as when he got good fame.
Johnson's Masques.

As nothing equals right to vertue done,
So is her wrong past all comparison:
Vertue is not malicious; wrong done her,
Is righted ever, when men grant they err.
Chapman's Monsieur d' Olive.

Tho' vertue be the same, when low she stands
   In th' humble shadows of obscurity,
As when she either sweats in martial bands,
   Or sits in court clad with authority;
Yet, madam, doth the strictness of her room,
   Greatly detract from her ability:
For, as inwall'd within a living tomb,
   Her hands and arms of action labour not;
Her thoughts, as if abortive from the womb,
   Come never born, tho' happily begot:
But where she hath, mounted in open sight,
   An eminent and spacious dwelling got,
Where she may stir at will, and use her might,
   There is she more herself, and more her own;
There in the fair attire of honour dight,
   She sits at ease, and makes her glory known.
Applause

Applause attends her hands, her deeds have grace :
  Her worth, new born, is ftraight as if fully grown.
With fuch a godly and refpected face
  Doth virtue look, that's fet to look from high ;
And fuch a fair advantage by her place
  Hath ftate and greatnefs to do worthily.
Daniel to the *Countefs of Bedford.*

A worthy mind needs never to repent,
The fuff'ring croffes for an honeft caufe.
Whilft trav'lling now with a contented mind,
The memory of this my fancy feeds ;
Though to great ftates their periods are affign'd,
Time cannot make a prey of vertuous deeds
E. of *Sterline*'s *Cræfus.*

Vertue, thofe that can behold thy beauties,
Thofe that fuck, from their youth, thy milk of goodnefs,
Their minds grow ftrong againft the ftorms of fortune ;
And ftand, like rocks, in winter gufts unfhaken ;
Not with the blindnefs of defire forfaken.
Lord *Brooke*'s *Muftapha.*

States may afflict, tax, torture, but our minds
Are only fworn to *Jove* : I grieve, and yet am proud
That I alone am honeft ; high powers ! ye know,
Vertue is feldom feen with troops to go.
Marfton's *Sophonisba.*

Man's wit doth build, for time but to devour ;
But vertue's free from time and fortune's pow'r.
Drayton's *Jane Grey*, to *Gilford Dudley.*

Others, whom we call vertuous, are not fo
In their whole fubftance ; but their vertues grow
But in their humour, and at feafons fhew.

For when, through taftlefs flat humility
In dough-bak'd man, fome harmlefsnefs we fee,
'Tis but his phlegm that's vertuous, and not he :

So is the blood sometimes; who ever ran
To danger unimportun'd, he was then
No better than a sanguine vertuous man :
So cloyster'd men, who in pretence of fear,
All contributions to this life forbear,
Have vertue in melancholy, and only there.

Spiritual cholerick criticks, which in all
Religions find faults, and forgive no fall,
Have, thro' this zeal, vertue but in their gall.

We're thus but parcel gilt ; to gold we're grown,
When vertue is our soul's complexion :
Who knows his vertue's name or place, hath none.

Vertue's but aguish, when 'tis several,
By occasion wak'd and circumstantial ;
True vertue's soul, always in all deeds all.

Dr. Donne.

Extraordinary vertues, when they soar
Too high a pitch for common sight to judge of,
Losing their proper splendor, are condemn'd
For most remarkable vices.

Massinger's Unnatural Combat.

Titles may set a gloss upon our name,
But vertue only is the soul of fame.

Shirley's Coronation.

Each must, in vertue, strive for to excell ;
That man lives twice, who lives the first life well.

Herrick.

What though he nor rewards, nor knows my pain ?
In vertuous acts the very doing's gain.

Barron.

To honour vertue, is to set it forth.

Ibid.

Vertue's no vertue whilst it lives secure ;
When difficulty waits on't, then 'tis pure.

John Quarles to Barron.

Black-side, long put, or standing opposite,
Doth use to add more lustre unto white :

pearl shines brighter in a negroe's ear :
ome ladies look more fair who patches wear :
o vice, if counterplac'd, or seated near,
lakes vertue shew more lovely, strong, and clear.

Howell.

'or vertue, though a rarely planted flow'r,
Vas in the seed by this wise florist known ;
Vho could foretel, ev'n in her springing hour,
Vhat colours she shall wear when fully blown.

Sir *W. Davenant's Gondibert.*

ertue's defensive armour must be strong,
o 'scape the merry, and malicious tongue.

Sir *W. Davenant's Law against Lovers.*

he frowns of heav'n are to the vertuous, like
hose thick dark clouds, which wandring seamen spy,
nd often shew the long expected land
near.

Sir *W. Davenant's Unfortunate Lovers.*

ate hath done mankind wrong ; vertue may aim
eward of conscience, never can of fame.
Edward Hyde, (E. of *Clarendon*,) on Dr. *Donne's Death.*
ertue doth man to vertuous actions steer ;
Tis not enough that he should vice forbear.

Denham.

Vhilst passion holds the helm, reason and honour
lo suffer wrack ; but they sail safe, and clear,
Vho constantly by vertue's compass steer.

Davenport's King John and *Matilda.*

Tis not to vertue that you now resort,
f it wants strength, its own self to support;
'is only sin not suff'ring that it fears,
: grows the stronger, the more weight it bears.

E. of *Orrery's Black Prince.*

e gods ! to what must I hereafter trust ;
ince you destroy me but for being just ?
f you of vertue only will admit,
Vhy am I ruin'd for pursuing it ?

E. of *Orrery's Tryphon.*

The

'The conful's loft! dreadful reverfe of fate!
It over turns my reafon, makes me doubt
If virtue ough to have regard from men,
Since it has none from heaven.

Crown's Regulus.

The gods in vain, plant vertue here below;
It ripens not by any fun, or time:
This world for virtue is too cold a clime.

Crown's Califto.

VICISSITUDE.

For what is it on earth,
Nay under heav'n, continues at a ftay?
Ebbs not the fea, when it hath overflown?
Follows not darknefs, when the day is gone?
And fee we not fometimes the eye of heav'n
Dimm'd with o'er flying clouds? there's not that work
Of careful nature, or of cunning art,
How ftrong, how beauteou, or how rich it be,
But falls in time to ruin.

Shakefpear's Sir John Oldcaftle.

Though land tarry in your heirs, fome forty,
Fifty defcents, the longer liver at laft yet
Muft thruft them out of it; if no quail in law,
Or odd vice of their own not do it firft.
We fee thofe changes, daily: the fair lands,
That were the clients, are the lawyers, now:
And thofe rich manners, there, of good man *Taylors*,
Had once more wood upon them, than the yard
By which they were meafur'd for the laft purchafe.
Nature hath thefe viciffitudes, fhe makes
No man a ftate of perpetuity

Johnfon's Devil's an Afs.

Ev'n like fome empty creek, that long hath lain
    Left or neglected of the tree by,
Whofe searching fides pleas'd with a wand'ring vein,
    Finding fome fofter way that clofe did lie,
Steal in at laft, then other ftreams again
    Second the firft, then more than all fupply;

VVill

ill all the mighty main hath borne at laſt
The glory of his chiefeſt pow'r that way ;
ing this new found pleaſant room ſo faſt,
'Till all be full, and all be at a ſtay :
id then about, and back again doth caſt,
Leaving that full to fall another way :

fares this hum'rous world ; that ever more
Wrapt with the current of a preſent courſe,
ins into that which lay contemn'd before ;
Then glutted, leaves the ſame, and falls t' a worſe :
w zeal holds all, no life but to adore ;
The cold in ſpir't and faith is of no force.

aight all that holy was, unhallow'd lies,
The ſcatter'd carcaſſes of ruin'd vows ;
hen truth is falſe, and now hath blindneſs eyes ;
Then zeal truſts all, now ſcarcely what it knows ;
hat evermore too fooliſh or too wiſe,
It fatal is to be ſeduc'd with ſhews.

Daniel's Muſophilus.

hus doth the ever-changing courſe of things
Run a perpetual circle, ever turning ;
nd that ſame day, that higheſt glory brings,
Brings us unto the point of back-returning.

Daniel's Cleopatra.

there no conſtancy in earthly things ?
No happineſs in us, but what muſt alter ?
o life, without the heavy load of fortune ?
What miſerys we are, and to ourſelves ?
v'n then when full content ſeems to ſet by us,
What daily ſores and ſorrows ?

Beaumont and *Fletcher's Monſieur Thomas.*

hus run the wheels of ſtate, now up, now down,
nd none that lives finds ſafety in a crown.

Markham and *Sampſon's Herod and Antipater.*

————————Oh ſad viciſſitude
f earthly things ! to what untimely end
re all the fading glories that attend

Vol. III.   M   Up

Upon the ſtate of greateſt monarchs, brought !
What ſafety can by policy be wrought,
Or reſt be found on fortune's reſtleſs wheel !
Toſt humane ſtates are here inforc'd to feel
Her kingdom ſuch, as floating veſſels find
The ſtormy ocean, when each boiſt'rous wind
Let looſe from *Eol's* adamantine caves,
Ruſh forth, and rowl into impetuous waves
The ſea's whole waters; when ſome times on high
The raiſed bark doth ſome time kiſs the sky,
Some times from that great height deſcending down,
Doth ſeem to fall as low as *Acheron*.
Such is the frail condition of man's ſtate.

May's Henry II.

V I C T O R Y.

1. Are not conqueſts good titles ?
2. Conqueſts are great thefts.
   Then would I rob for kingdoms, and if I
Obtain'd, fain would I ſee him that durſt call
The conqueror a thief ?
2. Thy council hath ſhed as much blood as would
Make another ſea : Valour I cannot
Call it, and barbarouſneſs is a word too mild.

Lilly's Midas.

Baſe ſeem'd the conqueſt, which no danger grac'd.

E. of Sterline's Darius.

Conqueſt by blood is not ſo ſweet as wit ;
For howſoe're nice virtue cenſures it,
He hath the grace of war, that hath war's profit.

Marſton's Sophonisba.

———————— Diſcretion
And hardy valour are the twins of honour,
And nurs'd together make a conqueror ;
Divided, but a talker.

Beaumont and *Fletcher's Bonduca.*

In all deſigns, this ſtill muſt be confeſt,
He that himſelf ſubdues, conquers the beſt.

Webſter and *Rowley's Thracian Wonder.*

The

is ours, tho' it coſt dear; yet 'tis not
to get a victory, if we loſe
: uſe of it.

Maſſinger's Baſhful Lover;

)er to choice ſpirits to relieve
ll as conquer men; and when they dye,
ore crown their memory, to leave
rs, than conqueſts in their diary,

Aleyn's Poictiers;

his numbers: victories conſiſt
ıds not multitudes: moſt of their part
)ur cauſe, and coldly will reſiſt:
ıot the hand, aſſured of the heart.

Aleyn's Henry VII.

ıot victory to win the field,
'e make our enemies to yield
our juſtice, than our force; and ſo
inſtruct, as overcome our foe.

Gomerſall.

deny your conqueſt, for you may
rtues to intitle 't yours; but otherwiſe,
f ſtrange and ill contriv'd deſires,
ı narrow or intemp'rate mind,
after of the field, I cannot ſay,
hath conquer'd, but that he hath had
hand of it; he hath got the day,
ʼubdu'd the men: victory being
ıne's gift, but the deſerving's purchaſe.
m doſt thou call deſerving?
who dares
t his heart in cold blood; him, who fights
of thirſt, or the unbridled luſt
fh'd ſword, but out of conſcience,
the enemy, not the man: who when
'rell's planted on his brow, ev'n then
hat ſafe protecting wreath, will not
ı the thunderer; but will
ledge all his ſtrength deriv'd, and in

A pious way of gratitude return
Some of the spoil to heaven in sacrifice;
As tenants do the first fruits of their trees,
In an acknowledgment that the rest is due.

Cartwright's Royal Slave.

1. To be o'ercome by his victorious sword,
Will comfort to our fall afford;
Our strength may yield to his, but 'tis not fit
Our virtue should to his submit;
In that, *Ianthe*, I must be
Advanc'd, and greater far than he.

2. Fighting with him who strives to be your friend,
You not with virtue, but with pow'r contend.

Sir W. Davenant's Siege of Rhodes.

Conquest of realms compar'd to that of minds,
Shews but like mischief of outragious winds;
Making no use of force, but to deface,
Or tear the rooted from their native place:
Who by distress at last are valiant made,
And take their turn invaders to invade:
From woods they march victorious back again
To cities, the wall'd parks of herded men
Victors by conqu'ring realms are not secure;
Nor seem of any thing, but hatred sure.
A king who conquers minds does so improve
The conquer'd, that they still the victor love.

Sir W. Davenant to the King.

He who commends the vanquish'd, speaks the pow'r,
And glorifies the worthy conqueror.

Herrick.

For he who conquests wisely has design'd,
Will never leave an enemy behind.
Beginnings should to th' end still useful be;
'Tis more to use, than gain a victory.

E. of Orrery's Mustapha.

What *Alexander* ne'er could reach, I won;
Had he subdu'd to the *Chinensian* shore,
They with some reason he had wept for more:

But,

k a froward child, at meals too great,
'd for want of ftomach, not of meat.
                    Sir *Francis Fane's Sacrifice.*

V I R G I N I T Y.

t not politick in the common-wealth
ure, to preferve virginity.
 virginity is national increafe;
iere was never virgin got, till virginity
rft loft.   Virginity, by being
oft, may be ten times found : by being
ept, it is ever loft; 'tis too
 companion, away with it.
ill ftand for it a little, though
ore I die a virgin.
ere's little can be faid in it : 'tis 'gainft
ile of nature.   To fpeak on the part
ginity, is to accufe your mother;
 is moft infallible difobedience.
t hangs himfelf is a virgin :
ity murthers itfelf, and fhould
y'd in highways, out of all fanctify'd
, as a defp'rate offendrefs againft
.   Virginity breeds mites; much like
fe, confumes it felf to the very
, and fo dies with feeding its own
h.   Befides virginity's peevifh,
 idle, made of felf-love, which is the
rohibited fin in the canon.
: not, you cannot chufe but lofe by't.
th't; within ten months it will make it
'o, which is a goodly increafe, and
incipal it felf not much the worfe.
ommodity will lofe the glofs
ring.   The longer kept, the lefs worth :
th't whilft 'tis vendible.   Anfwer the
of requeft. Virginity, like an
urtier, wears her cap out of fafhion;
futed, but unfutable; juft like

The

The brooch and the tooth-pick, which we wear not
Now ; your date is better in your pye and your
Porridge, than in your cheek ; and your virginity,
Your old virginity is like one of our
French wither'd pears ; it looks ill, it eats dryly ;
Marry, tis a wither'd pear : 'twas formerly
Better ; marry, yet 'tis a wither'd pear.
Will you any thing with it ?

Shakespear's All's Well that ends Well.

1. What an honest work it would be, when we find
A virgin in her poverty and youth,
Inclining to be tempted, to employ
As much perswasion, and as much expence
To keep her upright, as men use to do upon her falling.
2. 'Tis charity, that many maids will be unthankful for ;
And some will rather take it for a wrong,
To buy them out of their inheritance,
The thing that they were born to.

Beaumont and *Fletcher's* Honest Man's Fortune.

That which thy lascivious will doth crave,
Which if once had, thou never more canst have ;
Which if thou get, in getting thon dost waste it,
Taken is lost, and perish'd if thou hast it :
Which if thou gain'st, thou ne'er the more hast won ;
I losing nothing, yet am quite undone :
And yet of that, if that a king deprave me,
No king restores, though he a kingdom gave me.

Drayton's Matilda to King John.

A treasure 'tis, able to make more thieves
Than cabinets set open to entice ;
Which learn them theft, that never knew the vice.

Thomas Middleton's Mayor of Quinborough.

There's a cold curse laid upon all maids ;
Whilst others clip the sun, they clasp the shades.
Virginity is paradise lock'd up ;
You cannot come by yourselves without fee,
And 'twas decreed that man should keep the key.

Tourneur's Revenger's Tragedy.

ns would, mens words could have no pow'r;
honour is a cryſtal tow'r,
eing weak, is guarded with good ſpirits;
baſely yields, no ill inherits.

Tourneur's Revenger's Tragedy.

> number; maids are nothing then
the ſweet ſociety of men.
u live ſingle ſtill? one ſhalt thou be,
never ſingling *Hymen* couple thee.
ages that drink of running ſprings,
ater far excels all other things:
that daily take neat wine deſpiſe it.
 albeit ſome highly prize it,
d with marriage, had you try'd them both,
 much as wine and water doth.

Cook's Green's Tuquoque.

ne's your cloiſter, your beſt friends, your beads;
ſt and ſingle life ſhall crown your birth,
s a virgin, lives a ſaint on earth.
rewel world, and worldly thoughts adieu,
e chaſte vows, my ſelf I yield to you!

John Ford's Tis pity ſhe is a Whore.

dom that a virgin hath,
to be preferr'd; who would endure
nours of ſo excellent a thing
uſband? which of all the herd,
t poſſeſs'd with ſome notorious vice,
g or whoring, fighting, jealouſy,
a page at twelve, or of a groom
s horſes heels? is it not daily ſeen,
e wives but to dreſs their meat, to waſh
rch their linnen? for the other matter
g with them, that's but when they pleaſe;
atſoe'er the joy be of the bed,
ngs that follow procreation
ous, or you wives have gull'd your husbands
ur loud ſhriekings, and your deathful throes.

Field's Amends for Ladies.

1. What

1. What are you?
2. Sir, I am a chambermaid.
1. What are you damn'd for?
2. Not for revealing
My mistress secrets, for I kept them better
Than mine own; but keeping my maiden-
Head till it was stale, I am condemned
To lead apes in hell.
1. Alaſs, poor wench! upon condition
You will be wiſe hereafter, and not refuſe
Gentlemens proffers; learn pride ev'ry day,
And painting; beſtow a courteſy now
And then upon the apparitor to
Keep council, I releaſe you; take your apes
And monkeys away with you, and beſtow
Them on gentlemen and ladies that want play-fellow.
Shirley's School of Compliments

Virginity is but a ſingle good,
A happineſs, which like a miſer's wealth,
Is as from others, ſo from your own uſe,
Lock'd up, and cloſely cabin'd, ſince it not admits
Communication of it's good; when you
Shall, in the ſtate of marriage, freely taſte
Nature's choice pleaſure, the ſame happineſs
You were created for.
Glapthorne's Albertus Wallenstein

'Tho' you *Diana* like, have liv'd ſtill chaſt,
Yet muſt you not, fair, dye a maid at laſt:
The roſes on your cheeks were never made
To bleſs the eye alone, and ſo to fade;
Nor had the cherrys on your lips their being,
To pleaſe no other ſenſe than that of ſeeing:
You were not made to look on, tho' that be
A bliſs too great for poor mortality:
In that alone thoſe rarer parts you have,
To better uſes ſure wiſe nature gave,
Than that you put them to: to love, to wed,
For *Hymen's* rites, and for the marriage bed

Yo

ordain'd, and not to lie alone;
number, 'till that two be one.

Suckling.

:hing that we efpy
, faving you and I :
he fields, furvey the bow'rs,
   the bloffoms, and the flow'rs;
' they fo rich could be
bafe virginity.
t fo coy as you are now,
ʒly admits the plow:
ɪad man or beaſt been fed,
. kept her maidenhead ?

Randolph.

's are nothing ; they are fhy,
re what they deny.

Herrick.

f I have folemnly protefted
ɪd dye a virgin ?
ɪou muft
ɪly break that oath ; fuch temerarious
udent vows are better broke than
· none can by an ordinary way
 whether they have that fpecial gift
ency, as to be able to live
ɪɪnmarry'd.   What woman hath fo
ɪt the world of her own heart,
ach creek, furvey'd each corner, but
 there may remain much *terra incognita*
'? befides, concupifcences
ɪ reftrain'd will fwell the more ; had
: been kept in a brazen door,
y'd a harmlefs virgin, not a whore.
                    Nevile's Poor Scholar.
——— Suppofe
ɪirgin, alas poor green thing what
d for ! why to fteal goofeberrys,
'oung apricots in *May*, before

M 5   The

The stones are hard ; or pick the mortar
From an aged wall, and swallow it most greedily.
Sir W. Davenant's News from Plymouth.

———————— What's virginity?
A something nothing, singularity,
Unsociable, so slightly reckon'd of,
That either sex, but to thy number grown,
Has a desire to leave it.
Alexander Brome's Cunning Lovers.

V O W S.

Unheedful vows may heedfully be broken ;
And he wants wit, that wants resolved will
To learn his wit, t' exchange the bad for better.
Shakespear's Two Gentlemen of Verona.

1. He hath giv'n count'nance to his speech, my lord.
With almost all the holy vows of heav'n.
2. Ay, springes to catch woodcocks ! I do know,
When the blood burns, how prodigal the soul
Lends the tongue vows. These blazes, oh my daughter,
Giving more light than heat, extinct in both,
Ev'n in their promise, as it is a making,
You must not take for fire.   For lord *Hamlet*,
Believe so much in him, that he is young ;
And with a larger tether may he walk,
Than may be given you   In few, *Ophelia*,
Do not believe his vows ; for they are brokers,
Not of that die which their investments shew,
But meer implorers of unholy suits.
Breathing like sanctify'd and pious bawds,
The better to beguile.
Shakespear's Hamlet.

Are vows so cheap with women ? or the matter
Whereof they are made, that they are writ in water,
And blown away with wind ? or doth their breath
Both hot and cold at once, threat life and death ?
Who could have thought so many accents sweet
Tun'd to our words, so many sighs should meet
Blown from our hearts, so many oaths and tears
Sprinkled

Sprinkled among, all sweeter by our fears,
And the divine impression of stol'n kisses,
That seal'd the rest, could now prove empty blisses?
Did you draw bonds to forfeit? sign to break?
Or must we read you quite from what you speak,
And find the truth out the wrong way? or must
He first desire you false, would wish you just.

Johnson's Underwoods.

O they must ever strive to be so good;
Who sells his vow is stamp'd the slave of blood.

Tho. Middleton's Phœnix.

————These are feeble vows,
Made only by our fears: we ought to have
Our reason undismay'd, when e'er a promise
Can force performance.

Habbington's Queen of Arragon.

First, let me seek my vows where they were seal'd,
They were so strictly kept, that I shall find
Them warm, as if but newly breath'd——
These are the funeral rights of love.

Sir W. Davenant's Unfortunate Lovers.

Why, since you *Orgo's* words so soon believe,
Will you less civilly suspect my vows?
My vows which want the temple's seal, will bind
 (Though private kept) surer than publick laws;
For laws but force the body, but my mind
 Your virtue councels, whilst your beauty draws.

Sir W. Davenant's Gondibert.

. For 'tis in vain to waste
Thy breath for them: the fatal vow is past.
. To break that vow is juster, than commit
A greater crime, by your preserving it.
. The gods themselves their own will best express
To like the vow, by giving the success.

Sir Robert Howard's Indian Queen.

When vows with vows, altars with altars jarr,
It seems to breed in heav'n a civil war.

Crown's Juliana.

M 6   USUR-

USURPATION.

A scepter snatch'd with an unruly hand,
Must be as boistrously maintain'd, as gain'd:
And he, that stands upon a slipp'ry place,
Makes nice of no vile hand to hold him up.
Shakespear's King John.

Pirates may make cheap penn'worths of their pillage,
And purchase friends, and give to courtezans,
Still revelling, like lords, till all be gone;
While as the silly owner of the goods
Weeps over them, and wrings his hapless hands,
And shakes his head, and trembling stands aloof,
While all is shar'd, and all is born away,
Ready to starve, and dares not touch his own:
So *York* must sit, and fret, and bite his tongue,
While his own lands are bargain'd for and sold.
Shakespear's Second Part of K. Henry VI.

For tho' usurpers sway the rule a while,
Yet heav'ns are just, and time suppresseth wrongs.
Shakespear's Third Part of K. Henry VI.

To keep an usurp'd crown, a prince must swear,
Forswear, poison, murder, and commit all
Kind of villanies, provided it be
Cunningly kept from the eyes of the world.
Chapman's Alphonsus.

Think what the worst have done; what they enjoy,
That pluck down states to put up private laws,
Whom fame ennobles whilst she would destroy.
Lord *Brooke's Alaham.*

All usurpers have the falling sickness,
They cannot keep up long.
Middleton's Mayor of Quinborough.

Whilst you usurp thus, and my claim deride,
If you admire the vengeance I intend,
I more shall wonder where you got the pride
To think me one you safely may offend.
Sir *W. Davenant's Gondibert.*

'Tis

'Tis love, not faction, where the good
Conspire to kill usurping blood.

Killegrew's Conspiracy.

W A N T.

WANT of that torments us most,
    Whose worth appears in being lost.

Brandon's Octavio.

'Twere best, not call; I dare not call; yet famine,
Ere it clean o'erthrow nature, makes it valiant.
Plenty and peace, breed cowards; hardness ever
Of hardiness is mother.

Shakespear's Cymbeline.

It hath been taught us from the primal state,
That he, which is, was wish'd, untill he were;
And the ebb'd man, (ne'er lov'd, till ne'er worth love,)
Comes dear'd, by being lack'd.

Shakespear's Antony and Cleopatra.

Men ne'er are satisfy'd with what they have;
But, as a man match'd with a lovely wife,
When his most heav'nly theory of her beautys
Is dull'd, and quite exhausted with his practise,
He brings her forth to feasts; where he, alas,
Falls to his viands with no thought like others,
That think him blest in her; and they, (poor men)
Court, and make faces, offer service, sweat
With their desire's contention, break their brains
For jests, and tales, sit mute, and lose their looks,
Far out of wit, and out of countenance) :
So all men else, do, what they have, transplant,
And place their wealth in thirst of what they want.

Chapman's Second Part of Byron's Conspiracy.

The only plague, from men, than rest doth reave,
Is that they weigh their wants, not what they have.

E. of Sterline's Julius Cæsar.

Why

Why should we grieve at want?
Say the world made thee her minion, that
Thy head lay in her lap, and that she danc'd thee
On her wanton knee, she could but give thee a wh
World; that's all, and that all's nothing: the worl
Greatest part cannot fill up one corner of thy heart.
Say, the three corners were all fill'd, alas!
Of what art thou possest? a thin-blown glass,
Such as by boys are puft'd into the air.
Were twenty kingdoms thine, thou'dst live in cares
Thou could'st not sleep the better, nor live longer,
Nor merrier be, nor healthfuller, nor stronger?
If then thou want'st, thus make that want thy pleasu
No man wants all things, nor has all in measure.

Dekker's Second Part of the Honest Wbo

Your Wolf no longer seems to be a wolf,
Then when she's hungry.

Webster's White Da

Want made him feared more than his disgrace:
As 'tis observ'd, that *Catiline* ne'er meant
His country's ruin, 'till his means were spent.

Aleyn's Henry V.

What though the scribe of *Florence* doth maintain,
    To keep men quiet, is to keep them scant:
Crowds of examples, and all *Henry's* reign
    Refell him, whose rebellions sprung from want.
Want's a strange herald! For some men had bore
No arms at all, unless they had been poor.

To Men exhaust, and worn with penury,
    New things are pleasing, and the old ingrate,
And renovation is their remedy:
    Rebellions are the monsters of a state:
And nature shews, that they proceed no less
From the defect of matter, than th' excess.

They who to fortune's lowest form are thrown,
    To ruin, and confusion do aspire,
As if another's wound could salve their own:
    And when their own Estates are set on fire,

Then *Catiline*'s refolve is judg'd moft fit,
With fire, not water, to extinguifh it.

Aleyn's *Henry* VII.

Want is a fofter wax, that takes thereon,
This, that, and ev'ry bafe Impreffion.

Herrick.

Need is no vice at all; though here it be
With men, a loathed inconveniency.

Herrick.

For want's a real evil to mankind ;
What e'er we need, we languifh till we find.

Alex. Brome.

W A R.

It is the beft with foreign foes to fight
Abroad, as did the haughty *Hannibal*,
And not at home to feel their hateful fpight :
Of all the reft it is the greateft thrall,
That foes arriv'd fhould fpoil our fubjects all :
And for a truth this always hath been found,
He fpeedeth beft, which fights on foreign ground.

Mirrour for Magiftrates.

Laftly ftood war, in glitt'ring arms yclad,
   With vifage grim, ftern looks, and blackly hew'd ;
In his right hand, a naked fword he had,
   That to the hilts was all with blood embru'd :
   And in his left (that kings and kingdoms ru'd,)
Famine and fire he held, and there withal
He razed Towns, and threw down tow'rs and all.

Cities he fack'd, and realms that whilome flower'd
   In honour, glory, and rule above the beft,
He over-whelm'd, and all their fame devour'd,
   Confum'd, deftroy'd, wafted, and never ceaft,
   'Till he their wealth, their name, and all oppreft :
His face fore-hew'd with wounds, and by his fide
There hung his targe, with gafhes deep and wide :

In

In midſt of which depainted there we found
   Deadly debate, all full of ſnaky hair,
That with a bloody fillet was ybound,
   Out breathing nought, but diſcord ev'ry where
            Lord Dorſet in the *Mirrour for Magiſtrate.*
When thou famous victory haſt won,
   And high amongſt all knights haſt hung thy ſhield,
Thenceforth the ſun of earthly conqueſt ſhun,
   And waſh thy hands from guilt of bloody field:
For blood can nought but ſin, and wars but ſorrows yield.
                   Spenſer's Fairy Queen.

In thy faint ſlumbers I by thee have watch'd,
And heard thee murmur tales of iron wars:
Speak terms of manage to thy bounding ſteed;
Cry, courage! to the field! and thou haſt talk'd
Of ſallies and retires; of trenches, tents,
Of paliſadoes, frontiers, parapets,
Of baſilſks, of cannon, culverin,
Of priſoners ranſom, and of ſoldiers ſlain,
And all the current of a heady fight.
              Shakeſpear's Fiſt Part of K. Henry IV.
In peace, there's nothing ſo becomes a man
As modeſt ſtillneſs and humility:
But when the blaſt of war blows in our ears,
Then imitate the action of the tyger;
Stiffen the ſinews, ſummon up the blood,
Diſguiſe fair nature with hard favour'd rage;
Then lend the eye a terrible aſpect;
Let it pry through the portage of the head,
Like the braſs cannon; let the brow o'erwhelm it,
As fearfully, as doth a galled rock.
O'erhang and jutty his confounded baſe,
Swill'd with the wild and waſtful ocean.
Now ſet the teeth, and ſtretch the noſtril wide;
Hold hard the breath, and bend up every ſpirit
To his full heigth.
                Shakeſpear's K. Henry V.

              1. Methinks

. Methinks, I could not die any where so
contented as in the king's company;
His cause being just, and his quarrel honourable.
:. That's more than we know.
. Ay, or more than we should seek after; for
We know enough, if we know we are the
King's subjects: if his cause be wrong, our obedience
To the king, wipes the crime of it out of us.
2. But if the cause be not good, the king himself
Hath a heavy reck'ning to make; when all
Those legs, and arms, and heads chop'd off in a
Battle, shall join together at the latter
Day, and cry all, we dy'd at such a place;
Some swearing, some crying for a surgeon;
Some, upon their wives left poor behind them;
Some, upon the debts they owe; some, upon
Their children rawly left. I am afear'd
Their are few dye well, that dye in battle;
For how can they charitably dispose
Of any thing, when blood is their argument?
Now, if these men do not dye well, it will
Be a black matter for the king that led
Them to it, whom to disobey, were against
All proportion of subjection.
3. So, if a son, that is sent by his father
About merchandize, do fall into some
Lewd action and miscarry, th'imputation
Of his wickedness, by your rule, should be
Imposed upon his father that sent
Him; or if a servant, under his master's
Command, transporting a sum of money,
Be assail'd by robbers, and dye in many
Irreconcil'd iniquities; you may call
The business of the master, the author
Of the servant's damnation; but this is
Not so: the king is not bound to answer
The particular endings of his soldiers,
The father of his son, nor the master

Of his servant; for they purpose not their
Death, when they purpose their
Services. Besides, there is no king, be
His cause never so spotless, if it come
To the arbitrement of swords, can try it
Out with all unspotted soldiers: Some,
Peradventure, have on them the guilt of
Premeditated and contrived murther;
Some, of beguiling virgins with the broken -
Seals of perjury; some, making the wars
Their bulwark, that have before gored the
Gentle bosom of peace with pillage and
Robbery. Now if these men have defeated
The law, and out-run native punishment;
Though they can out-strip men, they have no wing
To fly from God. War is his beadle, war
Is his vengeance; so that here men are punish'd,
For before breach of the king's laws, in the
King's quarrel now: Where they fear'd the death,
They have born life away; and where they would
Be safe, they perish. Then if they die unprovided,
No more is the king guilty of their damnation,
Than he was before guilty of those impieties
For which they are now visited. Ev'ry
Subject's duty is the king's, but ev'ry
Subject's soul is his own. Therefore should ev'ry
Soldier in the wars do, as ev'ry sick man
In his bed, wash ev'ry moth out of his
Conscience: and dying so, death is to him
Advantage; or not dying, the time was
Blessedly lost, wherein such preparation
Was gained: and in him that escapes, it
Were not sin to think, that making God so
Free an offer, he let him out live that
Day to see his greatness, and to teach others
How they should prepare.

Shakespear's K. *Henr.*

Shame and confusion! all is on the rout:
Fear frames disorder; and disorder wounds,
Where it should guard. O War! thou son of hell,
Whom angry heav'ns do make their minister,
Throw in the frozen bosoms of our part
Hot coals of vengeance! Let no soldier flie.
He that is truly dedicate to war,
Hath no self-love; for he that loves himself,
Hath not essentially, but by circumstance,
The name of valour.

Shakespear's *Second Part of* K. *Henry* VI.

O war! begot in pride and luxury,
  The child of malice, and revengeful hate;
Thou impious good, and good impiety!
  Thou art the foul refiner of a state,
Unjust scourge of mens iniquity,
  Sharp easer of corruptions desperate!
Is there no means, but that a sin-sick land
Must be let blood with such a boist'rous hand?

Daniel's *Civil War.*

Now nothing entertains th' attentive ear,
  But stratagems, assaults, surprizes, fights:
How to give laws to them that conquer'd were;
  How to articulate with yielding wights.
The weak with mercy, and the proud with fear,
How to retain: to give deserts their right;
Were now the arts—and nothing else was thought,
But how to win, and maintain what was got.

Ibid.

Affection finds a side, and out it stands;
Not by the cause, but by her int'rest led:
And many urging war, most forward are,
Not that 'tis just, but only that 'tis war.

Ibid.

Who would make war, must not have empty coffers;
Where one for glory, thousands fight for gain.

E. of *Sterline*'s *Darius*.

Audit

Audit the end : How can humanity,
  Preserved be in ruin of mankind ?
Both fear and courage feel her cruelty,
  The good and bad, like fatal ruin find :
Her enemies do still provide her food,
From those she ruins, she receives her good.
Lord *Brooke of Wars.*

Scipio, advanced like the god of blood,
Leads up grim war, that father of foul wounds,
Whose sinewy feet are steep'd in gore, whose hideous
          voice
Makes turrets tremble, and whole cities shake ;
Before whose brows, flight and disorder hurry,
With whom march burnings, murder, wrong, wast,
          rapes ;
Behind whom, a sad train is seen, woe, fears,
Torture, lean need, famine, and helpless tears.
Marston's Sophonisba.

For all the murders, rapes, and thefts,
Committed in the horrid lust of war,
He that unjustly caus'd it first proceed,
Shall find it in his grave, and in his seed.
Webster's White Devil.

Some sharp their swords, some right their morions set,
  Their greaves and pouldrons others rivet fast,
The archers now their bearded arrows whet,
  Whilst ev'ry where the clam'rous drums are brac'd ;
Some taking view where they sure ground might get,
  Not one, but some advantage doth forecast :
With ranks and files each plain and meadow swarm,
As all the land were clad in angry arms.
Drayton's Barons Wars.

All wars are bad : yet all wars do good ;
And, like to surgeons, let sick kingdoms blood.
Dekker's Second Part of the Honest Whore.

He is unwise that to a market goes,
Where there is nothing to be sold but blows.
Aleyn's Henry VII.

These

hefe fair exordiums are the ways to win,
is war's rhet'rick bravely to begin.

Aleyn's Poictiers.

'or is it wifdom where no treafons are,
  To hope for fuccour from a ftrange fupply :
foney's the nerve and ligament of war,
  In makes them fight, and keeps from mutiny.
faders are fouls, armies the bodies, coin
he vital fpirits that do both combine.

Aleyn's Crefey.

—————————The fubject's large,
or can we there too much difpute, where, when
'e err, 'tis at a·kingdom's charges; peace
ad war are in themfelves indifferent,
ad time doth ftamp them either good or bad :
it here the place is much confiderable;
'ar in our own, is like to too much heat
'ithin, it makes the body fick ; when in
nother country, 'tis but exercife,
onveys that heat abroad, and gives it health.

Suckling's Brennoralt.

effation for fhort times in war, are like
all fits of health, in defp'rate maladies :
'hich while the inftant pain feems to abate,
atters into debauch and worfe eftate.

Ibid.

hough war's great fhape beft educates the fight,
  And makes fmall foft'ning objects lefs our care ;
it war, when urg'd for glory, more than right,
  Shews victors, but authentick murd'rers are.

Sir *W. Davenant's Gondibert.*

ow various are th' effects of war !
hat fury rules
'er human fenfe, that we fhould ftruggle to
eftroy in mangled wounds, our life, which
eav'n decreed fo fhort ? It is a myftery,
oo fad to be remember'd by the wife,

'That

That half mankind confume their noble blood
In caufes not belov'd, or underftood.

Sir *W. Davenant's Love and Honou*

To broach a war, and not to be affur'd
Of certain means to make a fair defence,
Howe're the ground be juft, may juftly feem
A wilful madnefs.

Hemmings's Jews Tragu

1. I ne'er thought fame a lawful caufe of war.
2. Wars are good phyfick, when the world is fick:
But he, who cuts the throats of men for glory,
Is a vain favage fool; he ftrives to build
Immortal honours upon man's mortality:
And glory on the fhame of human nature,
To prove himfelf a man by inhumanity:
He puts whole kingdoms in a blaze of war,
Only to ftill mankind into a vapour;
Emptys the world to fill an idle ftory:
In fhort, I know not why he fhould be honour'd,
And they that murder men for money hang'd.

Crown's Ambitious Statefm

War, is the harveft fir, of all ill men:
In war, they may be brutes with reputation.

Ib

W H O R E.

A hufwife, that, by felling her defires,
Buys her felf bread and cloth. It is a creature
That dotes on *Caffio*; as 'tis the ftrumpet's plague
To beguile many, and be beguil'd by one.

Shakefpear's Oth

'Tis there civility to be a whore;
He's one of blood and fafhion! and with thefe
The bravery makes, fhe can no honour leefe.
To do't with cloth, or ftuffs, luft's name might me
With velvet, plufh, and tiffues, it is fpirit!

Johnfon's Underwx

Farewell thou private ftrumpet, worfe than commo
Man were on earth an angel, but for woman!

7

ren-fold branch of hell from them doth grow ;
uft, and murther, they raife from below,
l their fellow fins. Women were made
d, without fouls : when their beauties fade,
:ir luft's paft, avarice or bawdery
hem ftill lov'd : then they buy venery,
damnation, and hire brothel flaves ;
their executors, infamy their graves.

Marfton's Infatiate Countefs.

ood creatures ! what would you have them do ?
you have them get their living by the
: man, the fweat of their brows ? fo they
ery man muft follow his trade,
ery woman her occupation :
decayed mechanical man's
ler husband is lay'd up, may not fhe
ly be lay'd down, when her husband's
fing is by his wife's falling ?
iin's wife wants means, her commander
open field abroad, may not fhe
:ivil arms at home ? a waiting
woman, that had wont to take, fay,
lady, mifcarrys, or fo ; the
nisfortune throws her down, may not the
urtefy take her up ? do you know
erman would pity fuch a woman's
why is charity grown a fin, or
ng the poor and impotent an
: ? you will fay beafts take no money
iir flefhly entertainment ; true, becaufe
ire beafts, and therefore beaftly ; only men
o loofe, becaufe they are men, therefore
; and indeed, wherein fhould they beftow
money better ? in land, the title
: crack'd ; in houfes, they may be burnt ;
arrel, 'twill wear ; in wine, alas for pity,
roat is but fhort : but employ your money
women, and a thoufand to nothing,

Some

Some one of them will bestow that upon you,
Which shall stick by you as long you live:
They are no ingrateful persons, they will
Give you *quid* for *quo* : do you protest, they'll swear;
Do you rise, they'll fall, do you fall, they'll rise?
Do you give them the *French* crown, they'll give
You the *French*————O *justus, justa, justum.*
They sell their bodies; do not better persons
Sell their souls? nay, since all things have been sold,
Honour, justice, faith, nay ev'n God himself,
Ay me, what base ignobleness is it
To sell the pleasures of a wanton bed ?
Why do men scrape, why heaps to full heaps join?
But for his mistress, who would care for coin ?
For this I hold to be deny'd of no man,
All things are made for man, and man for woman.
Marston's Dutch Courtezan.

Who keeps a harlot, tell him this from me,
He needs nor thief, disease, or enemy.
Middleton's Mad World my Masters.

Stand forth————thou one of those,
For whose close lusts the plague ne'er leaves the city.
Thou, worse th n common ; private, subtle harlot,
Thou doest deceive thrice with one feigned lip;
Thy husband, the world's eye, and the law's whip:
Thy zeal is hot, for 'tis to lust and fraud,
And dost not dread to make thy book thy bawd.
Thou'rt curse enough to husbands ill got gains,
For whom the court rejects, his gold maintains.
How dear and rare was freedom wont to be ?
How few but are by their wives copies free,
And brought to such a head, that now we see,
City and suburbs wear one livery.
Middleton's Phœnix.

Our term ends once a month ; we should get more
Than the lawyers, for they have but four terms
A year, and we have twelve, that makes them
Run so fast to us in the vacation.
Middleton's Michaelmas Term.

```
————:——You have no foul,
```
That makes you weigh so light : heav'n's treasure
    bought it,
And half a crown hath fold it :——for your body,
Tis like the common shore, that still receives
All the town's filth.   The sin of many men
Is within you ; and thus much I suppose,
That if all committers stood in a rank,
They'd make a lane (in which your shame might dwell)
And with their spaces reach from hence to hell :
Nay, I shall urge it more, there has been known
As many by one harlot maim'd and difmember'd,
As would have stuff'd an hospital : this I might
Apply to you, and perhaps do you right :
O y'are as base as any beast that bears,
Your body's ev'n hir'd, and so are theirs.
For gold and sparkling jewels, (if he can)
You'll let a *Jew* get you with *Christian* :
Be he a *Moor*, a *Tartar*, though his face
Look'd uglier than a dead man's scull ;
Could the devil put on a humane shape,
If his purse shake out crowns, up then he gets ;
Whores will be rid to hell with golden bits.
So that y'are crueller than *Turks*, for they
Sell *Christians* only, you fell your felves away.
Why those that love you, hate you; and will term you
Lickorish damnation : wish themselves half funk
After the sin is laid out, and ev'n curse
Their fruitless riot, (for what one begets
Another poisons): lust and murder hit;
A tree being often shook, what fruit can knit ?
         Dekker's First Part of the Honest Whore.

. A harlot is like *Dunkirk*, true to none,
swallows both *English*, *Spanish*, fulsome *Dutch*,
ack-door'd *Italian*, last of all the *French*,
and he sticks to you 'faith, gives you your diet,
rings you acquainted, first with monsieur doctor,
and then you know what follows.

———— 2. Misery.

Rank, stinking, and most loathsome misery!

1. Methinks a toad is happier than a whore,
That with one poison swells, with thousands more
The other stocks her veins: harlot, fie, fie!
You are the miserablest creatures breathing,
The very slaves of nature: mark me else,
You put on rich attires, other eyes wear them;
You eat, but to supply your blood with sin:
And this strange curse ev'n haunts you to your graves,
From fools you get, and spend it upon slaves:
Like bears and apes, y'are baited, and shew tricks
For money, but your bawd the sweetness licks.
Indeed you are their journey-women, and do
All base and damn'd works they list set you to:
So that you ne'er are rich; for do but shew me,
In present memory, or in ages past,
The fairest and most famous courtezan,
Whose flesh was dearest, that rais'd the price of sin
And held it up; to whose intemp'rate bosom,
Princes, earls, lords, the worst has been a knight,
The mean'st a gentleman, have offer'd up
Whole hecatombs of sighs, and rain'd in show'rs
Handfuls of gold, yet for all this, at last
Diseases suck'd her marrow, grew so poor,
That she has begg'd ev'n at a beggar's door.
And (wherein heav'n has a finger) when this idol
From coast to coast has leap'd on foreign shores,
And had more worship, than th' outlandish whores;
When sev'ral nations have gone over her,
When for each sev'ral city she has seen,
Her maidenhead has been new, and been sold dear:
Did live well there, and might have dy'd unknown,
And undefam'd; back comes she to her own,
And there both miserably lives and dies,
Scorn'd ev'n of those that once ador'd her eyes:
As if her fatal circled life thus ran,
Her pride should end there, where it first began.
                    Dekker's First Part of the Honest Whore.

A strumpet is one of the devil's vines;
All the sins like so many poles, are stuck
Upright out of hell, to be her props, that
She may spread upon them : and when she's ripe,
Every slave has a pull at her, then
Must she be prest : The young beautiful grape
Sets the teeth of lust on edge, yet to taste
That liquorish wine, is to drink a man's
Own damnation.

Dekker's Second Part of the Honest Whore.
Were harlots therefore wise, they'd be sold dear ;
For men account them good but for one year:
And then, like Almanacks whose dates are gone,
They are thrown by, and no more look'd upon.

Ibid.

She is a right strumpet; I ne'er knew any
Of their trade rich two years together: sieves
Can hold no water, nor harlots hoard up
Money; they have many vents, too many
Sluices to let it out; taverns, taylors, bawds,
Panders, fidlers, swaggerers, fools and knaves,
Do all wait upon a common harlot's
Trencher; she is the gally-pot to which
These drones fly; not for love to the pot, but
For the sweet sucket within it, her money, her money.

Ibid.

For to turn a harlot
Honest, it must be by strong antidotes ;
'Tis rare, as to see panthers change their spots :
And when she's once a star, fix'd and shines bright,
Tho' 'twere impiety then to dim her light,
Because we see such tapers seldom burn .
Yet 'tis the pride and glory of some men,
To change her to a blazing star again.

Ibid.

A drab of state, a cloath of silver flirt!
Her train borne up, her soul trails in the dirt.

A.b.

Ask but the thriving'st harlot in cold blood,
She'd give the world to make her honour good :
Perhaps you'll fay but only to the duke's fon
In private : why, the fift begins with one,
Who afterwards to thoufands proves a whore ;
Break ice in one place, it will crack in more.

Tourneur's Revenger's Tragedy.

Your punk is like your polititian ; for they
Both confume themfelves, for the common people :
And your punk of the two, is the better
Member ; for the, like a candle to burn
Others, burns herfelf.

Cupid's Whirligig.

Not fale-ware, mercenary ftuff, that ye may
Have i'th' fubburbs, and now maintain traffick with
Ambaffadors fervants ; nor with landreffes,
Like your ftudents in law, who teach her to
Argue the cafe fo long, till fhe find a
Statute for it ; nor with miftrefs filkworm
In the city, that longs for creams and cakes,
And loves to cuckold her hufband in frefh
Air, nor with your waiting gentlewoman,
That is in love with poetry, and will
Not part with her honour, under a copy
Of fine verfes, or an anagram ; nor
With your crafty Lady herfelf, that keeps a
Stallion, and cozens her old knight, and
His two pair of fpectacles, in the fhape
Of a ferving-man ; but with your rich, fair,
High-fled, glorious, and fpringing cat a mountains,
Full of blood, whofe eye will make a foldier
ftoop, and be were compos'd of marble ; whofe
Very fmile hath a magnetick force to
Draw up fouls, whofe voice will charm a fatyre,
And turn a man's prayers into ambition ;
Make a fermon fine to tell her at a touch
Of fin, and there hug his own damnation

Shirley's Grateful Servant.

Tha

: us be friends, and moſt friendly agree :
ip, and the punk, and the doctor are three ;
nnot but thrive, when united they be :

p brings in cuſtom ; the punk ſhe gets treaſure ;
h the phyſician is ſure of his meaſure,
t that ſhe makes him, in ſale of her pleaſure :

h, when ſhe fails by diſeaſes or pain,
ſtor new vamps and upſets her again.

Richard Brome's *City Wit.*

ſhould love a whore, a very
ı cocatrice ! my thoughts are drown'd in
ıf ſin ; ſhe's a very cannibal,
oth devour man's fleſh, and a horſe-leach
ks out mens beſt bloods perfection :
ıris'ners box that ope's for ev'ry
nevolence.

Sharpham's *Fluit.*

and whores are near ally'd,
h their tails maintain their pride.

Baron.

harlots fair, like gilded tombs,
vithout, within all rottenneſs :
: a painted fire upon a hill,
ure the froſt-nipt paſſengers,
ve them after hope : ſhe is indeed
as ſtrumpets are, angel in ſhew,
heart.

Hoffman's *Tragedy.*

ot is the broad way unto hell,
nth, a ditch, a poiſnous well :
nightly glow-worm, canker'd braſs,
on inn, a ſink, a broken glaſs :
is luſt, her lover is a ſlave,
s are fetters, and her bed's a grave.
own fountain ; ſtollen waters pleaſe
ıs minds, and breed the ſoul's diſeaſe.

Watkins.

W I L L.

And as this wit should goodness truly know,
  We have a will, which that true good should chuse,
Though will doth oft (when wit false forms doth shew)
  Take ill for good, and good for ill refuse :

Will puts in practice, what the wit deviseth :
  Will ever acts, and wit contemplates still :
And as from wit, the pow'r of wisdom riseth,
  All other virtues daughters are of will.

Will is the prince, and wit the counsellor,
  Which doth for common good in council sit ;
And when wit is resolv'd, will lends her pow'r
  To execute what is advis'd by wit.

Wit is the mind's chief judge, which doth controul
  Of fancy's courts the judgments false and vain ;
Will holds the royal scepter in the soul,
  And o'er the passions of the heart doth reign.

Will is as free as any emperor,
  Nought can restrain her gentle liberty :
No tyrant, nor no torment hath the pow'r
  To make us will, when we unwilling be.
                Sir *John Davies.*

What we would do,
We shou'd do, when we would ; for this would changes,
And hath abatements and delays as many,
As there are tongues, are hands, are accidents ;
And then this should, is like a spend-thrift sigh
That hurts by easing.
                Shakespear's Hamlet.

But orderly to end where I begun,
Our will, and fates do so contrary run,
That our devices still are overthrown ;
Our thoughts are ours, their ends none of our own.
                Ibid.

My will enkindled by mine eyes and ears,
Two traded pilots 'twixt the dang'rous shores
Of will and judgment
       Shakespear's Troilus and Cressida.

—The cloyed will,
tiate, yet unſatisfy'd deſire, (that tub
'd, and running ;) rav'ning firſt the lamb,
ſter, for the garbage.

Shakeſpear's Cymbeline.

not in my virtue to amend it.
ue ? a fig : 'tis in ourſelves that we
s. or thus. Our bodies are our gardens,
vhich our wills are gardiners: ſo
we plant nettles, or ſow lettice ;
ɔp, and weed up thyme ; ſupply it
ie gender of herbs, or diſtract it
any ; either have it ſteril with
, or manur'd with induſtry ;
he pow'r and corrigible authority
, lies in our will.

Shakeſpear's Othello.

rs are man's religion, pow'r his laws ;
. confuſion, and his will the cauſe.

Lord Brooke's Inquiſition on Fame and Honour.

ertainty is in our bloods, our ſtates ?
ʋe ſtill write, is blotted out by fates :
lls are like a cauſe, that is law-toſt,
ne court orders, by another's croſt.

Middleton's Game at Cheſs.

ſe you know my will is like
ſmooth and cold ; but being ſtrucken,
:s forth fire ev'n in the ſtriker's eyes.

Cupid's Whirligig.

:f is grown ſo deſp'rate, but the ill
way cured, if the party will.

Herrick.

man is puniſh'd, he is plagued ſtill,
: the fault of nature, but of will.

Ibid.

W I N T E R.

The wrathful winter hast'ning on apace,
   With blustering blasts had all ybar'd the treen,
And old Saturnus with his frosty face
   With chilling cold had pierc'd the tender green.
   The mantles rent wherein enwrapped been
The gladsome groves, that now lay overthrown,
The tapers torn, and ev'ry tree down blown.

The soil that erst so seemingly was seen,
   Was all despoiled of her beauty's hue,
And sothe fresh flow'rs (wherewith the summer's queen
   Had clad the earth) now Boreas blasts down blew,
   And small fowls flocking, in their song did rew
The winter's wrath, wherewith each thing defac'd,
In woeful wise bewail'd the summer past.

Hawthorn had lost his motley livery;
   The naked twigs were shiv'ring all for cold,
And dropping down the tears abundantly;
   Each thing (methought) with weeping eye me told
   The cruel season, bidding me withhold
Myself within, for I was gotten out
Into the fields, whereas I walk'd about.

*   Earl of Dorset in the Mirror for Magistrates.*

———————— *Somewhat*

My eye drawn in, so that I appear forlorn,
I am the certain sign of my fair parent earth
.... from the earth
My.................................
Thou.......... my beams, make the sky clear and fair:
And.............................. I me,
But I am.....................

*   Zuccaro's : Thomas Dekker's Sun's Darling*

....
And................................
When Hom...................................
....

Zuccaro

When ev'ry barn rung with the threshing flails,
And shepherds boys for cold 'gan blow their nails.

Brown's Pastorals.

————When winter doth the earth array
In silver suit, and when the night and day
Are in diffention, night locks up the ground,
Which by the help of day is oft unbound.

Ibid.

Fair *Flora's* pride into the earth again
Was sunk: cold winter had begun his reign,
And summon'd beauteous daylight to restore
To night, those hours, which he had stol'n before.

May's Henry II.

December rag'd, the northern winds did blow,
And by their pow'r had glaz'd the silver flood
Of near adjoyning *Thames,* whose waters stood
Congealed still; o'er which the snow around
Had fall'n, and with white fleeces cloath'd the ground.

Ibid.

Now shiv'ring winter fledg'd with feather'd rain,
  Cover'd the earth with beds of watrish down,
Which warns the prince to quit the open plain,
  And have his soldiers winter'd in a town;
Who unto *Bourdeaux* unimpeach'd retreats,
And for this year takes leave of martial feats.

The piercing frosts candy'd in *Gallick* skies,
  Against their countrys foes would so combine,
The tunicles should not secure their eyes,
  And all the humours would turn cristalline:
In their blue channels the red streams had flood,
And spirits been congealed in that flood.

Therefore the prince will not his men bestow,
  In fields unshelter'd, whilst the leagu'ring cold,
And batt'ring engines of chill ice and snow,
  Assault the spirits, and surprize their hold:
Who let their men i'th' field in winter lie,
Both combat nature, and the enemy.

N 5

Aleyn's Poictiers

W I S D O M.

And as from sense, reason's work doth spring,
　So many reasons understanding gain,
And many understandings knowledge bring,
　And by much knowledge, wisdom we obtain.

So many stairs we must ascend upright,
　Ere we attain to wisdom's high degree:
And if on earth we ripe our reason's light,
　Which else no mutants would like angels see.
                              Sir John Davies.

———————— Men wise,
By the same steps by which they fell, may rise.
                  Shakspear and Rowley's Birth of Merlin.

Wisdom wishes to appear most bright,
When it doth tax itself; as these black masques
Proclaim an enshield beauty ten times louder,
Than beauty could display'd
                      Shakspear's Measure for Measure.

A wise man's home is where'ere he's wise;
Now that, for a man, not from the place doth rise.
                  Marston's Second Part of Antonio and Mellida.

A wise man, wrongfully, but never wrong
Can take: the breath of such well temper'd proof,
It may be smooth'd, not pierc'd by savage tooth
Of foaming malice: show'rs of darts may dark
Heav'n's ample brow, but not strike out a spark;
Much less pierce the sun's cheek.
                              Ibid.

————————He that's a man for men,
Ambitious as a god, must like a god
Live free from passions; In full aim'd at end,
In mercy to others, sole self to comprehend;
Round in's own globe, not to be clasp'd, but holds
Within him all, his heart being of more folds,
Than shield of *Telamon*; not to be pierc'd, though struck:
The God of wise men is themselves, not luck.
                              Marston's Sophonisba.

All

All things are lawful that do profit bring ;
A wife man's bow goes with a two-fold ftring.
John Day's Ifle of Gulls.

The opinion of wifdom, is a foul tetter,
That runs all over a man's body : if fimplicity
Directs us to have no evil, it directs us
To a happy being, for the fubtileft folly
Proceeds from the fubtileft wifdom.
Webfter's Dutchefs of Malfy.

This is the wife man's cure,
That any thing, fate wills, he can endure.
Daubourne's Poor Man's Comfort.

Let a wife man place his ftrength
Within himfelf, nor truft to outward aids :
That whatfoever from the gods can come,
May find him ready to receive their doom.
May's Cleopatra.

Move on then ftars, work your pernicious will :
Only the wife rule, and prevent your ill.
Maffinger and *Field's Fatal Dowry.*

True wifdom, planted in the hearts of kings,
Needs no more glory than the glory't brings ;
And like the fun, is view'd by her own light,
J'ing, by her own reflection, made more bright.
Quarles.

Wealth, without wifdom, may live more content,
Than wit's enjoyers can, debarr'd of wealth ;
All pray for riches, but I ne'er heard yet
Of any fince *Solomon* that pray'd for wit :
He's counted wife enough in thefe vain times,
That hath but means enough to wear gay cloaths,
And be an outfide of humanity; what matters it a pin,
How indifcreet fo e'er a natural be,
So that his wealth be great ? that's it doth caufe
Wifdom in thefe days to give fools applaufe.
And when gay folly fpeaks, how vain foe're ;
Wifdom muft filent fit, and fpeech forbear.
Tailor's Hog hath loft his Pearl.

N 6

——In such like affairs,
Which do concern th' uncertain rule of states,
Wife men should always be above their fates.
          Glapthorne's Albertus Wallenstein.

——————But let
Ev'n the plotting destinies contrive,
And be themselves of council ; all their malice
Shall only shew an idle fruitless hate,
While wisdom takes the upper hand of fate.
          Cartwright's Royal Slave.

Excellent morality ! O the vast extent
O'th' kingdom of a wise man ! such a mind
Can sleep secure, when the brine kisses the moon,
And thank the courteous storm for rocking him !
          Baron's Mirza.

The wise men were but seven : now we scarce know
So many fools, the world so wise doth grow.
          Heath's Clarastella.

Your wisdom hath the skill to cure
Distempers, stronger than your fortune feels.
          Sir W. Davenant's Unfortunate Lovers.

The wise I here observe,
Are wise tow'rds God ; in whose great service still,
More than in that of kings, themselves they serve.
          Sir W. Davenant's Gondibert.

I can but smile to think how foolish wise
Those women are, that chuse their loves for wisdom.
Wisdom in man's a golden chain, to tie
Poor women in a glorious slavery.
          Sicelides.

Justice and faith never forsake the wise,
Yet may occasion put him in disguise ;
Not turning like the wind, but if the state
Of things must change, he is not obstinate ;
Things past, and future, with the present weighs,
Nor credulous of what vain rumour says ;
Few things, by wisdom are at first believ'd ;
An easy ear deceives, and is deceiv'd.
          Denham.

But feven wife men the antient world did know ;
We fcarce know feven, who think themfelves not fo.

Denham.

Wifdom of what her felf approves, makes choice ;
Nor is led captive by the common voice.
Clear fighted reafon wifdom's judgement leads,
And fenfe, her vaffall, in her footfteps treads.

Ibid,

All human wifdom to divine, is folly ;
This truth, the wifeft man made melancholy.

Ibid.

Greatnefs we owe to fortune, or to fate ;
But wifdom only can fecure a ftate.

Denham's Sophy.

1. Are there divinities below ?
2. There are ; ev'ry wife thing is a divinity,
That can difpofe, and check the fate of things.

Sir Robert Howard's Great Favourite.

1. Confult a little with your prudence.
2. Wifdom's too froward to let any find
Truft in himfelf, or pleafure in his mind ;
She takes by what fhe gives ; her help deftroys ;
She fhakes our courage, and difturbs our joys :
Rafhnefs allows unto the fudden fenfe
All it's own joys, and adds her confidence.

Sir Robert Howard's Veftal Virgins.

'or 'tis the fate of wife men, to be thought
To act what int'reft, not juftice, bids them :
And Hiftories do oft'ner palliate crimes,
Than publifh them.

Fane's Sacrifice.

Were all things of one temper,
The univerfe would not fubfift one minute :
Were all men wife, the world would be at a
ftand, whilft each do prove unmalleable
Into others defigns.

Hectors.

The

The wife do always govern their own fates,
And fortune with officious zeal attends
To crown their enterprizes with success.

Abdicated Prince.

W I T.

Wit not avails, late bought with care and cost;
Too late it comes, when life and all is lost.

Mirror for Magistrates.

The wit, the pupil of the soul's clear eye,
   And in man's world the only shining star:
Look in the mirror of the fantasy,
   Where all the gath'rings of the senses are:

From thence, this pow'r the shapes of things abstracts,
   And them within her passive part receives,
Which are enlightned by that part which acts,
   And so the forms of single things perceives:

But after, by discoursing to and fro,
   Anticipating, and comparing things,
She doth all universal natures know,
   And all effects into their causes brings:

When she rates things, and moves from ground to ground,
   The name of reason she obtains by this:
But when by reason she the truth hath found,
   And standeth fix'd, she understanding is.

When her assent she lightly doth encline
   To either part, she has opinion's light:
But when she doth by principles define
   A certain truth, she hath true judgment's sight.

Sir John Davies.

But they that know that wit can shew no skill,
   But when the things in senses glass doth view,
Do know, if accident this glass do spill,
   It nothing sees, or sees the false for true:

For if that region of the tender brain,
   Where th' inward sense of fantasy should sit,
And th' outward sense's gath'rings should retain,
   By nature, or by chance, become unfit.

Either at firſt uncapable it is,
    And ſo few things, or none at all receives:
Or marr'd by accident, which haps amiſs,
    And ſo amiſs it ev'ry thing perceives.
Sir *John Davies.*

As the moſt forward bud
Is eaten by the canker, ere it blow;
Ev'n ſo by love, the young and tender wit
Is turn'd to folly, blaſting in the bud;
Loſing his verdure, ev'n in the prime,
And all the fair effects of future hopes.
Shakeſpear's Two Gentlemen of Verona.

The only ſoil of his fair vertue's gloſs,
If vertue's gloſs will ſtain with any ſoil,
Is a ſharp wit, match'd with too blunt a will;
Whoſe edge hath pow'r to cut, whoſe will ſtill wills,
It ſhould ſpare none that come within his pow'r.
Shakeſpear's Love's Labour's loſt.

Short-liv'd wits do wither as they grow.
Ibid.

Your wit makes wiſe things fooliſh; when we greet
With eyes beſt ſeeming heaven's fiery eye,
By light we loſe light; your capacity
If of that nature, as to your huge ſtore
Wiſe things ſeems fooliſh, and rich things but poor.
Ibid.

Good wits are greateſt in extremities.
Johnſon's Volpone.

But as of lions it is ſaid, and eagles,
That when they go, they draw their ſeres and talons
Cloſe up, to ſhun rebating of their ſharpneſs:
So our wit's ſharpneſs, which we ſhould employ
In nobleſt knowledge, we ſhould never waſte
In vile and vulgar admirations.
Chapman's Revenge of Buſſy D'ambois.

Her wit ſtings, bliſters, galls off the skin
With the tart acrimony of her ſharp quickneſs:
By

By sweetness she is the very *Pallas*
That flew out of *Jupiter's* brain-pan.
Marston's First Part of Antonio and Mellida.

One excellence to many is the mother:
Wit doth as creatures, ore beget another.
Drayton in the Mirror for Magistrates.

The wit of man wanes and decreases soon;
But woman's wit is ever at full moon.
Middleton's Mad World my Masters.

When she has reapt what I have sown,
She'll say one grain tasts better of her own,
Than whole sheaves gather'd from another's land:
Wit's never good, till bought at a dear hand.
Dekker's First Part of the Honest Whore.

———————'Tis most fit,
He should have state, that riseth by his wit.
Barrey's Ram Alley.

He's a good husband, who so buys his wit,
That others, not himself, doth pay for it.
Mayn's Henry VII.

When wit makes not abuse it exercise,
The use of it then are truly wise:
But 'tis a foolish vanity, not wit,
When conscience bounds are broke to practice it.
Nabbs's Covent Garden.

In meaner wits that proverb chance may hold,
That they who soon are ripe, are seldom old.
Epitaph on Tho. Randolph's Death.

Dread not the shackles; on with thine intent:
Good wits get more fame by their punishment.
Herrick.

Wit's an unruly engine, wildly striking
  Sometimes a friend, sometimes the engineer:
Hast thou the knack? pamper it not with liking:
  But if thou want it, buy it not too dear.
Many affecting wit beyond their pow'r,
Have got to be a dear fool for an hour.
Herbert.

As

As buds to blossoms, blossoms turn to fruit;
So wits ask time to ripen and recruit,

Howell.

Thy wit's chief virtue, is become it's vice;
  For ev'ry beauty thou hast rais'd so high,
That now coarse faces carry such a price,
  As must undo a lover that should buy.

Sir *W. Davenant* to *Tho. Carew.*

The nimble packing hand, the swift
Disorder'd shuffle, or the slur, or his
More base employment, who makes love for bread,
Do all belong to men that may be thought
To live, sir, by their sins, not by their wits.

Sir *W. Davenant's Wits.*

These are the victories of wit: by wit
We must atchieve our hopes; which to refine
And purify, with paces doubled let us
Descend a marble vault: there taste the rich
Legitemate blood of the mighty grape:
It magnifies the heart, and makes the agile
Spirits dance;
It drowns all thoughts adulterate and sad,
Inspires the prophet, makes the poet glad.

Sir *W. Davenant's Just Italian.*

Wit flies beyond the limit of that law,
By which our sculptors 'grave, or painters draw,
And statuarys up to nature grow;
Who all their strokes of life to poets owe.
Their art can make no shape for wit to wear,
It is divine, and can no image bear:
None by description can that soul express;
Yet all must the effects of it confess:
States boast of those effects, when they relate,
How they in treatys foil'd a duller state:
And warriors, shewing how they gain'd the day,
How they drew up, and where their ambush lay:
And lovers, telling, why a rival fail'd,
Whilst they but whisper'd beauty, and prevail'd:

And

And cloifter'd men, when they with fmiles declare
How rigidly they are confin'd from care,
And how they let the world plough troubled feas,
Whilft they for penance muft endure their eafe.

Sir *W. Davenant* to the E. of *Orrery.*

A- fullen heirs, when waftful fathers dye,
Their old debts leave for their pofterity
To clear ; and the remaining acres ftrive
T'enjoy, to keep them pleafant whilft alive :
So I (alas !) were to my felf unkind,
If from that little wit, he left behind,
I fimply fhould fo great a debt defray ;
I'll keep it to maintain me, not to pay.
Yet, for my foul's laft quiet when I dye,
I will commend it to pofterity :
Although 'tis fear'd, 'caufe they are left fo poor,
They'll but acknowledge, what they fhould reftore.

Sir *W. Davenant* to Doctor *Duppa.*

You can't expect that they fhould be great wits,
Who have fmall purfes, they ufually
Sympathize together ; wit is expenfive,.
It muft be dieted with delicacies,
It muft be fuckled with the richeft wines,
Or elfe it will grow flat and dull.

Nevile's Poor Scholar.

Time runs, love flies ;
He that thinks leaft, is the moft wife :
And fortune ever did approve
A prefent wit, in war, or love.

Fane's Love in the Dark.

W I V E S.

I will rather truft a *Fleming* with my
Butter, parfon *Hugh* the *Welchman* with my
Cheefe, an *Irifhman* with my *aqua vitæ*
Bottle, or a thief to walk my ambling
Gelding, than my wife with her felf : then fhe
Plots, then fhe ruminates, then fhe devifes :

And

And what they think in their hearts they may effect,
They will break their hearts but they will effect.

Shakespear's Merry Wives of Windsor.

We'll leave a proof, by that which we will do,
Wives may be merry, and yet honest too;
We do not act, that often jest and laugh:
'Tis old, but true, still swine eat all the broth.

Ibid.

Such duty as the subject owes the prince,
Ev'n such a woman oweth to her husband:
And when she's froward, peevish, sullen, sower,
And not obedient to his honest will,
What is she but a foul contending rebel,
And graceless traytor to her loving lord?
I am asham'd, that women are so simple
To offer war, where they should kneel for peace;
Or seek for rule, supremacy, and sway,
When they are bound to serve, love, and obey.
Why are our bodies soft, and weak, and smooth,
Unapt to toil and trouble in the world,
But that our soft conditions, and our hearts
Should well agree with our external parts?
Come, come, you froward and unable worms,
My mind hath been as big as one of yours,
My heart as great, my reason happly more,
To bandy word for word, and frown for frown;
But now I see, our lances are but straws,
Our strength as weak, our weakness past compare:
That seeming to be most, which we indeed least are.
Then vale your stomachs, for it is no boot,
And place your hands below your husbands foot:
In token of which duty if he please,
My hand is ready, may it do him ease.

Shakespear's Taming of the Shrew.

After you are marry'd, sir, suffer valiantly;
For I must tell you all the perils that you are
Obnoxious to. If she be fair, young, and
Vegetous, no sweetmeats ever drew more
Flies; all the yellow doublets, and great rose-

In the town will be there : if foul and crooked,
She'll be with them, and buy those doublets and
Roses, sir; if rich, and that you marry
Her dowry, not her, she'll reign in your house,
As imperious as a widow : if noble,
All her kindred will be your tyrants : if
Fruitful, as proud as *May*, and humorous
As *April* ; she must have her doctors, her
Midwives, her Nurses, her longings ev'ry
Hour ; though it be for the dearest morsel
Of man : if learned, there was never such
A parrot ; all your patrimony will
Be too little for the guests that must be
Invited, to hear her speak *Latin* and *Greek :*
And you must lie with her in those languages
Too, if you will please her : if precise, you
Must feast all the silenc'd brethren once in
Three days, salute the sisters, entertain
The whole family, or woo'd of them, and
Hear long-winded exercises, singings,
And catechisings, which your not giv'n to,
And yet must give for, to please the zealous
Matron your wife; who, for the holy cause,
Will cozen you over and above : then, if
You love your wife, or rather doat on her,
O, how she'll torture you, and take pleasure
In your torments ! you shall lye with her but
When she lists ; she will not hurt her beauty,
Her complection, or it must be, for that
Jewel, or that pearl, when she does ; ev'ry
Half hour's pleasure must be bought anew, and
With the same pain and charge you woo'd her at first.
Then, you must keep what servants she please, what
Company she will ; that friend must not visit
You without her license ; and him she loves
Most, she will seem to hate eagerliest
To decline your jealousy, or feign to be
Jealous of you first ; and for that cause go
Live with her she-friend, or cozen at the

College, that can inftruct her in all the
Myfterys of writing letters, corrupting
Servants, taming fpies; where fhe muft have that
Rich gown for fuch a great day, a new one
For the next, a richer for the third; be
Serv'd in filver, have the chamber fill'd with
A fucceffion of grooms, footmen, ufhers,
And other meffengers; befides embroiderers,
Jewellers, tire-women, femfters, feather-men,
Perfumers; whilft fhe feels not how the land
Drops away, nor the acres melt; nor forefees
The change, when the mercer has your woods
For her velvets: never weighs what her pride
Cofts, fir, fo fhe may kifs a page, or a
Smooth chin, that has the defpair of a beard;
Be a Statefwoman, know all the news, what
Was done at *Salisbury*, what at the *Bath*,
What at court, what in progrefs: or, fo fhe
May cenfure poets, and authors, and ftiles,
And compare them, *Daniel* with *Spencer*,
Johnfon with th'other youth, and fo forth; or
Be thought cunning in controverfies, or
The very knots of divinity, and have often
In her mouth the ftate of the queftion:
And then skip to the mathematicks, and
Demonftration and anfwer in religion
To one, in ftate to another, in bawdry
To a third.   All this is very true, Sir.
And then her going in difguife to that
Conjurer, and this cunning woman; where
'The firft queftion is, how foon you fhall dye?
Next, if her prefent fervant love her? next,
That if fhe fhall have a new fervant? and
How many? which of her family would
Make the beft bawd, male or female?
What precedence fhe fhall have by her next
Match? and fets down the anfwers, and believes
Them above the fcriptures. Nay, perhaps fhe'll

Study

Study the art : and then comes reeking home
Of vapour and sweat, with going a foot,
And lies in a month of a new face, all
Oil, and bird-lime; and rises in asses
Milk, and is cleans'd with a new sucus: God
Be with you sir, one thing more (which I had
Almost forgot)   This too, with whom you are
To marry, may have made a conveyance
Of her virginity aforehand, as
Your wise widows do of their estates, before
They marry, in trust to some friend, sir; who
Can tell? or if she have not done it yet,
She may do, upon the wedding day, or
The night before, and antidate you cuckold.

Johnson's Silent Woman.

He that will choose
A good wife from a bad, come learn of me,
That hath try'd both, in wealth and misery.
A good wife will be careful of her fame,
Her husband's credit, and her own good name,
And such art thou : a bad wife will respect
Her pride, her lust, and her own name neglect,
And such art thou ; a good wife will be still
Industrious, apt to do her husband's will ;
But a bad wife, cross, spightful and madding,
Never keep home, but always be a gadding,
And such art thou ; a good wife will conceal
Her husband's dangers, and no thing reveal
That may procure him harm, and such art thou:
But a bad wife corrupts chast wedlock's vow,
On this side vertue, and on that side sin,
On this who strive to loose, or this to win:
Here lives perpetual joy, here burning woe.
Now husbands choose on which hand will you go?
Seek vertuous wives, all husbands will be blest;
Fair wives are good, but vertuous wives are best.
They that my fortunes will peruse, shall find
No beauty's like the beauty of the mind.

How a Man may choose a good Wife from a bad.

————My dear lord's wife, and knows
That tinfel glitter, or rich purfled robes,
Curled hairs, hung full of fparkling carcanets,
Are not the true adornments of a wife:
So long as wives are faithful, modeft, chaft,
Wife lords affect them.   Vertue doth not waft
With each flight flame of crackling vanity.
A modeft eye forceth affection,
Whilft outward gaynefs, light looks but entice;
Fairer than nature's fair, is fouleft vice.
She that loves art, to get her cheek more lovers,
Much outward gawds, flight inward grace difcovers:
I care not to feem fair, but to my lord.
Thofe that ftrive moft to pleafe a ftranger's fight,
Folly may judge moft fair, wifdom moft light.

Marfton's Second Part of Antonio and Mellida.

In the election of a wife, as in
A project of war, to err but once, is
To be undone for ever.   You are a man
Well funk in years, and to graft fuch a young
Bloffom into your ftock, is the next way
To make ev'ry carnal eye befpeak your injury.
Troth I pity her too; fhe was not made
To wither and go out by painted fires,
That yields her no more heat than to be lodg'd
In fome bleak banquetting houfe in the dead
Of winter; and what follows then? your fhame,
And the ruin of your children; and there's
The end of a rafh bargain.

Middleton's Any thing for a quiet Life.

'Tis not enough for one that is a wife
   To keep her fpotlefs from an act of ill,
But from fufpition fhe fhould free her life,
   And bare her felf of pow'r as well as will:
'Tis not fo glorious for her to be free,
As by her proper felf reftrain'd to be.

When

When she hath spacious ground to walk upon,
   Why on the ridge should she desire to go?
It is no glory to forbear alone
   Those things, that may her honour overthrow:
But 'tis thank-worthy, if she will not take
All lawful liberties for honour's sake.

That wife, her hand against her fame doth rear,
   That more than to her lord herself will give
A private word to any second ear;
   And though she may with reputation live,
Yet, though most chast, she doth her glory blot,
And wounds her honour, though she kills it not.

When to their husbands they themselves do bind,
   Do they not wholly give themselves away?
Or give they but their body, not their mind,
   Reserving that though best for others, pray?
No sure, their thoughts no more can be their own;
And therefore should to none but one be known.

Then she usurps upon another's right,
   That seeks to be by publick language grac'd:
And though her thoughts reflect with purest light,
   Her mind, if not peculiar, is not chast.
For in a wife it is no worse to find,
A common body, than a common mind.

And ev'ry mind though free from thought of ill,
   That out of glory seeks a worth to shew:
When any's ears but one therewith they fill,
   Doth in a sort her pureness overthrow.
                   Lady *Carew*'s *Mariam*.
Let all young sprightly wives that have
Dull foolish coxcombs to their husbands,
Learn by me their duties, what to do;
Which is, to make them fools, and please them too.
           Beaumont and Fletcher's *Noble Gentlemen*.

——————————————I know
The sum of all that makes a man, a just man happy,
Consists in the well choosing of his wife;
And there well to discharge it, does require
Equality of years, of birth, of fortune;
For beauty being poor, and not cry'd up
By birth or wealth, can truly mix with neither:
And wealth, where there's such difference in years,
And fair descent, must make the yoke uneasy.

Massinger's New Way to pay old Debts.

A witty wife, with an imperious will,
Being crost, finds means to cross her husband still.

Richard Brome's Mad Couple well match'd.

If e'er I take a wife, I will have one,
Neither for beauty nor for portion,
But for her vertues; and i'll marry'd be
Not for my lust, but for posterity:
And when i'm wed, i'll never jealous be,
But make her learn how to be chast by me:
And be her face what 'twill, i'll think her fair,
If she within the house confine her care:
If modest in her words and cloaths she be,
Not daub'd with pride, and prodigality:
If with her neighbours she maintains no strife,
And bears her self to me a faithful wife;
I'd rather unto such a one be wed,
Than clasp the choicest *Hellen* in my bed:
Yet though she were an angel, my affection
Should only love, not doat on her perfection.

Randolph.

Suspicion, discontent, and strife,
Come in for dowry with a wife.

Herrick.

Oh servile state of conjugal embrace!
Where seeming honour covers true disgrace.
We with reproaches, mistresses defame;
But we poor wives endure the greatest shame:

O

We to their slaves are humble slaves, whilst they
Command our lords, and rule what we obey:
Their loves each day new kindnesses uphold,
We get but little, and that little cold.;
That a poor wife is with her state reproach'd,
And to be marry'd, is to be debauch'd.

Crown's Caligula.

W O M E N.

———— It is thought wonderful
Among the seamen, that mugill, of all
Fishes the swiftest, is found in the belly
Of the bret, of all, the slowest: and shall
It not seem monstrous to wise men, that the
Heart of the greatest conqu'ror of the world,
Should be found in the hands of the weakest
Creature of nature? of a woman! of
A captive! Ermines have fair skins, but foul
Livers; sepulchers fresh colours, but rotten
Bones; women fair faces, but false hearts.

Lilly's Alexander and Campaspe.

Mens due deserts each reader may recite,
　For men of men do make a goodly shew,
But womens works can never come to light;
　No mortal man their famous acts may know;
　No writer will a little time bestow,
The worthy acts of women to repeat;
Though their renown and due deserts be great.

Mirror for Magistrates.

1. You're pictures out of doors,
Bells in your parlours, wild cats in your kitchens,
Saints in your injuries, devils being offended,
Players in your housewifry, and housewives in your beds!
2. O, fie upon thee, slanderer!
1. Nay, it is true, or else I am a *Turk*;
You rise to play, and go to bed to work,

Shakespear's Othello.

If

: be black, and thereto have a wit,
find a white that shall her blackness fit.

Shakespear's Othello.

's none so foul and foolish thereunto,
oes foul pranks, which fair and wise ones do.

Ibid.

man sometimes scorns what best contents her;
her another, never give her o'er;
corn at first, makes after love the more:
: do frown, 'tis not in hate of you,
ither to beget more love in you:
: do chide, 'tis not to have you gone;
hy, the fools are mad, if left alone:
no repulse, whatever she doth say;
get you gone, she doth not mean away:
:r, and praise, commend, extol their graces;
ne'er so black, say they have angel's faces.
man that hath a tongue, I say is no man,
th his tongue he cannot win a woman.

Shakespear's Two Gentlemen of Verona.

woman reads another's character,
out the tedious trouble of decyphering.

Johnson's New Inn.

at holds religious and sacred thoughts
woman; he that bears so reverend
pect to her, that he will not touch
but with a kiss'd hand and a timerous
; he that adores her like his goddess,
im be sure, she'll shun him like her slave.
good souls, women of themselves are
able and tractable enough, and
l return *quid* for *quod* still, but we are
that spoil them, and we shall answer for't
ier day; we are they that put a
of wanton melancholly into them,
makes them think their noses bigger than
faces, greater than the sun in brightness;

O 2

And

And whereas nature made them but half fools,
We make them all fools.

Chapman's May Day.

'Trust women! ah *Myrtillus*, rather trust
'The summer's winds, th' ocean's constancy;
For all their substance is but levity:
Light are their wav'ring veils, light their attires,
Light are their heads, and lighter their desires:
Let them lay on what coverture they will
Upon themselves, of modesty and shame,
They cannot hide the woman with the same.
'Trust women! ah *Myrtillus*, rather trust
'The false devouring crocodile of *Nile*,
For all they work is but deceit and guile:
What have they but is feign'd? their hair is feign'd,
Their beauty feign'd, their stature feign'd, their pace,
Their gesture, motion, and their grace is feign'd:
And if that all be feign'd without, what then
Shall we suppose can be sincere within?
For if they do but weep, or sing, or smile,
Smiles, tears, and tunes, are engines to beguile;
And all they are, and all they have of grace,
Consists but in the outside of a face.

Daniel's Arcadia.

But how durst he of one the glory raise,
  Where two contemn'd would needs the wrong repair?
It spite our sex, to hear another's praise;
  Of which, each one would be thought only fair.

Earl of *Sterline's Julius Cæsar.*

A woman's hate is ever dipp'd in blood,
And doth exile all councils that be good

Lord *Brooke's Alaham.*

Alas, fair princess! those that are strongly form'd,
And truly shap'd, may naked walk; but we,
We things call'd women, only made for shew
And pleasure, created to bear children,
And play at shuttle-cock; we imperfect mixture,
Without respective ceremony us'd,

And

ver compliment, alas, what are we?
from us formal cuſtom, and the courteſies
h civil faſhion hath ſtill us'd to us,
.ll to all contempt. O women! how much,
much are you beholden to ceremony?

Marſton's Sophonisba.

· be a, virgin of a modeſt
ſhame ſac'd, temp'rate aſpect, her very
ſty inflames me, her ſober bluſhes
ne: If I behold a wanton, pretty,
ly, petulant ape, I am extreamly
e with her, becauſe ſhe is not clowniſhly rude,
hat ſhe aſſures her lover of no
int, dull, moving *Venus:* Be ſhe
ly ſevere, I think ſhe wittily counterfeits,
love her for her wit: If ſhe be
ed and cenſures poets, I love her ſoul,
or her ſoul, her body: Be ſhe a
of profeſt ignorance, oh I am
ely taken with her ſimplicity;
lur'd to find no ſophiſtication
her! Be ſhe ſlender and lean, ſhe's
Greek's delight: Be ſhe thin and plump, ſhe's
talian's pleaſure: If ſhe be tall, ſhe's
goodly form, and will print a fair
rtion in a large bed: If ſhe be
and low, ſhe's nimbly delightful,
rdinarily quick witted: Be ſhe young,
or mine eye: Be ſhe old, ſhe's for my
irſe, as one well knowing there is much
olenefs in a grave matron: But be
oung, or old, lean, fat, ſhort, tall, white, red,
I, nay even black, my diſcourſe ſhall find.
n to love her, if my means may procure
rtunity to enjoy her.

Marſton's Fawn.

hen that ſex leave vertue to eſteem,
greatly err, which think them what they ſeem.

'Their

Their plighted faith, they at their pleasure leave,
   Their love is cold, but hot as fire their hate ;
On whom they smile, they surely those deceive ;
   In their desires, they be insatiate :
Them of their will, there's nothing can bereave,
   Their anger hath no bound, revenge no date :
They lay by fear, when they at ruin aim,
They shun not sin, as little weigh they shame.
Drayton's Barons Wars.

To dote on weakness, slime, corruption, woman!
What is she, took asunder from her cloaths ?
Being ready, she consists of hundred pieces,
Much like your *German* clock, and near ally'd ;
Both are so nice, they cannot go for pride :
Beside a greater fault, but too well known,
They'll strike to ten, when they should stop at one.
Middleton's Mad World my Masters.

When there comes a restraint upon flesh, we
Are always most greedy upon't ; and that
Makes your merchant's wife often times pay so
Dear for a mouthful : give me a woman
As she was made at first, simple of herself,
Without sophistication, like this wench :
I cannot abide them, when they have tricks,
Set speeches, and artful entertainments :
You shall have some so impudently aspected,
They will out-cry the forehead of a man,
Make him blush first, and talk him into silence ;
And this is counted manly in a woman ;
It may hold so, sure womanly it is not : no,
If e'er I love, or any thing move me,
'Twill be a woman's simple modesty.
Ibid.

———— Oh hapless creatures!
There is in woman a devil from her birth ;
Of bad ones we have shoal, of good a dearth.
Dekkers Match me in London.

She

t bad that hath defire to ill,
hat hath no pow'r to rule that will.

Beaumont and *Fletcher's Woman Hater.*

lat are call'd women, know as well
it were a far more noble thing,
: where we are grac'd, and give refpect
here we are refpected; yet we practife
· courfe, and never bend our eyes
with pleafure, till they find the way
us a neglect: then we, too late
, the lofs of what we might have had,
t to death.

Beaumont and *Fletcher's Scornful Lady.*

me, what is that only thing,
hich all women long:
ng what they moft defire,
ive it, does them wrong?
not to be chaft, nor fair,
:s, malice may impair;
rimm'd, to walk or ride,
inton unefpy'd;
:rve an honeft name,
to give it up to fame;
·e toys: in good or ill,
fire to have their will;
n they have it, they abufe it,
/ know not how to ufe it.

Beaumont and *Fletcher's Women Pleas'd.*

orious women that are fam'd
culine vertue, have been vitious;
lappier filence did betide them:
, no faults, who hath the art to hide them.

Webfter's White Devil.

are caught as you take tortoifes:
t be turn'd on her back.

Ibid.

Thi

This is the tyranny we men endure;
Women can make us mad, but none can cure.
Webſter and *Rowley's Thracian Wonder*

——————————It ſhall ſuffice;
By women man firſt fell, by them I'll riſe.
Maſon's Mulcaſſes.

Women and honeſty are as near ally'd,
As parſons lives are to their doctrines,
One and the ſame.
Barry's Ram Alley.

Never regard the paſſions of a woman:
The're wily creatures, and have learnt this wit,
Where they love moſt, beſt to diſſemble it.
Smith's Hector of Germany.

How have I wrong'd thee! oh who would abuſe
Your Sex, which truly knows ye! O women,
Were we not born of ye? ſhould we not then
Honour ye? nurs'd by ye, and not regard
Ye? begotten on you, and not love ye?
Made for ye, and not ſeek ye? and ſince we
Were made before ye, ſhould we not love and
Admire ye as the laſt, and therefore perfect'it work
Of nature? Man was made, when nature was
But an apprentice, but woman, when ſhe
Was a skilful miſtreſs of her art; therefore
Curſed is he that doth not admire thoſe
Paragons, thoſe models of heav'n, angels
On earth, goddeſſes in ſhape: by their loves
We live in double breath, even in our
Offspring after death.   Are not all vices
Maſculine, and vertues feminine? are
Not the *Muſes* the loves of the learned?
Do not all noble ſpirits follow the *Graces*,
Becauſe they are women? there's but one phœnix,
And ſhe's a female: is not the princeſs
And foundreſs of good arts, *Minerva*, born
Of the brain of higheſt *Jove*, a woman?
Have not theſe women the face of love, the

'Tongue

Tongue of perfuafion, the body of delight ?'
O divine perfection'd woman, whofe praifes
No tongue can full exprefs, for that the matter
Doth exceed the labour ! O, if to be
A woman be fo excellent, what is
It then to be a woman enrich'd by
Nature, made excellent by education,
Noble by birth, chaft by vertue, adorn'd
By beauty ! a fair woman which is the   .
Ornament of heaven, the grace of earth,
The joy of life, and the delight of all fenfe,.
Ev'n the very *fummum bonum* of man's life.

Cupid's Whirligig.

——————————————What a plague
Of vary'd torture·is a woman's heart ?
How like a peacock's tail, with diff'rent lights·
They differ from themfelves ! the very air
Alters the afpen humours of their bloods,
Now excellent good, now fuper-excellent bad.

Sir *Giles Goofe-Cap.*

Creatures the moft imperfect, nothing of
Themfelves, only patch'd up to cozen and
Gull men, borrowing their hair from one, and
Complexions from another ! nothing
Their own that's pleafing ; all diffembled, not
So much, but their very breath is fophifticated
With amber-pellets, and kiffing caufes.
Marry a woman!——'Thou undergo'ft an
Harder task, than thofe bold fpirits, that did
Undertake to fteal the great *Turk* into *Chriftendom.*
A woman ! fhe's an angel at ten, a
Saint at fifteen, a devil at forty,
And a witch at fourfcore.

Swetnam the Woman Hater.

——————————————We are all
But flefh and blood ; the fame thing that will do
My lady good, will pleafe her woman too.

John Ford's Lover's melancholy.

O 5   Here

Here's th' unhappiness of woman ftill,
That having forfeited, in old time, their truft,
Now makes their faith fufpected, that are juft.

Maffinger, Middleton, and *Rowley's Old Law.*

O never love, except thou be belov'd!
For fuch an humour ev'ry woman feizeth,
She loves not him that 'plaineth, but that pleafeth.
When much thou lovett, moft difdain comes on thee,
And when thou think'ft to hold her, fhe flies from thee:
She follow'd flies, fhe fled from, follows poft,
And loveth beft, where fhe is hated moft.
'Tis ever noted, both in maids and wives,
Their hearts and tongues are never relatives:
Hearts full of holes (fo elder fhepherds feign)
As apter to receive, than to retain.

Brown's Paftorals.

Women, as well as men, retain defire,
But can diffemble more than men, their fire.

Ibid.

Truft not a woman! they have found the herb
To open locks; not brazen towers can hold 'em;
Or if they get not loofe, they have the vertue
Of loadftones; fhut up in a box, they'll draw
Cuftomers to them; nay, being dead and bury'd,
There is a Sufpicion they will break the grave;
Which puts fo many husbands to the charge
Of heavy ftones to keep their bad wives under.

Shirley's Conftant Maid.

——————————————It is
The nature of women to be vext,
When they know any of their fervants court
Another; and that love they thought not worth
Their own reward, will fting 'em to the foul,
When 'tis tranflated where it meets with love:
And this will either break her ftubborn heart,
Or humble her.

Shirley's Brothers.

All

All mankind are alike to them;
and though we iron find
That never with a loadstone join'd,
    'Tis not the iron's fault,
Si, because the loadstone yet was never brought.

So where a gentle bee hath fall'n
    And labour'd to his pow'r,
A new succeeds not to that flow'r,
    But passes by;
'Tis to be thought, the gallant elsewhere loads his thigh.

For still the flowers ready stand,
    One buzzes round about,
One lights, one tastes, gets in, gets out,
    All, all ways use them,
Till all their sweets are gone, and all again refuse them.

Suckling.

I will not love one minute more, I swear,
No, not a minute; not a sigh or tear
Thou gett'st from me, or one kind look again,
Tho' thou should'st court me to't, and would'st begin.
I will not think of thee, but as men do
Of debts and sins; and then, I'll curse thee too:
For thy sake, woman shall be now to me
Less welcome, than at midnight ghosts shall be:
I hate so perfectly, that it shall be
Treason, to love that man that loves a she;
Nay, I will hate the very good, I swear,
That's in thy sex, because it does lie there:
Their very vertue, grace, discourse, and wit,
And all for thee: —what, wilt thou love me yet?

Ibid.

——These silly women, when they feed
Their expectation so high, do but like
Ignorant conjurers, that raise a spirit,
Which handsomly they cannot lay again.

Suckling's Aglaura.

He is a parricide to his mother's name,
And with an impious hand murthers her fame,

That wrongs the praise of women ; that dares write
Labells on saints, or with foul ink requite
The milk they lent us : Better sex, command
To your defence, my more religious hand
At sword, or pen ; yours was the nobler birth ;
For you of man were made, man but of earth,
The son of dust : and tho' your sin did breed
His fall, again you rais'd him in your seed :
Adam in's sleep again full loss sustain'd,
That for one rib, a better self regain'd ;
Who had he not your blest creation seen,
An *Anchorite* in *Paradise* had been.
Why in this work did the creation rest,
But that eternal providence thought you best
Of all his six days labour ? Beasts should do
Homage to man, but man shall wait on you :
You are of a comelier sight, of daintier touch,
A tender flesh, and colour bright, and such
As *Parians* see in marble ; skin more fair,
More glorious head, and far more glorious hair ;
Eyes full of grace and quickness ; purer roses
Blush in your cheeks ; a milder white composes
Your stately fronts ; your breath more sweet than his
Breaths spice, and nectar drops at ev'ry kiss.
Your skins are smooth, bristles on theirs do grow
Like quills of porcupines ; rough wooll doth flow
O'er all their faces ; you approach more near
The form of angels, they like beasts appear :
If then in Bodies where the souls do dwell
You better us ; do then our souls excel ?
No, we in souls equal perfection see,
There can in them, nor male nor female be.
Boast we of knowledge ? you are more than we,
You were the first ventur'd to pluck the tree :
And that more rhet'rick in your tongues do lie,
Let him dispute against, that dares deny
Your least commands ; and not persuaded be
With *Sampson's* strength, and *David's* piety.

To

To be your willing captives : vertue sure
Were blind as fortune, should she choose the poor
Rough cottage, man, to live in, and despise
To dwell in you, the stately edifice :
Thus you are prov'd the better sex ; and we
Must all repent, that in our pedigree,
We chose the father's name ; where should we take
The mother's, a more honour'd blood, twould make
Our generation sure and certain be,
And i'd believe some faith in heraldry.
Thus perfect creatures, if detraction rise
Against your sex, dispute but with your eyes,
Your hand, your lip, your brow, there will be sent
So subtle and so strong an argument,
Will teach the stoick his affection too,
And call the cynick from his tub to wooe.
Thus must'ring up your beauteous troops go on,
The fairest, is the valiant *Amazon*.

Randolph.

Let them imagine, who did ever know
What misled womens wild desires will do,
When they extremely do, or lust, or loath ;
Cruel alike, alike unjust in both,
And from their worst desires most hardly chang'd.

May's Edward III.

The wanton nymph doth more delight me far ;
The modest nymphs do more seem chast than are :
Women are all alike ; the diff'rence this,
This seems and is not, that both seems and is ;
Or if some are not, as they call it, ill ;
They want the pow'r and means, but not the will.

Sicelides.

Women in the beginning (as 'tis said)
To be an help to man was chiefly made :
Then ought not women much to be commended,
Who answer th' end for which they were intended ?
Women were made to help men, so they do ;
Some unto sorrow, grief, diseases too :

Others,

Others, do their kind husbands help to spend
Their whole estates; thus answer they their end:
Some help men unto more than they were born
To have, I mean *Acteon's* head and horn.
Crooked condition'd nature made her, when
She form'd her of the crooked'st parts in men:
Nature first fram'd her of a man's rib, she
Then can't chuse but a cross-grain'd creature be:
And ever since (it may not be deny'd)
Poor man hath subject been t'a stich i' th' side.

Clevelai

For shame you pretty female elves,
Cease thus to candy up your selves:
No more you sectarys of the game,
No more of your calcining flame.
Women commence by cupid's dart,
As a king hunting dubs a hart.

Ib

She shew'd that her soft sex contains strong minds,
   Such as evap'rates through the coarser male:
As through coarse stone, elixir passage finds,
   Which scarce through finer chrystal can exhale.

Sir *W. Davenant's Gondibe*

———A woman's will
Is not so strong in anger, as her skill

Sir *W. Davenant's Albovi*

Oh what a feeble sort's a woman's heart,
Betray'd by nature, and besieg'd by art!

Fane's Love in the Da

Dangers and business are cut out for men;
Women are spar'd, to stock the world again.

Fane's Sacrif

No woman takes her self to be a monster;
Yet she would be so, if her eyes were stars,
Her lips of roses, and her face of lilies.
Why, traps were made for foxe, gins for hares,
Lime-twigs for birds, and lies and oaths for women.

Ib
C

Oh women, mens subduers!
Natures extreams! no mean is to be had;
Excellent good, or infinitely bad.

> *Davenport's King John and Matilda.*

Womens sweet words
As far are from their hearts (though from their breasts
They flie) as lapwings crys are from their nests.

> *Davenport's City Night Cap.*

He is a fool who thinks by force, or skill,
To turn the current of a woman's will.

> *Tuke's Adventures of Five Hours.*

Seek for the star that's shot upon the ground,
And nought but a dim gelly there is found:
Thus foul and dark our female stars appear,
If fall'n or loosned once from vertue's sphere.

> Bishop *King.*

Women, like china, should be kept with care;
One flaw debases her to common ware.

> *Crown's Sir Courtly Nice.*

Poor womankind——
Heav'n for our ruin, gifts on us bestows,
Charms to allure, no power to oppose.
In passion we are strong, in reason weak,
Constant alone, to error and mistake;
In vertue feign'd, in vanity sincere;
Witty in sin, and for damnation fair.

> *Crown's Darius.*

These are great maxims, sir, it is confest;
Too stately for a womans narrow breast.
Poor love is lost in mens capacious minds;
In ours, it fills up all the room it finds.

> *Crown's Second Part of the Destruction of Jerusalem.*

From men we only seem to fly,
To meet them with more privacy.

> *Crown's Calisto.*

W O R D S

Ev'n as the vapour which the fire repells,
Turns not to earth, but in the mid air dwells;

Where

Where while it hangs, if *Boreas*' frofty flaws,
With rigour rattle it, not to rain it thaws,
But thunder, light'nings, ratt'ling hail or fnow
Sends down to earth, whence firft it rofe below:
But if fair *Phœbus* with his count'nance fweet
Refolve it, down the dew, or manna fleet:
The manna dew, that in the eaftern lands,
Excel the labour of the bees fmall hands.
Elfe for her *Memnon* grey *Aurora*'s tears
On the earth it ftill; the partner of her fears.
Or fends fweet fhow'rs to glad their mother earth,
Whence firft they took their firft inconftant birth:
To fo great griefs, ill taken words do grow:
Of words well taken, fuch delights do flow.
Mirror for Magiftrates.

———— His plaufive words
He fcatter'd not in ears, but grafted them
To grow there and to bear.
Shakefpear's *All's well that ends well.*

Your words are ear-wigs to my vexed brains,
Like hen bane juice, or aconite diffus'd,
They ftrike me fenfelefs.
True Trojans.

Words are the foul's embaffadors, who go
Abroad upon her errands to and fro;
They are the fole expounders of the mind,
And correfpondence keep 'twixt all mankind.
They are thofe airy keys that ope (and wreft
Sometimes) the locks and hinges of the breaft.
By them the heart makes fallies: wit and fenfe
Belong to them: They are the quinteffence
Of thofe ideas which the thoughts diftil,
And fo calcine and melt again, until
They drop forth into accents; in whom lies
The falt of fancy, and all faculties.
The world was fram'd by the eternal word,
Who to each creature did a name afford;

And

And such an union made 'twixt words and things,
That ev'ry name a nature with it brings.
Words do involve the greatest mysterys :
By them the *Jew* into his *Cabal* pries.
The chymick says, in stones, in herbs, in words,
Nature for ev'ry thing a cure affords :
Nay, some have found the glorious stars to be
But letters, set in an orthography,
The fate of kings and empires to foretell ;
With all things else below, could we them spell.
That grand distinction between man and brute,
We may to language chiefly attribute.
The lion roars, the elephant doth bray ;
The bull doth bellow, and the horse doth neigh ;
Man speaks : 'Tis only man can words create,
And cut the air to sounds articulate
By nature's special charter. Nay, speech can
Make a shrewd discrepance 'twixt man and man :
It doth the gentleman from clown discover ;
And from a fool the grave philosopher :
As *Solon* said to one in judgment weak,
I thought thee wise until I heard the speak.
For words in man bear the most critick part ;
We speak by nature ; but speak well by art.
And as good bells we judge of by the sound,
So a wise man by words well plac'd is found :
Therefore it may be call'd no vain pretence,
When 'mongst the rest the tongue would be a sense.
The tongue's the rudder which man's fancy guides,
Whilst on this world's tempestuous sea he rides.
Words are the life of knowledge ; they set free,
And bring forth truth by way of midwif'ry :
The activ'st creatures of the teeming brain,
The judges who the inward man arraign :
Reason's chief engine and artillery
To batter error, and make falshood fly :
The cannons of the mind, who sometimes bounce
Nothing but war, then peace again pronounce.

The

The *Pen* or the ... turn ... the ... of words,
... have made deeper wounds than spears or swords.
>   *Howell.*

...
...
...
...
...
Some men ... ... nature's as
...
Are ... many ... from their first source.
>   *....'s Poor Scholar.*

W O R L D

How weary, stale, flat, and unprofitable
Seem to me all the uses of this world?
... on't! ... 'tis an unweeded garden,
That grows to seed; things rank, and gross in nature,
Posses it merely.
>   *Shakespear's Hamlet.*

This world's a city full of straying streets,
And death's the market-place where each one meets.
> *Shakespear, Beaumont and Fletcher's Two noble Kinsmen.*

Lo, how the stormy world doth worldlings toss,
    "I mean sandy pleasures, and a rocky will!
Whilst them that court it most, it most doth cross,
    To vice indulgent, vertue's step-dame still.
>   *E. of Sterline's Crœsus.*

Who to the full, thy vileness, world, e'er told!
    What is in thee, that's not extremely ill?
A loathsome shop, where poison's only sold,
    Whose very entrance instantly doth kill:
Nothing in thee but villany doth dwell,
And all thy ways lead head long into hell,
>   *Drayton's Legend of Pierce Gaveston.*

This world is like a mint, we are no sooner
Call into the fire, taken out again,
Hammer'd, stamp'd, and made current, but
Presently we are chang'd.
>   *Dekker and Webster's Westward Hoe.*

As mankind, so is the world's whole frame
Quite out of joint, almost created lame:
For before God had made up all the rest,
Corruption enter'd, and deprav'd the best:
It seiz'd the angels, and then first of all
The world did in her cradle take a fall,
And turn'd her brains; and took a general maim,
Wronging each joint of th' universal frame:
The noblest part, man, felt it first; and then,
Both beasts and plants, curst in the curse of man;
So did the world from the first hour decay,
That evening was beginning of the day;
And now the springs and summers, which we see,
Like sons of women after fifty be:
And new philosophy calls all in doubt,
The element of fire is quite put out:
The sun is lost, and th' earth, and no man's wit
Can well direct him where to look for it.

Dr. *Donne.*

——————The world contains
Princes for arms, and counsellors for brains,
Lawyers for tongues, divines for hearts, and more,
The rich for stomachs, and for backs the poor;
The officers for hands, merchants for feet,
By which remote and distant countries meet.

Bid.

They say the world is like a byass-bowl,
And it runs all on the rich mens sides: others
Say, 'tis like a tennis ball, and fortune
Keeps such a racket with it, as it tosses
It into time's hazard, and that devours all.

Cupid's Whirligig.

This world's the chaos of confusion:
No world at all, but mass of open wrongs,
Wherein a man, as in a map may see
The high road way from woe to misery.

Willy beguil'd.

1. What

1. What other is the world than a ball,
   Which we run after with hoop and with hollo,
He that doth catch it, is sure of a fall,
   His heels tript up by him that doth follow!
2. Do not women play too?
3. They are too light, quickly down.
1. O yes, they are the best gamesters of all;
   For though they often lie on the ground,
Not one amongst a hundred will fall,
   But under her coats the ball will be found.

Shirley's Bird in a Cage.

No marvel, thou great monarch didst complain,
And weep, there were no other worlds to gain:
Thy griefs and thy complaints were not amiss;
Hea's grief enough, that finds no world but this.

Quarles.

Thus having travers'd the fond world in brief,
The lust of th' eyes, the flesh, and pride of life;
Unbiass'd and impartially we see,
'Tis lighter in the scale, than vanity.
What then remains? But that we still should strive
Not to be born to die, but dye to live.

Cleveland.

Well hath the great creator of the world
Fram'd it in that exact and perfect form,
That by itself unmoveable might stand,
Supported only by his providence.
Well hath his pow'rful wisdom ordered
The in nature disagreeing elements,
That all affecting their peculiar place,
Maintain the conservation of the whole.
Well hath he taught the swelling ocean
To know his bounds, left in luxurious pride
He should insult upon the conquer'd land
Well hath he plac'd those torches in the heav'ns
To give light to our else all darkned eyes:
The chrystal windows thorough which our soul
Looking upon the world's most beauteous face,

t with fight and knowledge of his works.
hath he all things done : for how, alas !
any ftrength or wit of feeble man
ied have that greater univerfe
veak an *Atlas* for one commonwealth ?
could he make the earth, the water, air,
ire, in peace their duties to obferve,
idle up the headftrong ocean,
cannot rule the wits and tongues of men,
keep them in ? It were impoffible
ve light to the world, with all his art
kill, that cannot well illuminate
darkned underftanding.

Sophifter.

s grand wheel, the world, we're fpokes made all ;
: that it may ftill keep its round,
mount while others fall.

Alex. Brome.

looks upon this world, and not beyond it,
e abodes it leads to, muft believe it
oloody flaughter-houfe of fome ill pow'r,
r than the contrivance of a good one.
thing here breeds mifery to man ;
fea breeds ftorms to fink him : If he flies
ore for aid, the fhore breeds rocks to tear him :
arth breeds briars to rend him, trees to hang him ;
: things that feem his friends, are falfe to him :
air that gives him breath, gives him infection ;
takes his health away, and drink his reafon.
eafon is fo great a plague to him,
ever is fo pleas'd as when he's robb'd on't
ink or madnefs.

Crown's ambitious Statefman.

——Oh curfed troubled world !
e nothing without forrow can be had,
tis not eafy to be good or bad !
orrour attends evil, forrow good,
plagues the mind, and vertue flefh and blood.

Crown's Darius.

The world is a great dance, in which we find
The good and bad have various turns assign'd ;
But when they've ended the great masquerade,
One goes to glory, th' other to a shade.
Crown's Juliana

Y O U T H.

BE affable and courteous in youth, that
You may be honour'd in age.   Roses that
Lose their colours, keep their favours, and pluck'd
From the stalk, are put to the still.   *Cotonea*,
Because it boweth when the sun riseth,
Is sweetest when it is oldest : and children,
Which in their tender Years sow courtesy,
Shall in their declining states reap pity,
Lilly's Sapho and Phao

————Let me not live (quoth he)
After my flame lacks oil ; to be the snuff
Of younger spirits, whose apprehensive senses
All but new things disdain ; whose judgments are
Meer fathers of their garments ; whose constancies
Expire before their fashions.
Shakespear's All's well that ends well

- ---- For Youth no less becomes
The light and careless livery that it wears,
Than settled age his sables, and his weeds
Importing health and graveness.
Shakespear's Hamlet

I'll serve his youth, for youth must have his course,
For being withstain'd, it makes him ten times worse :
His pride, his riot, all that may be nam'd,
Time may recall, and all his madness tam'd.
Shakespear's London Prodigal

I will

I'll not practice any violent means to stay
Th' unbridled course of youth in him : for that
Restrain'd, grows more impatient; and, in kind,
Like to the eager, but the gen'rous grey-hound,
Who, ne'er so little from his game withheld,
Turns head, and leaps up at his holder's throat.
Johnson's Every Man in his Humour.

What Stoick strange, who most precise appears,
Could that Youth's death with tearless eyes behold ?
In all perfections ripe, tho' green in years;
A hoary judgment under locks of gold.
E. of Sterline's Crœsus.

——————————The heat
Of an unsteady youth, a giddy brain,
Green indiscretion, flattery of greatness,
Rawness of judgment, wilfulness in folly,
Thoughts vagrant as the wind, and as uncertain.
John Ford's Broken Heart.

——————————Folly may be in youth :
But many times 'tis mixt with grave discretion
That tempers it to use, and makes its judgment
Equal, if not exceeding that, which palseys
Have almost shaken into a disease.
Nabbs's Covent Garden.

I love to see a nimble activeness
In noble youth; it argues active minds
In well shap'd bodies, and begets a joy
Dancing within me.
Ibid.

1. Though youthful blood be hot,
Yet it must be allay'd and cool'd by snowy age;
And those of elder years ought to restrain
Its violent and impetuous course.
2. Ay, but with this caution and proviso,
That the restraint be not unseasonable :
'Tis a receiv'd opinion 'mong anatomists,
That the ligature and binding of a member,
If seasonably apply'd, preserves the heart

From

From violent influxes of the blood ;
But if the application be untimely, it caufes
Gangreens and hæmorrhagies ;
So youthful blood if checkt unfeafonably,
Becomes more infolent and impetuous,
More vitiated and corrupt, than if
Its natural courfe had not been hinder'd ;
The age of youth is the ftrong rein of
Paffion, and vice does ride in triumph
Upon the wheels of vehement defire,
Which run with infinite celerity,
When the body drives the chariot,
They can't be ftopp'd on a fudden ;
Art and deliberation muft be us'd.

Nevile's Poor Scholar.

All hardy youths ! from valiant fathers fprung,
   Whom perfect honour he fo highly taught,
That th' aged fetch'd examples from the young,
   And hid the vain experience which they brought.

Sir *William Davenant's Gondibert.*

Something of youth, I in old age approve ;
But more the marks of age in youth I love.
Who this obferves, may in his body find
Decrepit age, but never in his mind.

Denham.

And they whofe high examples youth obeys,
Are not defpifed, though their ftrength decays ;
And thofe decays, to fpeak the naked truth,
Though the defects of age, were crimes of youth :
Intemp'rate youth, by fad experience found,
Ends in an age imperfect and unfound.

Denham.

And to rafh youth 'tis an unhappy fate,
To come too early to a great eftate.

Crown's Calisto.

F I N I S.

Lightning Source UK Ltd.
Milton Keynes UK
UKHW010003160219
337399UK00011B/947/P